Fighting For You

Fighting For You

A New Adult Romance Novel

By

January Valentine

Printed in the United States of America

ISBN: 13: 978-0615958101
ISBN: 10: 0615958109

Book Design by Victoria Valentine
Edited by: Phaedra Valentine
Proofreader: Shellie Hedge

Water Forest Press Books
PO Box 295, Stormville, NY 12582
waterforestpress.com

January Valentine Books

Wheel Wolf (Werewolf Horror) Amazon bestselling paranormal werewolves & shifters.
Thanks to a blood moon at Phantom Lake, Jack Bailey will never be the same. Wheel Wolf is a story of unconditional love that lives beyond the grave, and a relentless fight for retribution. An Amazon bestseller in Werewolves/Shifters/Horror/Suspense.

Love Dreams Contemporary Romance
Michael is in a wheelchair. Sienna has been emotionally damaged. They keep having accidental run-ins, but can they find love?

Sweet Dreams in the Mind of a Serial Killer
He plants roses ... in dead women. A witness says: He doesn't look human.

Fighting For You New Adult Contemporary Romance
Jewelia wants to work for the NYPD. Indigo is a medical student with baggage. They come from two different worlds. Can they beat the odds? Watch for: *Running From Regret* Indigo's POV in 2014.

Beautiful Experiment Paranormal Romance Book One of The Island of Defiance Trilogy
Six unruly teens are kidnapped, sent to an uncharted island. Caretaker, Brook, is hot. Father is mysterious. Will they find a way home before the island is overrun with demons?

Newly Bred With Magic (erotic fantasy short)
Seven Day Wonder (erotic fantasy novella) (Lana Lundon)
Snowed In (5 author erotic anthology)

All titles are available on Amazon, B & N and through other booksellers in print and ebook format.

Dedication

Have you ever loved someone so much you're positive breathing without him or her is impossible? Had to fight so hard you lost sense of yourself? This book is dedicated to everyone who has felt the pangs of love. Suffered, fought, and recovered. May you find your dream and hold onto it. Sometimes love takes more than a first chance. Never give up.

Love is the beauty which clings to life, binds hearts together, leaving them hollow without it. – JV

January Valentine

"Life isn't perfect. Think of it as a designer dress you pull out of the closet. Beautiful, except for that one little wrinkle where it was crushed. When you try to iron it out, you end up making more. Choices are a bitch. Making the right one takes time, patience."
– Indigo

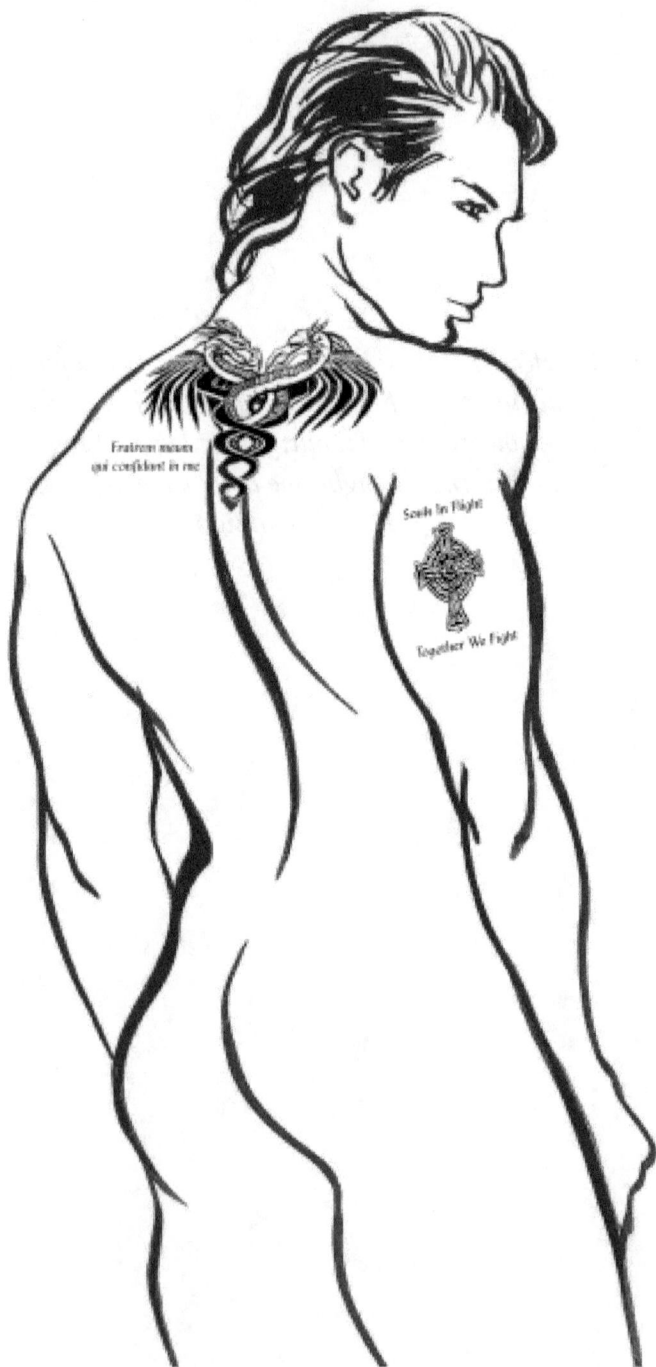

Mi Rosa Mi Joya

January Valentine

If Dreams Came True

When I strutted into Kelly's Café, all heads turned my way, fiery eyeballs flashing like beacons. Had my flowing chestnut hair caught the crowd as it did daylight? Perhaps my eyes, which at times held a similar hue; soft golden brown flooding an emerald-green forest. Or was I the main attraction because I happened to be wearing a fuchsia bikini my body rejected by spilling my curves all over the place?

A rush of horror washed over me. My brain disengaged, the streets outside filled with chaos. Without my cuffs and firearm, I'd be a victim. I was helpless!

January Valentine

Kelly's Cafe

Manhattan was in its usual Monday morning panic. Shielding my eyes from a blinding sunrise, I crossed Tenth Avenue as a sign flashed a green *walk*, my body weaving through a mob of blue and white-collar comrades like a knitting needle through yarn. Before punching the time clock at AMA (Abigail Mitchell Apparel) – the elegant department store where I worked part-time security – I slid past a few utility workers congregating under Kelly's awning. The open glass door welcomed an early spring, and more pushy customers than I would have liked to have seen, as I was already seriously late.

I hadn't slept well the night before. Tossing and turning was one thing, but God, how I missed Nikos, my Mediterranean mistake. It's been over six months, I told myself. Time to get on with your life, girl. He turned out to be a conniving bastard and you're a freak for letting him get to you this way. But the familiar pressure of those strong arms folding around me, drawing our bodies close, was a mood killer, to say the least. The thought of him back in his homeland – soaking up the same sun my purple lenses filtered – on a pristine beach with another woman in his bear hug, made me want to vomit. Not only was he roll-over-stop-your-heart-gorgeous, but so was the island he lived on. It was paradise. I'd seen it firsthand.

Before I entered Kelly's, I looked down at my jeans, ribbed tank top and half-zipped hoodie. I wasn't dressed to kill, but the circle of guys parted for me like gentleman, although their facial expressions were anything but. The wiggle room they left me to squeeze through was so tight I felt hot breath on my neck as I passed. If I had eyes in the back of my head, instead of a long, messy braid, I'd probably have caught them gaping at my rear end.

Once inside the café, the dream bounced across my mind and I had to choke back laughter. If dreams came true, would I be in trouble. I'd be feeling more than hot breath on my neck and eyes on my rump roast, that's for damn sure.

Like a kid with a secret, I couldn't keep a straight face. And that's how I looked when my eyes caught his. There I stood, like a grinning idiot. Solo. Stalled in the middle of the place, with a tooth-baring smile.

Our eyes locked.

Did I detect a glimmer of recognition in his?

Surely not on my end. I'd never forget anything so scrumptious. My mouth felt like cardboard, and a sinking sensation accompanied my awkward lips as they shrank back into their normal shape. At least I held my jaw in place.

Madre de Dios.[Mother of God.] He was fine. Finer than the to-die-for 18K gold sparkly flat rope necklace displayed in AMA's guarded jewelry case; the one I drooled over but would never be able to afford. The only gold I owned was plated. Then my fingers slipped over the slender crucifix, centered with a brilliant diamond, suspended from a delicate chain around my neck ... Shame set in. Grandma had left me one of her few precious possessions, blessed by a Cardinal, passed on to me with her love. The cross had meaning, sentiment, emotions a lump of cold metal could never have, regardless of its lure ... and cost.

My moment of guilt dissolved as I melted into his gaze,

conscious of the skate of my lips which blotted my creamy lipstick, willing them not to quiver.

A step up from Nikos, hell – twenty steps up from Nikos was more like it. From the distance, I couldn't gauge the color of his eyes, but they were wide, translucent. A surge of sunlight flared through the window, striking his face, and he squinted as his stare endured ... dared. My elevator stomach dropped ten floors.

The beckoning barista broke our trance. Gorgeous did a forward head-swoop, faced the impatient guy in the green smock, and placed his order. I saw his lips move, but had to imagine the sound of his voice. Smooth and mellow, of course. It had to be ... deep and sexy. As sexy as his masculine profile, and defined trapezius and shoulder muscles bulging through his pullover. I strained to see more of him; unable to through the crowd. Still, with a top half like that, how could the bottom be disappointing?

Stricken with a sudden bout of immobility, my ballets still glued to the same two floorboards, I found myself drawing in too many breaths. Wondering if he felt the same connection, I consciously wiped expectation from my face.

After he finished speaking to the barista, his head moved in my direction, sweeping smoothly from side to side as though focusing on imaginary objects around me. By some unexplained force, our eyes would connect, meet, hold. Then he'd break free, look over his shoulder.

We seemed to be involved in a hide and seek game, two rubbernecking strangers, well aware of the crudeness of staring. Still, I couldn't fight the urge. And apparently, he experienced the same fascination.

Suddenly he grew bolder, and it was my turn to focus on blurred faces around him, up and over his head, pretending to study the menu hanging on the wall. Each time I dared a peek, he'd be glancing my way. Our eyes kept brushing with more than curiosity, and I became quite uncomfortable. Finally, the corner of his questioning eyes crinkled, his lips pursing with a hint of a smile.

The gaze we shared sent messages, and I thought he might be contemplating a walk in my direction. *Oh no, please don't. I mean, yes, yes. I'm over here ...*

At the thought of standing beside him, my legs grew weak, my body tingly. *Guapo! [Handsome.]* He was drop-dead hotter than a Ghost Pepper. My reaction to this guy was puzzling. My preference had always been for the dark and mysterious type. He might have been borderline jock — but not your typical college Joe. But, mysterious ... oh yeah. Esthetically, he'd be considered *late summer*. And the look on his face made mine react ...

The impatient barista, suspending a steaming coffee cup in his wobbling hand, grumbled, once again breaking the spell. There was something compelling about college Joe's change of expression a moment before his head swung back to the guy: Brooding. Soul digging. A chill ran down my spine. I couldn't take it ... and I couldn't take my eyes off him.

His hair was thick and appealingly messy; he must have been facing a hectic morning, or his sun-tipped locks had been pillow-brushed and finger-combed. Mmm, to run my fingers through that would be amazing.

The v-neck sweater expanded for his broad neck, the smooth black knit a striking contrast against his sandy hair. His bronzed face hinted there might be a sailboat tan beneath his clothes. Speedboat maybe ...

I wondered if I'd have noticed him had he not initiated the staring contest. But Lord, those eyes drew me right in. Captivating ... I needed backup. I reached for my cell phone.

Me: Kelly's
Em: When?
Me: NOW!
Em: Working U ok?
Me: Sending pic
Em: OMG. Who *is* that?
Me: Idk don't show Pete

Roommate and Best Friend

He's hotter than my Honda before the engine blew." Emma pulled in a breath.

"You think?" My threaded brows shot up.

"Holy shit, Jewel. How many pics did you sneak?" Emma laughed light and airy, like wind chimes. She dropped her shoulder bag on the table and grabbed my phone. With satin ebony hair, shoulder length and straight, she appeared a perfect work of anime art. I watched his delicious photos flash across the smudged screen as her fingers slid over it. She shoved my phone back into my hand before dropping onto the sofa. "He gave you *the eye*, huh? How did you not jump him?"

"Not easy. He made a big deposit into my memory bank, that's for sure." In an instant, I relived the split second our stares met and held. "He didn't give me *the eye*, not like ours." My laugh resonated, deeper than Em's, but every bit as musical. "But it was sure as hell invitational. Whatever ..." The sigh I drew rose from my gut.

"Hopefully now you'll realize there *are* other baskets for your eggs ..."

My eyes widened. "What the hell are you talking about?"

I choked out a laugh. "Baskets and eggs? I'm not the Easter bunny, and certainly not ready for mating."

"One of my mother's expressions," Emma giggled. "You know what I mean. Maybe now you'll forget the gigolo and start sleeping. I'm tired of sleep deprivation because of your bathroom runs, or wherever it is you go fifty times a night."

"Nikos who?" I shot her a snarky grin. Over the past months I'd spent so much time thinking of my ex, my memory bank had been almost depleted of juicy visuals. "Let's put it this way. Nikos was a piggybank. This guy's Fort Knox. I wonder if I'll ever see him again?"

"You have to, Jewel. From what you described, it's a love story in the making."

"Yeah, but in this crowded city," I blew out an exasperated groan, "maybe we're just two Manhattanites passing in a café."

"That's what I love about you," Emma's voice followed her over-the-head arm stretch, "you keep us in drama."

I searched the fridge for dinner. Finding nothing of interest, I leaned a rounded hip against one of the four counter stools. Sliding onto the seat, I half draped myself over the Formica top, supporting my head with a palm, slipping into my *oh, misery* position. "We need to shop. This kitchen looks poverty-stricken. Wanna go out for food?"

Emma brushed thick bangs from her forehead, her body, suspended on the three cushions of our burgundy sofa, barely making a dent. "I'm beat. You go though. Bring me back the usual."

"How did your day go?" I habitually asked.

"Multi dimensional neurosis. Phobias, panic attacks, delusions of grandeur. You name it." Emma closed her eyes, took in a breath, expelling a gust of air.

"I don't know how you do it." I shook my head. "I have enough trouble figuring out my own brain, without trying to dissect someone else's."

"That's why I sweated out five years at Columbia." Pointing a lean leg, she kicked a high-heeled pump across the room, nailing one of the club chairs in front of the living room picture window. The chair rocked, rippling the vanilla drape hanging behind it. For a petite girl, Emma was strong; she was also impulsive and burning with ambition.

I met Emma Kim when I was pre-college apartment hunting in Manhattan. I answered her ad and within a few days we were roommates, forming an instant bond and lasting friendship. Sweet and compassionate, she had chosen the perfect profession: Mental Health Professional. While she saved enough cash to go into private practice, she worked for the State of New York.

It wouldn't be long and I'd have my B.S. and launch my career. From my first day at John Jay, I'd flown through every single class with a 3.8 until my life fell apart. That occurred during the year of Nikos Loukas, the hunk with the accent that cracked the core of the *never let your guard down* ice queen. I guess it was bound to happen, and probably did to every girl. For me, once was enough.

Nikos had dumped me during midterms, forcing me close to depression, something foreign to me, as foreign as the man. Thank heavens for Emma. I was one of her most difficult cases, and with twenty-four hour access, should have been her easiest success. But nothing could pull up my grades, or push me through the two classes I inevitably flunked. So, I'd registered for the same said courses again this semester. Thankfully, my second run of Forensic and Political Science were proving to be successful. I'd graduate soon, and hopefully land a permanent position in law enforcement.

But until graduation, the closest I could come was catching shoplifters in one of the finest upscale stores in Manhattan.

"How was *your* day?" Emma yawned out in her soft voice.

"I nabbed two old ladies who tried to smuggle out three-hundred-dollar swimsuits." I chuckled. Lifting myself off the stool I stretched, stood in the center of the room, then dropped into a chair across from Emma.

"Speaking of shopping. Did you pick up a helmet?"

"They had to order one. My head didn't fit anything in the store." I twirled my hair around a finger.

"Must be all those brains." Emma laughed and rolled lithely to her feet. "Okay. I'm recharged. Let's go out to eat."

I shook my head. "I should be used to you by now. No means an eventual yes. Do you do this with men?"

She shot me a smirk and went to her room to change. When she walked back in, we looked pretty close to twins. Both wearing jeans and T-shirts, sandals and handbags slung over a shoulder, the main difference between us was our builds and hair texture.

Emma and I ate at Landon's Bistro. We ended up pigging out on veggie wraps and iced coffee. We skipped dessert. Both on health kicks, wasted calories meant extra time at the gym, something Emma would love. I would not. Dancing was all the exercise I needed.

"So." Em pushed her plate aside. "What are you going to do about the hunk?"

I scrunched my mouth and raised a brow. "I'll probably never see him again, so why would I even entertain such ridiculous thoughts?" I drained the last drop of coffee through my straw, then pulled lip gloss and a small mirror from my bag. "Shit," I groaned. "I was supposed to meet Pete at seven."

I didn't have to check my cell to realize seven p.m. had come and gone. The sun had vanished behind the skyline, and the only light came from stores and street lamps.

"If talking about this dude makes you lose time ... forget about Pete ..."

I sighed. "Yeah ... imagine being with him? I could lose more than time. That's the frightening part."

Emma rolled her eyes. "I should have such problems."

"Let's get going," I dropped two dollars on the table, stood, and slung my bag over a shoulder.

As we headed for home, the rent controlled apartment Em's aunt owned, I pulled out my cell and texted Pete an apology.

"You two have the weirdest relationship. It's like you're married without benefits," Emma, two strides ahead of me, said as she swung her head around.

"Or restrictions." I laughed.

"There's such a thing as negative dependency." Her eyes followed her straight nose, pointing right at me.

"He's like a big brother, and don't act like I'm a patient." I stood with hands on hips. "I don't have to rely on anyone or anything but myself. And I don't second guess myself, either, which I know you're about to accuse me of. I know exactly what I'm doing and where I'm heading."

"Oh, so now you're a mind reader too." She laughed. "I didn't know they taught clairvoyance at Jay."

"Insight is not taught." I smirked. "It's a natural born talent."

Emma rolled her eyes, fished into her bag for her jangling keychain, and unlocked the door.

"I call shower," I said, dropping my gear onto a chair, and headed to the linen closet.

With so much on my mind, concentration didn't come easy, but I did my best self-analysis under water.

"Crap." On my way out of the shower, I complained, "It's almost midnight. I'll have bags under my eyes tomorrow. Great way to start a mission."

Emma stood at the doorway. I paused for her to bolster my morale. "Well, at least you won't be bloated." She wiped steam off the bathroom mirror and stared at herself. "Unlike problems, veggie wraps disintegrate in a matter of hours."

Hunting College Joe

Before sunrise, I headed out the door in a turquoise bra top and black Capri leggings, lugging a sweater and racing thoughts, wondering if my perfectly planned stalk would have a positive outcome. If I timed it right I'd reach Kelly's at the same time as college Joe. Feeling thoroughly prepped, I hoped for a repeat of history.

As I walked down the street anxiety built and my head filled with "what ifs". Then it hit me: *really ... what if? What was I doing?*

It wasn't even rush hour and the place was a mob scene. *Couldn't some of these people find somewhere else to buy their morning coffee?* My stomach quivered, along with my jaw, both rebelling, gripping tighter than my pants.

My brain went into non-stop-nag mode. What am I gonna do – walk around the entire café inspecting faces? Examine the top half of every guy's torso while searching for the special one that had almost knocked me off my feet?

Attempting to scour the place discreetly, I didn't see the chair leg that tripped me. I lost my balance, but thankfully grabbed onto a guy whose jaw dropped when I hung onto him for dear life. Not thankful for *him* though, as the shoulder I commandeered was attached to the arm I accidentally jerked into the air. A nightmare unfolded when the cup of steaming coffee he clutched flew out of his hand.

"Save me, Lord," I whispered as black liquid saturated the front of his suit jacket.

"Oh my God ... did you get burned?" I gushed while reaching for a handful of napkins, ready to swab him off. "It's so ... crowded ... in ... here ..." My cheeks didn't need the burgundy blush I'd patted on less than an hour earlier.

I must have looked about to cry, or beg, or faint, maybe all three, because the anger in his hazel eyes disappeared and a smile sprouted. Then he slowly assessed my shirt, my hips. *Stop right there buddy ...*

"Grab a seat. I'll buy us a cup of coffee." His approving eyes worked their way back up to mine, which were still wide and straining as he shrugged a pretty damn nice pair of shoulders out of his jacket, and flung it over a chair.

The guy was gracious. Smooth. Suave. He could have been a professional, maybe an attorney, and he was being nice, maybe too nice. I knew the incident had attracted stares. Eyes all over me, I feared a coronary. Oh merciful heaven. Had I eaten breakfast, I might have hurled it over the poor guy's chest. Even worse, his impeccably styled head of hair.

"You look like you could use something stronger than this." He held up his empty cup like a trophy, and winked. "Come on. Have a seat." He dragged out the chair beside him.

"That's okay." I managed a smile that didn't seem to go along with my internal turmoil. "I'm late for class. I have to run."

Kelly's was buzzing, faces a blur. The café seemed to shrink around me, then everything started to spin. I had to get out of there. Pronto.

That's when it happened. Of course, at the most inopportune time. I knew schemes rarely unraveled as planned, but things couldn't have been worse. My mission had been canceled by an unknown force. Maybe it was meant to be this way. I lifted my face to the ceiling. *Grandma, is that you trying to tell me something? Maybe I'm not supposed to ever see him again. Is that it? Couldn't you have tipped me off earlier? Before I walked into this mess?*

There he was. Standing in line. Exactly like the day before, the look on his face a startling replica. My hands trembled. My legs began to buckle. I felt the blood drain from my tingling face which would then turn stark white for the first time in my life.

The speech Em and I had concocted was spilled all over the expensive jacket of some amorous stranger. My heart was in overdrive, skipping beats. And to make matters worse, I'd have to walk right by gorgeous to get out the door. So I did the next best thing. I hid in the ladies' room for five minutes. That would give him enough time to grab his coffee and vacate the premises. Please be gone, I prayed as I stepped out of the bathroom, blotting the ice-cold water I'd thrown at my cheeks, my eyes darting every which way.

Just my luck. A single barista handling two lines. What the hell? Punished. I was being punished for something I must have done. It must have been horrendous for heaven to impose such a dreadful sentence.

Okay, Jewel. You can do this. Quietly skim by. Brace those legs. Look calm. BE calm. Deep breath. That's it. In and out. In and out. Soft breaths. I moved as if in a dream, a sleepwalking basket case, not feeling my arms, my legs, my slinking footsteps. I busied myself, digging into my bag for nothing while looking straight ahead. But ... as fate would have it, the line he was on merged with the other, altering his position, bringing him even closer to the insignificant space I was trying to sneak through. And then he turned. Why? I had no clue, but this time, when his eyes reached out to mine, a shadow of a smile crept across his lips, and I swore his gaze did a head to toe sweep ... of me.

I steadied myself, ready to cast him my dimpliest smile, willing my voice to return, along with my confidence; of course

I was thinking ahead, planning an opening conversation. But there it was again ... that troubling expression on his face. Moody? God, I hoped not. Solemn? Heartbroken – that was the look. Please don't let him be crushing on someone who didn't love him back. What girl in her right mind wouldn't have loved him back?

My heart skipped a few more beats. Rushing adrenaline shot through my limbs, jellifying my brain. I couldn't believe it. I hadn't felt this way since my first high school crush, which ended in disaster when I slid across the cafeteria floor thanks to the banana peel that adhered to the sole of my shoe.

Maybe the look in his eyes hastened my recovery.

As though I'd grown wings, my body turned fluid and capable. Next thing I knew, my ballet flats slid across the floor, bringing me close enough to see his eyes were green, no, blue, wait, gray? They looked versatile, changing with the colors he wore. In tan Khakis and peach pullover, they appeared turquoise: big, bright, tropical seas.

Skimming past bodies, drawing looks from customers acting as if I were a line-cutter, heated my face, but I didn't care. I was back on course. And this was a mission. The adrenaline I thought I'd depleted surged. Hopefully, the rush would remain hidden beneath my olive complexion.

A second barista appeared and the snaking line divided in two, stealing him further from my planned invasion. In a final attempt I closed in and stuck an arm between two women, excused myself, slipped up to the counter and snatched a couple of packets of sugar to go with my invisible coffee. I couldn't just glide up to him, but I could angle my body just the right way ... and that's precisely what I did.

Apparently, he noticed my maneuvers. "Mocha latte?" The slight curl of his lips angelic, but oh so sexy.

I found my voice, about to accept his gracious offer – when for some reason, as he gazed over my head the smile slid from his face like a dying sun. Then his luscious lips drew into a brittle line and his eyes were no longer on mine. The *reason* turned out to be a scrawny blonde who wedged herself between us, shot me a dirty look, then turned her back, completing the takeover in a slithering second. Talk about insults. Stuck up bitch, I wanted to scream as I slammed her in the jaw. With what had to be Divine Intervention, I kept my hands from balling at my sides and did neither. The pulse of my cell phone had to have been my saving grace.

Pete: Reminder. Movie night

Of course, I'd forgotten.

Me: Can't wait

Liar.

Pete: Dinner first @ Six

Me: Already starving

Pete: Laters

Me: Pete?

Pete: Yeah Kit Kat?

Me: Miss U

Pete: Miss u 2 babe

So, that was that. I left Kelly's without my latte fix, even more devastating, without making actual contact. I jogged ten blocks to the class for which I was about to be late. All for nothing! My ballets flew, coming to a squeaking halt before my classroom door. After this, I'd have cause to skip the gym. By the time I collapsed in my seat my feet ached, but my ballerinas bore the brunt of the mad dash. Professor Eidlehorn was in the middle of explaining why acid wouldn't permanently erase fingerprints. No one seemed to notice that I was panting. Maybe they just didn't care. I fought to focus, and ward off my professor's lethal breath when he leaned into me as he dropped an assignment in my lap.

"Highest grade in the class, Miss Delarosa." *Did he eat raw onions every morning?*

"Thank you, Jarrod." I felt odd calling him by his first name, but since he insisted ...

College Joe and our hijacked meeting haunted me: his face, her face, my agitation, clumped into a boiling knot in the pit of my stomach. But I couldn't let it eat me alive. If I was getting back in the game, about to deal with a bitch like her, I'd need to grow thick skin ... hard and fast ... show her – no him – who the better woman was.

Me & Pete

After class I went straight to work. Despite the hectic morning, the afternoon dragged.

I was decked out in finery. Dripping of someone else's money, I strolled up and down the luxurious aisles of AMA. Stilettos sinking into three inch thick carpet, I sifted through racks of designer originals, gorgeous fashions I'd love to own, but got to wear for free. It was part of my job. I had to look fantastic so I'd fit in with the wealthy. The wealthy whose clothes covered their inadequacies. Or so my grandma would say whenever I complained about my wardrobe. I'd never forget her words: "Jewelia ... you remember. It's not the clothes that make you who you are. Your beauty is on the skin you were born with ... and also beneath that lovely surface."

My grandparents were the most in love couple I'd ever known in my entire life. Totally opposite in ethnicity and disposition, they were mad about each other until the day they died, three months apart. I wondered if I'd ever find a love so strong that I'd want to die, like my grandpa did, if I lost my true soul mate.

"Always make sure he loves you more." I remembered

Grandma telling me with a nod and wink. By surrendering to death so close to hers, my physically fit grandpa proved he'd loved her more than life. I sighed and wiped a brimming tear from my duct before it had a chance to trace the curve of my nose.

Following my reverie, I felt a pang and needed a change of scene, so I took the escalator to the second floor, pausing to admire a rack of slinky dresses recently added to a spotlight display. After fingering silk, sequins and tulle, I moseyed into the hair salon where I grabbed a natural bristle hairbrush, then picked up a striking red lipstick instead.

Thanks to AMA, I'd become an impulse buyer. I had more odds and ends in my room than I had space for. Four p.m. finally rolled around and I was on my way home – in my own clothes and ballet flats, running for the bus.

When I walked through the door, Emma was in the kitchen making a stir fry. It smelled delish, but since I was eating out with Pete, I had to pass.

"Save me some leftovers. I'm taking a shower."

"You look beat." Her eyes were sympathetic, then their almond shape rounded. "So?"

"So what?" I huffed.

"How did it go? I half expected you to call ... or text. But when you didn't ... well, I guess I assumed ..."

The expression on my face must have warned, because she backed off.

I flopped into a chair in the living room. After munching on an apple while watching *Judge Judy* reruns, I hopped into the shower. Unable to hear the doorbell which Em answered, I paraded out with a towel slung low around my hips, hair dripping spray-on conditioner down my back, shoulders and chest. I figured I must have glistened like an icicle in a thaw, because Emma's eyes widened. Then her hand flew to her mouth, covering a gasp. Sitting beside her on the sofa, Pete sucked in a long breath, then returned a burst of air to the room in the form of a low wolf whistle.

"You have the body of a goddess, Jewel," he groaned, throwing a forearm across his forehead to fake a faint.

I cupped my breasts. "Eat your heart out."

"Oh, don't think I don't." He lifted a brow.

"Maybe if you'd wear your uniform you'd have a better chance," I teased, then padded into my bedroom to dress. He had a way of lifting my mood. But definitely not in the same way college Joe did.

Pete Williams was an NYPD rookie. Also a Criminal Justice major, he'd settled on the first job offer after graduation, which was a stepping stone to his career choice: Plain Clothes Detective. In his blues, Pete could knock anything or anyone off his feet, literally. Standing six three, and over two-hundred-twenty pounds of lean muscle, with a Latin look, he was hotter than August pavement at high noon. He was all American, but second generation Sicilian mixed well with Brit and Scot.

Emma and I ran into Pete one afternoon while he was on his corner beat. He tried to nail us for jaywalking, but ended up buying us drinks instead of issuing tickets. From that day on we forged the perfect triangle. Pete's loving soul was hard to resist, blending easily with Emma's compassion, and my lust for life and need to control every aspect of it. Our personalities may have ricocheted now and then, but we never really clashed.

Pete turned to Emma, who was dressed in workout sweats. "You coming with us?"

"Nah." Magazine on lap, she slid to the floor and stretched her hamstrings.

Besides being absolutely adorable, Pete had a definitive nature. Life was broken down categorically – cut and dried – yes or no. He wouldn't take *nah* for an answer.

"Get off the fence and come with us. Bring someone, Em. We'll make it a foursome."

"Scott's working and there's really no one else ..."

"Are you two an item yet?" Pete was relentless.

Emma pruned her lips. "Scott's an emergency escort.

Nothing more."

"Like Pete?" Standing beside the hunk occupying almost half of the sofa, I giggled, tweaked his bristly chin, then fell into his soft brown eyes.

"Not at all." Emma didn't move from her lotus position.

I grabbed Pete's arm and yanked. "Let's go. We're gonna be late."

Emma tore her stare away from *Elle* long enough to swipe a once-over. "You make the cutest couple." She winked. "Have fun."

We stopped at an Italian restaurant for pasta with marinara sauce, garlic bread and salads. Afterward, we hit up a candy store to bag some goodies to munch on during the show. As we strolled down West 54th, headed for the theater, I must have unconsciously been thinking about college Joe, because I barely absorbed Pete's jabber about work, complaining about the system, his salary, his temporary assignment on the corner of Madison.

"Hey," he said, flinging an arm around my shoulders, pulling me close. "So, what do you think, beautiful?"

"About what?"

"About my parents' cabin in Maine?"

Oops. His droning must not have been all about work. "Maybe. Why don't we talk about it later?"

"You can be such a drag sometimes. But I still love you." He planted a kiss atop my head.

Looking up at him, I smiled. I was lucky to have him. "I love you back, Pete. I always will." I slowed his stride, reached up and aimed my cherry red lips for his cheek.

During the two hour comedy, we put on our own show, laughing like idiots – at each other – not the flick. As usual, we sat in the back row.

"Open," Pete chirped.

Before I could turn, a buttery piece of popcorn slid down my cheek. "Pete, you'll get us kicked out. Again," with a mouthful, I mumbled as I swiped my face with a napkin.

"I'm a cop. I can do whatever I want." His next pitch landed in the row in front of us, making us giggle more.

A flash light beam hit our faces, and an usher stood before us, scowling. "Knock it off you two, or you're outta here."

I covered a laugh with my palm, while Pete said, "Sorry, man. It won't happen again." The moment the usher stepped away, Pete chuckled. "...until you leave," as he threw popcorn at the usher's back.

Sinking into my seat, I covered my face, giggling. "I don't know how I stand you. You're such a ball buster."

"Cause you love me." He batted his eyelashes, then his arm tightened around my shoulders, his head resting against mine. "You're fun to be with, Jewel. Helps take the load off life."

"Hey, are you doing alright? I mean, the job and all?"

"Sure." He kissed my cheek. "But I can't wait to lose the uniform."

"Shit. You heat those blues, baby," I teased, patting his thigh which felt solid beneath his jeans. "I'm having a great time, too." I pressed my cheek firmly against his, then settled back into the seat.

The movie ended and as we exited the theater the first thing to hit me was the invigorating smell of rain. Without hesitation, I led us into the middle of a thunderstorm. The sky flashed above us, thunder accompanying each bolt of lightning.

"Want to wait it out?" Pete was so thoughtful. "How convenient. There's a bar two doors away." He eyed me, shrugging one of his caterpillar brows.

"Hmm. I'm tempted." Damn early mornings. Whatever happened to freedom and irresponsibility? "I'd like to, Pete, but I'm beat. Let's make a run for it."

Pete's guiding arm went around me, shoving me under awnings, close to buildings we scooted past. When we ran out of overhead shelter, he held a big hand over my head.

By the time we reached my apartment, my hair was glued to my scalp, my clothes to my skin.

I fumbled through my bag, found my key and opened the door. Palms over mouths we fell through the doorway and into the foyer. The apartment was silent and dim. Emma's door was closed, no reading lamp bleeding from the bottom inch of white painted wood.

On my way to the shower, I offered Pete one of my tees, as he was as soaked to the skin as I was.

The door cracked open, and Pete poked his head in, stare glued to my foamy face. "I'll make us some tea. Lemon and honey?"

"Don't forget to scrub the lemon before you slice it. And just give it a good squeeze. Don't drop the rind in my cup."

He let out a good-humored sigh. "Of course, dear. I know you and bacteria don't mix." He rolled his eyes and shut the door.

Grinning, I lathered with scented wash and shampooed my hair, then padded into the kitchen, comfy and dry, sporting *Hello Kitty* sleep shorts and tank top.

Pete greeted me with a chuckle. "You look like a little kid."

"Sometimes I feel like one. Too bad life doesn't realize this."

"What are you talking about? Something wrong?"

I was tempted to vent my emotions, then decided against it. Pete was understanding, but I didn't feel comfortable confiding in him about college Joe. For sure he'd start the third-degree, which I wasn't up to. I had no idea what was going on, so how could I explain it to someone else?

Sitting at our small table, we shared tea and gossip we hadn't had a chance to dish during the movie. Cop talk was usually interesting, not to mention occasionally shocking.

"So you were the first one to find the victim?" Even though my body was tired, my eyes were wide awake. So was my mind.

"Yep. First on the scene." Cop talk always sobered Pete.

"Oh my God. How awful was it?" I remembered my grandmother resting in a casket and shuddered. Experiencing a natural passing was a far cry from witnessing a gunshot victim left bleeding to death in an alley.

"Hey. Don't flinch. You'll be encountering this stuff soon."

"With luck." With moist pink lips, I shot him a duck face to lighten the mood.

Reaching across the table, he patted my hand. "You'll get in, Jewel. Just flash that smile of yours." He winked then laughed. "And that dumb looking face."

"Hey," I protested his crude remark, throwing a spoon at him, then got serious. "Score high, you mean."

"Yeah, babe. You've got to. Lots of competition out there."

I scrunched my mouth and sighed. "Ugh. Forensic Science tomorrow. With Professor Blooming Onion."

Pete burst out laughing. "Who?"

"Eidlehorn. I swear, that guy must search for the most offensive breakfast foods on the market. His breath is a knockout."

"So are you." Pete grinned. "I remember that dude. Listen, doll. I'm gonna hit the road." He went to the sink, washed and dried his cup and placed it on a shelf. "Let you get some rest. You look beat."

I met him at the doorway and ruffled his hair. "You too, big guy." I poked one of his pecs straining through my borrowed shirt. "Lavender is your color. Keep the shirt."

His dramatic posedown stressed the shoulders and back. He tugged at the sleeves. "Geez. I'm about to burst through the seams. I don't know how you manage to squeeze into this, Jewel."

"Very funny." I swatted him. "Unlike you, mine's all up front."

"Haven't we all noticed." He peered over my shoulder. "Hmm. Not to underestimate the backside."

"Sometimes I think you just like me for my body." I backed him into the living room.

"And all this time, I've felt the same about your intentions."

Laughing, he followed me to my room, waited until I

crawled into bed, then tucked me under the covers. His lips were warm on my forehead. Plush and gentle. "Nite, sweetie." His breath was raspberry tea scented.

"You're so good to me, Petey." A sigh of contentment warmed my pillow. I curled up on my side. "I don't know what I'd do without you."

With a palm sinking into my mattress, he leaned in for a good night kiss. "You're the doll I always wanted. Someday I'll walk you down the aisle." His face took on the strangest look. "You're the only woman I've ever loved."

I knew Pete and his family weren't close, but until that moment, I never realized just how distant he and his mom were. What the hell was wrong with her? Pete was a sweetheart. To imagine him anything other than jovial made me sad. How could she not treasure him? I wanted to pull him down beside me, cuddle away every worry. But Nikos was the only man who had ever shared my bed.

"If I'm ever lying in some alley, I hope you're my first responder," whispering, I looked deep into his eyes. "I feel safe with you."

"You really know how to get to a guy."

My lids began to flutter. "Night, Pete," I mumbled, as a peaceful wave of sleep engulfed me. "I had a great time tonight."

"Ditto. I'll lock the door on my way out." His voice moved to the other side of the room.

My First Bike-A-Thon

The *bum bum* beat, blasting from the living room, jarred me from a scrumptious dream about college Joe.

"Oh God, Em!" I screamed.

Grumbling, I rolled out of bed.

The aroma of breakfast lit a fire under me as I dressed and entered the kitchen, carrying my helmet.

"Ready for the bike-a-thon, I see," Emma chirped, pouring orange juice into two glasses.

"As I'll ever be." I rolled my eyes. "How did I get into this anyway?" I grabbed a glass and let the cold O.J. flow down my dry throat, then looked down at my sleep-ravaged *Hello Kitty's*. "I haven't been on bicycle since I was a kid."

"Stop complaining. You're on the back of Pete's motorcycle all the time." Emma cracked two eggs into a sizzling frying pan. "You'll be fine." She swung her head to check out my spandex. "Make sure you're covered from head to toe. I don't want to be patching you up tonight, listening to you spout off profanity in Spanish."

"Who gives a shit about a few scrapes and bruises," I plucked a piece of toast from the toaster. "So what if I fall off my bike and look like an ass. It's for a good cause. Kids and illness should never be synonymous." The image of sick children made my heart sink.

***

Emma and I rode our bikes through city streets, bringing us uptown and into the park entrance, the starting point of the event. Emma was right. The day turned out to be perfect for outdoor activities. A cool breeze made the bright sun tolerable. And the humidity was low, thank goodness, because coated in sweaty spandex might prove as uncomfortable as holding a pee on a packed train car.

"Weee," I squealed, gaining the confidence to scoot in front of her. She laughed when my front wheel began to wobble as it sideswiped a rock in its path and I eased off the pedal to coast beside her.

"Careful, Jewel. Seems to be a traffic jam ahead. With so many bikes, concentration is essential. None of your classic clowning today." She twisted her head for an instant, shooting me a phony scowl.

Just ahead of us, two mountain bikes rested against trees, as far off the trail as shrubbery permitted. Masses of others pedaled past them. Emma and I appeared to be the only rubberneckers, gawking out of general curiosity, then stalled by the striking bodies of the two hot cyclists with the best butts I'd ever seen. Or was it the padding? Either way, these guys were impossible to ignore.

Without the need for words, Emma and I were in tune. We rolled up on our bikes a safe distance behind theirs and hopped off, prepared to offer our help should they need it.

"Holy shit." I tried to be as inconspicuous as possible while trying to fit my words between Emma's blue helmet and one of her ears. "It's him," I whispered. My sneakers sinking into spongy grass, I took a quick step back.

We whipped off our helmets simultaneously and set them on our bikes, ogling college Joe who lifted his buddy's rear wheel off the ground while the guy reattached the chain that hung loose at ground level.

"What did you say?" Emma whispered back.

My lips pressed to her ear. "College Joe. You know, the memory bank guy from Kelly's? Damn, I sent you his pic!"

"I'm not looking at his face." She grinned. "Are you gonna just stand there or do something already?"

"What would you like me to do?" I demanded. All I needed was for him to turn and see Em and me arguing. Why did things turn catastrophic whenever he was around? I looked toward heaven. "Grandma, is it you again?"

"What are you talking about?" Em cocked an ear.

"Nothing." My whisper came out harsh. "We can't just stand here, Em. Think of something, will you? Because I just spaced, and we look like two idiots posing here like this, mumbling to each other."

At that, we burst into stifled laughter, and things began to fall into place. We balanced our bikes against bordering trees, discreetly discussing exactly how to approach the opportunity.

"I can't believe this is happening." My heart bounced in my chest. "There's no way I'm gonna blow this chance." I managed to slow the rapid beats, but my stomach fluttered. "I feel like I have to take a ..."

"Don't." Emma held a hand over her mouth. "The look on your face is killing me."

"Thanks, friend."

"Well, pull yourself together, girl. I've never seen you this way."

"That's because I've never *been* this way, wise-ass."

"Don't get flippant, biatch."

During our entire exchange we lurked behind them, arms folded over our chests, looking like petite imitations of Pete when he leaned casually on his Harley. Only I wasn't casual. I was practically frantic. "How can I pull this off?"

He'd appeared interested at Kelly's coffee house, where from across a crowded room, my confidence level had soared. But we were now in the wide open park. Nothing around us but cyclists, sprouting foliage, and clear blue skies. I took a quick survey of the surrounding area. No blonde bimbo. *Yes! Okay, Jewel. You've got one shot at this.*

"First of all, stay cool." Emma looked comically bug-eyed.

"I'm trying." I grit my teeth. "Don't you know it's a scientific fact that people get angrier when you tell them to chill? So give me some good advice instead, before I explode."

Emma laughed at my exasperation. "Just do your thing, girl. I know you've got it in you."

I jabbed her arm and lifted a brow, making a mental note: do not suck on the inside of your cheek, or worse, chew on either one of your lips. "Here goes. Wish me luck."

"Good luck already." She gave me a send-off pat on my butt.

Taking a deep breath, faking cool and casual, I moseyed toward him. He must have sensed my approach, because he turned before I arrived at his side.

Still holding the bike off the ground gorgeous did a double-take as I approached, then quickly recovered from his state of shock. My heart thumped a few times, and my swallow went so deep it almost reached my stomach, which threatened to growl. Concerned about another banana peel incident, I became overly aware of the terrain and kept checking my feet, but each time I surfaced, his eyes were aimed at me.

I saw his head hitch left, hook right, even swing around behind him. Then I was the target again. He had the most talkative eyes I'd ever seen: come on, baby ‾ keep your distance ‾ move it, will you? ‾ hold it right there. Hell, his eyes wouldn't have let me take another direction if I'd wanted to.

His lips finally decided to spring into a grin. And there they were, up close and unfathomable ... those elusive eyes, trained on me as though I were a late flight. My legs could have buckled, but I was too stubborn to let them.

"Hey there," he said. The voice. I finally heard the voice without the interference of chattering customers. And just as I'd imagined: indulgent, saturating, a perfect match for the guy who'd left me speechless in Kelly's a few days earlier. But today I was determined to chew his ear off. Well ... at least be able to respond to him.

"Hey. Need help?" As if ... The only thing I knew about bikes was that they had two wheels and pedals.

"Sure. Whatcha got in mind?" One side of his grin grew more than the other, then he moved his attention from me to his friend who was wrapping the chain around the crank. "Let me know when you're ready. Need it higher?"

The way his biceps tightened, bulging through his shirt when his arms strained, was mind-blowing. And just looking *was* blowing my mind.

"Nah. It'll only take a minute," the friend replied, shooting a glance at me.

As if inspecting, I moved closer to the disabled bike, and Joe's side. "Broken chain, huh?" So dumb. It's obvious, you nitwit.

"Didn't snap." He faced me again, this time his eyes slipping from my smile to the skin-tight spandex I wore. "Just loosened up a bit."

I sensed his approval, but there was so much more going on behind his stare. I brushed my fingers through my helmet-headed hair attempting to fluff it into some sort of feminine aura. God, could this get any worse? "Oh. That's good. Can you fix it?"

He studied me for a moment, eyes sinking so deep, I almost fainted. "If not, what are the chances of snagging a ride on the back of yours?"

I felt my eyes bulge. "Um, well, I guess, uh ..."

He burst into laughter, and shook his head. "My buddy just needs to catch the teeth, then backpedal to lock it in place. We'll be back on the trail in a few minutes."

I shared his gaze with the tire. "I figured it was something like that."

He angled his head, one eye closed to block out the sun, the other squinting at me. "Sure you did." The tone of his voice was knee-weakening. Was he trying, or was he just naturally irresistible? My thoughts gave me no peace. Does he have a girlfriend?

In the distance a clear stream poured over rocks, around curves, disappearing behind a knoll. I longed to strip off my spandex, douse every inch of my body with cool water. By that point in our journey, I'd have been heading home for an ice-cold shower had it not been for college Joe.

His charcoal shirt deepened the gray in his eyes, highlighting the blue. He really *was* a gorgeous specimen: tall and powerfully built, with tousled hair, tanned skin, straight nose and full lips.

Shifting from foot to foot I watched him, feeling like gravel on a sidewalk, trying to drum up interesting conversation. "It's starting to get pretty hot," I said as I innocently gripped the bottom hem of my clinging T-shirt. I shook it away from my body, not intending to show off any part of my D cups, or skin. But from his angle, he might have caught a slice of my bare midriff. His double-take told me he liked every inch of what he saw.

"Sure is." Smiling, his gaze moved from my stomach to my face, and his lashes fanned those smoldering eyes, drawing me too close for comfort. "Yeah ... " he nodded, "I remember you from Kelly's," slipped easily through his lips, and I almost fainted on the spot. "Who could forget someone like ... a fellow mocha latte drinker." Then his expression grew guarded, and he turned away, fidgeting with the tire before lowering it to the ground. I thought he flushed, but it could have been the rising heat of the day.

He had to be used to girls flocking to his side on a daily basis. Daily? How about hourly.

He was like the 18K gold necklace I longed for, something I might be able to caress, but never call my own. Why was I even bothering? Then I heard my dad's words, with the utmost affection and pride, telling me, "Jewelia, you're a scrapper. A survivor." What the hell? I was here. Why not? I might as well live up to my name and make him proud ... but the thoughts brewing in my head made me cringe. Don't listen, Dad

Perspiration glistened on college Joe's forehead and neck. He must have finger-brushed his hair again, because it fell in disarray. I longed to reach up and run my fingers through it, but instead, cleared my throat.

"Would you like a bottle of water? I have some ..." I motioned to my bike, and Emma, who hadn't moved from beneath the cover of an elm branch.

"Sure. I could use a break. We've been riding since sunrise."

"Sunrise?" I gulped. "Either you wanted to get an early start ... or we're very late."

He chuckled. "I rode my bike down from Westchester. We hit some trails before heading over here."

The wheels inside my head started spinning, scheming another accidental run-in. Being near this guy wiped every ounce of reason from my mind. I had to make sure this moment turned into more than just a fleeting conversation. "Oh, so you must bike a lot then."

"Every chance I get." When he slowly rocked his head, he looked so sexy. "But you ... something tells me you'd rather be cruising in your Porsche, right?" He winked, and swiped his forearm across his hairline.

"Yeah, sure. That would be me. Touring Manhattan in my 911." I giggled.

He chuckled again, then his face lit up. "Cycling's amazing. Fresh air. Great for the body. Perfect for getting as close to nature as possible."

As close to *you* as possible ... I pictured myself in his arms, and butterflies filled my stomach. "Keeps you healthy. Like taking long walks after dinner, I guess. Good for digestion and all." I shrugged. *Talking about bodily functions? Next you'll be telling him you sometimes pass gas when you do sit-ups.*

"Yeah, a nice jog is a good alternative." He winked. "After digestion."

I felt my cheeks flush, and had to pull myself together

before I started babbling more nonsense. *Deep breath. Cute smile.* "Now if you were talking beaches," I pressed my lips together, showing off my dimples, "salty breeze, watching moonlit waves," I nodded, "yeah, then I'd be more likely to go further

... jogging, I mean."

"So you're a beach bunny, huh?" His arms crossed his chest, and he lifted a brow.

I tossed my head, then twirled a lock of hair around my finger. "I guess you could say that."

Indigo

College Joe's friend stood and stretched his back, then brushed his hands off. "I think it'll hold." His attention turned to me, his eyes taking the same path Joe's had taken not more than five minutes earlier. "Hey," he said. "How's it going?" As he spoke he flexed the muscles of his neck, creating a flirty head-jerk. I couldn't help but notice how Joe observed his every move, kind of calculating, but remained silent.

"Hey. I'm Jewelia." I held out my hand. Ready to do Emma the biggest favor of her life, and let him know he wasn't my choice, I bopped my head in her direction. "That's Emma up there, holding up that tree."

He chuckled and his eyes followed mine. Apparently Emma had been watching, because the smile I'd left her with lingered, but now her brow arched. I gave her *the eye*, hoping she'd hurry over before the opportunity died.

"How are you doing, Jewelia? I'm Bill." He gripped my hand. His attention, suddenly captured by Em, seemed to tighten his expression, along with his fingers that almost crushed mine. *Am I missing something here?*

"I'm great," I replied, although I seemed to be the last thing on his mind.

College Joe stood at his side, still taking it all in, then dropped himself into the conversation. "I'm Indigo." He took a step forward and reached for my hand. I scrutinized his gaze, imagining him to be thinking, "Where have you been all my life?"

The concept, and physical contact, jolted me. "Nice to meet you." My voice was as light as the breath I was holding.

"Jewelia ..." Surrounded by his deep voice, I'd just been airbrushed by my own name. "Jewelia ..." he deliberated, "very pretty." The purse of his lips made it sound prettier than ever.

"Indigo ... unusual." I must have appeared confused, because he immediately pointed out with a grin, "My name is James Ballou ... properly pronounced, *blue*, which obviously morphed into Indigo," he let out the cutest combination of a humph and chuckle, "and it stuck. My friends rarely call me James."

"Then Indigo it is." I was lost in his eyes. "My friends call me Jewel."

Aware of the grip of our hands even after we'd finished speaking, our fingers loosened, hesitated, then grudgingly unlocked.

Emma appeared at my side and I grabbed her arm, offering an enthusiastic introduction. However, Emma needed no intro. Neither did Bill.

"Emma?" After breathing out her name, Bill's entire face broke into a smile.

"Billy..." She choked his name as though it had been lodged deep in her throat, like a caged butterfly finally free to fly.

"Billy Arkana." She seemed to be struggling with her lips.

Indigo's brows crunched. "Billy Arkana? What happened to William Addison?"

Tearing his eyes from Emma's, Bill turned to Indigo and smirked. "Texas rock star days."

Arms folded over his chest, Indigo burst out laughing. "Arkana. Creative."

Bill fanned out his arms. "What can I say?"

"No need to explain ... Billy." Indigo turned to me and

grinned. His stance was relaxed, his long legs slightly spread in the masculine way that made women drool, creating such a stir in my tummy I had to fight the urge to close in on him.

"How long has it been, Billy?" Emma shifted his attention back to her, and only her.

"Too long." Excitement edged Bill's voice. "It's so good to see you. I can't believe I ran into you in New York, Em. How have you been?"

"Life's been good. I'm a clinical psychologist." She let out a quick breath. "I work for the State."

"I always knew you could do it ..." Bill was behaving as though Emma had invented the coffee bean.

"Yup." She beamed. "What about you?" Before he could reply, she held up a hand. "Don't tell me. Science teacher. Am I right?"

"I'm into drugs," Bill said, brushing a hand through his hair. The other dropped onto his hip.

Em stiffened, then took a step back.

I recoiled. "Huh?"

"He just pushes them." Arms still folded across his chest, legs still spread in that enticing stance, Indigo appeared calm and in control, obviously amused by our reactions to Bill's statement. Or was it an admission? I was totally confused ... and concerned. Em's face said she agreed. And did she look disappointed.

"Pharmaceutical rep." Bill smirked.

I felt the sigh of relief Em let out.

"He likes to shock people with the drug line." As he watched his friend in action, Indigo kept shaking his head. "In reality, he's a nerd."

"Look who's talking. I'm surprised you left the kids long enough to ride today." Bill wore a perpetual grin. When Indigo's eyes cut into him, he palmed his forehead. "I forgot, you're the organizer."

The kids? Don't tell me he's married, and Bill slipped.

Indigo's expression clouded. Angling his head over my

shoulder, his stare fixed on the cyclists.

Bill took a bottle of hand sanitizer from his pack and offered it to Indigo, who still hadn't recovered from his mood swing. Maybe the tag, Indigo, was appropriate for more than one reason ... *dark blue ... dark side.*

Perspiration drizzled across Bill's forehead, the line of his wavy dark hair that fringed his ears. "I could use a break," he said, reaching for his water bottle. "Join me?" he directed to Emma, who joyfully obliged, following him to an area shaded by willows.

"You haven't changed." I heard her giggle. "Do you still rock out with the band?"

"Nope. Haven't in forever." He sounded bummed.

Indigo shot me a questioning glance. My eyes unintentionally lowered, and I managed to control a quiver in my bottom lip. He tilted his head, then took my hand, and we tagged along, clutching our water bottles. We found a shady spot beside a sparkling stream, and the four of us dropped onto the grass in a loose circle.

"So, you girls live in the city?" Indigo's eyes moved from me to Emma, then dove back into mine.

Em and I nodded. "Uh huh."

"And you?" I asked, addressing both guys, but focusing openly on Indigo.

When we all established we had apartments within a ten mile radius we laughed.

"I can't believe we're almost neighbors and have never run into each other before," Bill marveled. "And girls like you two would be difficult to miss, even in a crowded city. So how did this happen?" He slung an arm around Emma's shoulder.

"It must be fate." I'd never seen Emma flirt before. It was refreshing. "Tears you apart ... brings you back together again. Kind of how the ocean drags shells out to sea, then brings them back to shore ... dredging up what could have been buried forever had it not been for the strength of the tide."

"I actually *almost* met Jewel." Indigo's side glance looked apprehensive.

"So, this is the mysterious beauty I've been hearing about for weeks?" Bill slapped his knee. "I'll be damned."

Mysterious beauty? What the hell? Listening to Bill, my eyes widened, and if capable of sound they would have snapped, *Huh?* directly into Indigo's ... but his stunned stare was not pointed at me.

Indigo looked like he wanted to sew Bill's mouth shut, his glare bringing his friend's perfunctory disclosure to a halt. With a grinning shrug, Bill turned to concentrate on Emma, whose eyes roamed over every inch of him, pulling him back each time his gaze shifted even slightly. Bill whispered something in her ear, and the next thing I knew, they disappeared.

Indigo and I sat side by side. The brush of his leg against mine caused a shockwave. I unleashed my ponytail, shaking out my hair, then palms on the ground I stretched my arms behind my back, tossed my head up, drank in the day. I could feel Indigo's eyes absorb the lines of my elongated neck, the exaggerated arch of my spine which in turn emphasized my chest. I wondered if my sprouting nipples could be detected through my cotton sports bra and lightweight T-shirt.

Beneath me the grass felt like velvet. I watched Indigo's fingers pluck blades, tossing them idly into the air, and imagined how his touch would feel on my skin. I almost shuddered.

"What did he mean?" I swung my head in Bill's direction. "When he said something about leaving the kids?" As I asked, my stomach lurched, worrying about what his answer might be.

"Hospital rotation ... I'm in the children's wing this month." His stare cooled, shifting to the cloudless sky.

There was that distressing look again. Was he hardened by life or just overburdened by it?

"Tough, huh? Not much free time and all that ..." I was already gauging how many leftover hours, and how much energy, there'd be for me.

He blew out a sigh that sounded unanticipated, then drew

a deep breath. "Yup. Occupies almost twenty-four-seven." His words were steady, matter of fact, as if industrious was his accepted way of life and would never be debated. "Exams in a couple of months. Then I have some downtime until I start my residency."

He looked at me. Really looked at me, and his expression softened so drastically, I felt as though he wanted me to share his innermost thoughts. To listen. Understand. Confide in me? Was I getting to him?

"So what do you do in your free time?" I gazed at him with lowering lids.

"I spend a lot of time at the Hamptons. Correction. I used to." The way he tilted his head, his ever-changing expressions, his fingers stroking the blades of grass cropping up between us, was driving me insane.

"Nice." My nose pointed skyward. I closed my eyes, giving my imagination free reign.

"It's a great place to relax. Have fun. Whatever ..." His voice trailed off. "My family has a summer home there."

"Ah. A rich boy. So, you must be used to getting what you want." I smirked.

His glare cut right through me. "Not everything in this life has a price tag."

"I ... I'm sorry. I was teasing. I didn't mean to sound ..."

"Don't worry about it." His lips broke into a heart-melting grin. "I'm sure a girl like you can say just about anything and get away with it. You have a face that would be hard to get mad at."

This guy came off as so cool, he could charm every layer of skin off a snake till he hit bone. But his eyes. Those crystal eyes were deceptive. They were anything but cool. They were deep, they were clear, then they were guarded, sweltering with secrets.

"Stay right there ..." the tone of his voice startled me, and I almost freaked when he brought his face in for a kiss. Keeping my composure, I didn't purse or part my lips, but I did lift my head and close my eyes, waiting for his mouth to crush mine.

However, his thumb didn't tug down my bottom lip; his lips didn't cover mine. Instead, his thumb and forefinger snatched a stray lash from my cheek. When my lids sprang open, he held it to my lips. "Make a wish."

For more than one reason, I let out a puff of air.

He tucked a lock of hair behind my ear. "I hope it comes true."

"Not as much as I do." My eyes glued to his, I grinned.

As I gazed, I contemplated. Of course I'd been immediately attracted to the challenge that had to come with a guy like him. But there was something beyond the occasional ice in his blue eyes. Something that cried to break free of the broodiness. I wanted to be the one to open the door. Find out what was hidden deep inside him.

"You have the most amazing eyes, Jewel; like dusk sprinkled with rays of sunshine."

"Funny. I was just admiring yours."

From somewhere in the distance, I heard Emma call out my name. The sight of Bill's arm around her waist gave me goose bumps.

"Guess break time's over." Sighing, Indigo stood and brushed grass from his butt. He grasped my hands and pulled me up and against his chest. His scent, something like an ocean breeze, took my breath away. I wanted to be crushed in his arms and kissed until time stopped. To make him want me as much as I wanted him. To sink back onto the blanket of grass. Light his skin on fire. Make him moan with ecstasy. I lifted my eyes to his, and for a split second, felt as though I'd dipped into his soul. He held me for a long moment while his eyes filled with longing, then he released me abruptly.

I stifled the tremor that threatened my limbs, and mumbled a weak, "Thanks." Feeling the rise of a flush, I drew a deep breath.

"Any time." He smiled down at me, but something had changed. Our moment had ended. "Hold on," he called to

Bill. "I've got to lose one of these shirts." In a smooth, crisscross maneuver, he brought his gray Henley up and over his head. His blue tee slid with it, but was snagged by the span of his shoulders, exposing a sleek physique. It appeared I'd been right: a delicious tan covered every inch of visible skin, even dipping into the waistband of his shorts. With a twist of his torso he shook free of both shirts, in the process showing off his ink. That's when my internal flutters began tripping over one another, working their way to my throat.

A few ribs below his own heart was a tattoo of a bright red bleeding heart. The tat was beautiful ... sad. Was he sad? Who was she? I wondered. The girl who'd been such an important part of his life that he'd tattooed her heart beneath his. Or was it *his* heart turned inside out? Was he still bleeding for her?

I strained to examine it further, but in a moment he replaced the tee shirt, cloaking the tattoo as he tugged the cotton fabric down over his muscular chest. But I did notice a black Byzantine cross on his right arm before he shrugged everything back into place. The guy was delish. I wondered what else might be hidden under his clothes. He was the gift I was dying to unwrap.

He stared down at me, his eyes now heather, faceted by afternoon sunshine. Mine felt like saucers, unblinking. It was as though neither of us knew what to say. Still, our eyes spoke. Mine roamed every inch of his face again and again, while his worked slowly ... only once.

After this ... how could we just say goodbye?

From a side glance I glimpsed Emma and Bill, in the process of strapping on their helmets, the entire time talking. Emma wore a coy smile; she seemed to be doing her thing. It was obvious today was their beginning. He towered over her slight, but curvy frame. Picking up her bike, he steadied it as she slipped onto the seat. Their actions seemed to be our cue: make a move or leave.

I was captured by a flurry of wind that intoxicated me with Indigo's scent. "It's beautiful here. I'll have to use this trail again." I gazed up at him, expectation clinging to my jaw line. "I think I'm going to be doing a lot more cycling."

"Maybe we'll run in to one another again. Bill and I ride most weekends, if time permits." His eyes were shaded, even in bright daylight, they shadowed.

"Mabes." My shrug was careless.

I had just been blown off. My heart sank. I turned to take a step, intending to finish this ride, then hit the first frozen yogurt stand to cross my path. But would extra fudge and whipped cream erase my memory of him?

Things moved in slow motion. Emma began flagging me, and the next thing I knew I felt Indigo's hand on my shoulder. I couldn't move. There I stood like a lamp post, until his fingers tightened and he eased me around to face him.

"Jewel ..." My name was an airy rush. "I doubt we'd be able to hang together out there," he motioned to the wheels spinning past us, "but Bill and I usually stop at Kelly's after riding." Those deeply faceted eyes were vibrant as they caressed my face, slowly, seductively.

Holy shit. He didn't have to speak, or move. Just standing before me – the look on his face, the purse of his lips still molded with my name – was enough to push me over the edge. *Grandma, how much more can I take? Did Grandpa have this effect on you?* I so wished I could text her.

Indigo was incredibly handsome and totally irresistible ... and he was standing inches away, making my legs weaker than a cup of tea brewed with a used tea bag. Talk, Jewel. For shit sake, you've never been tongue-tied in your life.

"Race you back." I was breathless.

He grinned. "You're on."

Kelly's

Everything happened so fast I didn't remember walking away, but I must have looked like a neon flash as I stuck my head into my helmet and lifted my bike.

"We're meeting up with them later." With a racing heart, I told Emma.

"I know." She smiled slyly.

I flipped Indigo a wave as he and Bill merged into the lane of other cyclists, then confronted Em. "You little bitch. What's going on?"

"I'm so psyched." Her cheeks looked like ripe apples.

"Yeah. I can see that. Spill it."

"It's a long story ... let's not waste time now. I'll tell you about it tonight."

"I already get it. He's someone out of your deep, dark past. I just need the whys and hows."

Her eyes were shooting off crazy sparks. "I knew him ... we ... I ..."

"Oh, Em." Reaching out, I patted the side of her helmet. "It's squashed all over your face. Come on." I squeezed her arm, then threw a leg over the uncomfortable seat. "Let's not let them get too far ahead of us." My words held a double meaning.

By the time our wheels rounded the familiar streets of Manhattan, I was exhausted. A drooping flower, I needed refreshment.

"What do you think about quick showers?" I asked Em. I wanted to look, and smell, my best when I met up with Indigo. "Should we risk it?"

"Absolutely not. I don't want to miss them."

"Don't you think Billy Arkana," I couldn't resist teasing, "will wait for you?"

"I'm not taking any risk of losing him again."

"You're in love. I can't believe it. Just remember, I can't afford the rent on my own. Not yet, anyway."

"Oh, stop it." Her apple cheeks bulged.

Em and I locked our bikes into the rack a few doors down from Kelly's and quickly lost the helmets. We shook out our hair, dabbed our faces with tissues and, helmets cradled, sauntered into the café, cool as two ripe cucumbers ready for peeling.

Still fluffing my flattened locks, I elbowed her. "How do I look?"

"Sexy and overheated. How about me?"

"Hot and sweaty."

"Do I smell?" Em's face twisted with panic.

I sniff-tested the air around us, praying our deodorant had survived the day. "Hmm. Nothing out of the ordinary, but why didn't I spray on something enticing this morning?" After evaluating her distress, I reconsidered. "Nah. We're good."

I zeroed in on them first, sitting across from one another at a booth near a back window of the café. The Henley Indigo had removed once more covered his pale blue T-shirt, and his hair was neatly combed.

Conscious of dreaded helmet-head, I swept a few loose strands back into my ponytail, but let the springy tendrils dangle in front of my ears, and didn't touch the baby soft wisps above each temple.

Indigo watched our approach attentively. As we neared, his shoulders lifted with an inhale and I could have sworn he blew out relief. His lips curled slightly, his eyes sending messages. My stomach tightened. By the time Em and I reached the table, both guys were standing like gentlemen, motioning for us to slide into the booth first.

"Hey." I tried to sound breezy.

"Hey." The tone of his voice was rich.

I followed the sweep of his arm and slid onto the padded bench. Indigo settled beside me and spoke to my profile. "So, does this mean you two are buying?" He took my helmet from my lap and reached over me, setting it on the window ledge next to his.

When his arm brushed my boobs, a chill shot down my spine. The side of his chest felt warm, firm but caressible. The day had brought such surprises, I felt like I was dreaming. His fresh, nautical scent wafted into my nostrils, snapping me into reality.

I made a quarter turn in the direction of his voice. "Sure. A round of water for everyone."

Bill let out a laugh.

"She's not joking," Emma chuckled, looking snuggly beside Bill who stowed her helmet with his.

Indigo pressed his index fingers to his temples. "Don't tell me. You took the scenic route."

"What, did you two get here like, five minutes ago? Because the gears on your bikes are still warm." Gears are still warm? I had no idea what I was talking about, but it sounded good.

Indigo laughed. "Oh, a gear-watcher. Thanks for the heads up. I'm really going to have to watch those gears from now on ... make sure they don't overheat again. I don't want to break down in the park, or in the middle of Madison Avenue."

Bill and Emma started cracking up.

A heavyset guy who looked in his fifties approached, giving me a chance to cope with my awkward moment.

"Hey, Indigo." He paused beside us, big hands on hips, his gaze zigzagging the table.

"How are you doing, Mike?" Indigo put out a hand.

"Can't complain. How are the classes coming?"

"I'm doing rotations." Indigo's face lit with a grin.

"Geez, time flies. Soon to be a licensed MD. Bet your folks are overjoyed. How are they?"

A brief disturbance dimmed Indigo's light. If something had troubled him, he recovered well. "They're great. Just got back from the British Virgin Islands."

"Must be nice." Mike grinned and shook his head. For a moment his eyes looked vacant. "Your dad had the right idea. Too bad I didn't take a similar path. Who are your friends?"

Indigo rested his hand on my shoulder; his touch felt lighter than in the park, but every bit as electric. "Jewel, this is Mike Kelly, the owner of this rockin' coffee house." His forearm tensed just long enough to make the introduction, then drifted back to the table top, aligning with his other. For a casual meeting, there was a lot of physical contact going on. Imagine a date? I wondered if he was feeling it too.

"Hello, Mike." I was formal, but warm. "This is Emma."

"Nice to meet you ladies." Mike smiled. "I'll get a waiter over here." He swung his gaze back to Indigo. "Tell your folks I send my best, and next trip, I'd like an invite." He winked at me, then with a straight back, strode away.

"So he's close with your family?" I asked.

Indigo's stare followed Mike until he disappeared behind the counter, then he turned to me. "He and my dad spent eight years together in the Marines. They touch base now and then."

"Do your parents ever come here?" I wanted to know if I should be looking over my shoulder.

The look on his face was strained. "My parents don't go many places together."

"I thought they just got back from the Virgin Islands?"

"It was a business trip. They don't do much for pleasure." A hint of a frown reshaped his beautiful lips.

A waiter appeared, took our order, then in hushed tones, we fell into private conversations.

"What do you do, Jewel?" Indigo asked.

"Finishing school." I shifted, bringing the side of my leg onto the seat so I could face him. "And I work at AMA."

He did a slight recoil and gaped. "You're in the medical profession?"

I instantly made the connection. Was he pulling a snobatude with me? "Hell no. I work security at Abigail Mitchell Apparel while I finish two classes at Jay. I hope to be part of NYPD soon." My words bounced through the narrow space between us.

His eyes widened further. "Awesome. Can you take care of a few hundred parking tickets?" he teased.

"Time will tell." I grinned. "So are you specializing?"

"I am. In pediatric medicine ... possibly research."

"Wow. No wonder your parents are thrilled," I tried not to gush. "That's some accomplishment."

"Yeah, I guess. But it was a given. My dad's a surgeon. I have two uncles who are physicians." His face filled with conviction. "I grew up knowing I'd be a doctor."

"Regimented, huh? So, you come here same time every morning?" I tilted my head.

"A few minutes before ... sometimes a minute or two after seven. Either way, I have to check in at the hospital by seven-thirty."

"Well you know what they say ..." What does *who* say? I was winging it.

Half of his mouth curved, like the first day I saw him, and I almost melted. "What do they say?" He cocked his head.

Our faces were so close, I could have sucked in his breath if I raised my head, which I finally did. His eyes bore into mine; clear gray, glimmering with amusement.

I shrugged my brows, becoming philosophic, "A minute too early ... a minute too late ... either way ... you won't catch the train." *Great save. Thank you, Grandma.*

"True. Which proves timing is everything." With a curved brow, he smiled and nodded. His elbow rested on the table, thumb and forefinger cupping his chin. "Does that slice of wisdom apply to all modes of public transportation? Because now I'll be thinking of you whenever I'm waiting for a cab, or trying to find a seat on the bus."

"How flattering." I smirked.

"I try my best."

"Was that your sister the other morning?" I was dying to know what part the possessive blonde played in his life.

His face went blank, his brows forming the elevens I staved off with glycolic facials, and by avoiding expressions like the one that claimed his face after I asked the question.

"The other morning when we were in line together. I was getting sugar ... you mentioned mocha latte ..." Come on, Jewel. You can do better than that. "The tall girl with the long blonde hair ..."

His elevens deepened. Then his face took the same troubled shape as the day the bitch wedged her body between us.

"You're talking about Vanessa."

"I don't know her name ... well I didn't ..."

"Vanessa's far from my sister." Rolling his eyes, he chuckled.

Go on ... my stare, and my silence, both shouted.

His eyes searched my face, which I knew looked grim. "Vanessa and I go way back. We were next door neighbors ... kind of close growing up. You know, kid stuff and all."

"Yeah. I have siblings ... and childhood friends ..."

"Vanessa was a tomboy, always trying to fit in with the boys."

"Or between," I couldn't stop the crude remark.

He looked surprised, then apologetic. "She's got a way about her."

"She sure does. Almost took the tips of my toes off." I faked a laugh that was way too stiff.

"In her defense, she's been through a lot." His tone mimicked mine. "I'm sure she didn't realize."

I'm sure she did, my brain echoed, but go on, my gaze said.

"Her parents passed away when she was fourteen, and she was shipped off to the Midwest to live with an aunt and uncle. Her world was torn apart."

He was defending her rude behavior ... what ... ten years later? Were her childhood claws still embedded? Was the heart tattooed to his chest *hers*?

"She managed to pull her life together though," he continued, almost admiringly, "moved back a couple of years ago and seems to be doing well."

"That's nice." I so didn't mean my polite words. "Are you still close?" Stop now, before you stick your foot in your big mouth.

He drew a deep breath, like the world was so weighty, and breathing would ease the strain. His eyes were almost constantly shadowed, which saddened me.

"She's closer with my mother. I don't see her often. Just when she stops by the house."

Great. Vanessa and Mrs. Ballou were tight. Vanessa obviously still had a deep-seeded interest in Indigo, and Mother was no doubt her cheerleader. Better to let the subject drop, like my face.

I watched the waiter emerge from the kitchen, a tray on his shoulder bearing our burgers, chicken fajitas, fries and drinks. The food smelled delish and I was starving. I had to remind myself to smile – and take small bites.

Indigo broke the silence when he let out a laugh. He dabbed his lips with a paper napkin. "Ah, the pleasant sounds of munching." He trailed a fry across a splatter of ketchup on his plate, then popped it into his mouth. "Somebody say something, please. All I hear is Arkana over there, gobbling his burger." He flipped another fry across the table. It bounced off Bill's arm.

Sealing my lips with a napkin, I giggled. "Be careful of what you ask for." I drew a sip of iced tea through my straw. "We'll be spitting food all over each other if we forget our table manners. Emma knows what I'm talking about."

A hand flew to Emma's mouth, subduing a bite of chicken. She nodded in double-time. "Umm," was all she could mumble. I knew she was visualizing the food fights in our kitchen whenever Pete was around.

Bill snorted. "I'll be sure to talk with my mouth full next time I'm having dinner at your house, Ballou. I'm sure your mother would appreciate that."

Indigo frowned. "You wouldn't be the first of my friends she tossed out of the house."

Not Vanessa, that was for sure. Oh, God. What was Indigo's mother like? The thought of the *mother challenge* had never occurred to me until that moment. At the concept of a future meeting, my fries began attacking my fajita ... inside my tum. With Vanessa up her butt, dear Lord, for sure his mother would look down her nose at me. On the flip side, I wondered if she was one of those: *no woman is good enough for my son,* mothers. Sort of like my dad was with anyone I dated, but in that antagonistic way in which dads were so proficient; frightening the hell out of a date without uttering a word.

Intruder Alert

*T*he meal was over. I sank into the booth, emotionally drained from overanalyzing everything, and sighed. "This turned out to be quite a day."

"Yeah, it was a good ride ... enjoyable ..." Indigo neatly arranged his glass and utensils on his plate, then tossed his balled-up napkin on top. "You should think about signing up for the next one." His words were more of a request than suggestion.

"The next one?" I gulped.

"We're riding for Juvenile Diabetes next month."

"Are you a promoter or something?" My eyes strained.

"Yep. It's the last semester of med school and rather than behaving like drunken savages," he chuckled, "some of us decided to put our free time, although limited, to a better use. Cycle For Health. An organization we cooked up." He grinned. "Doing things for sick kids, keeping healthy ones on the right track." His eyes were soft, his voice genuine.

"That's really amazing, Indigo."

"Kind of like you being a cop, Jewel. We'll both be public servants." He winked.

Without trying, this guy kept blowing me away, piece by piece. How much more could I take before I crawled into his lap and planted a kiss on those inviting lips? It was said, the way to a man's heart was through his stomach. In my female opinion, tenderness was more masculine than bulk. And this guy had both. I analyzed his hands, so clean, so strong, so steady. Precise: that was it.

Those sensitive hands would love a woman. Heal sick children. The girl who landed Indigo would be fortunate. He seemed to be everything anyone with half a brain could ever want. And I wanted him with all of my brain, all of my body. From the first moment I set eyes on him, something said, "He's the one." But I doubted he'd be in the market for a serious relationship for a long time.

I saw Bill lean close to Em's ear and figured he was asking for her number. Sure enough, as her mouth moved, his fingers pushed buttons on his phone. I wondered if Indigo would ask for my number. The day was winding down. So was I. A gnawing letdown began to dampen my mood, but I maintained the grin that felt pasted on my face as I pushed my plate closer to the center of the table.

"Looks like it's time to hit the trail." I handed Indigo his helmet, then reached for mine.

"Thanks. I really had fun today." His eyes scrolled over my face, as though he was memorizing every feature he studied.

"Me too. I hope you know this meal calls for three more hours of suffering at the gym." I grimaced.

"Or another day of cycling." His eyes stalled on mine.

I waited for an invitation, but all he said was, "I ..." and hesitated as he held his helmet on his thigh, flipping the strap back and forth as though contemplating one of the biggest decisions of his life. Then without notice he slid from the seat and stepped aside, waiting for me to slip out.

The sun, diving behind high-rise buildings, burned streaks of purple and red in the fading blue sky. Shoulder to shoulder, Emma and Bill strolled to their bikes. Separated by mere inches, Indigo and I tagged along. He cradled his helmet. I swung mine.

When Indigo tilted his head, his eyes were once more clear

blue. "So, what do you do on weekends?"

I blinked up at him. "Umm. Church and ... sometimes I visit my family in Poughkeepsie."

Eyes never leaving mine, he nodded slowly.

"You?" I tried to relax my facial muscles.

"Dinner with the family now and then. Sometimes an early movie for downtime before the chaos strikes again."

"With your parents?" My voice hitched.

He chuckled. "I don't go to the movies with my parents." With the softest touch, he lifted strands of hair caught in my lashes. "Do you have plans for tomorrow?"

"I don't normally plan." *Liar* ... "I'm spontaneous."

He laughed. "I should have seen that coming." His tone deepened. "Maybe you're on to something. I imagine acting on impulse can be a lot more exciting than plans that don't always work out."

We walked toward our bikes, our bodies so close our arms brushed. Indigo took my hand, gently bringing me to a halt. "Jewel ..." When I angled my head, his eyes bore into mine. "I'd really like to ..."

When he began lowering his face to mine, my heart started thudding. I wondered if he could feel the pulse through my hand. The emotion cutting through his gaze was enough to make me tremble. But my mouth relaxed, while my lips parted, waiting for the best *first* kiss of my life.

Maybe it was the falling dusk, the warmth of Indigo's fingers clutching mine, the overpowering sensation flowing between us. Whatever it was, it was magic.

Indigo inched closer, and my stomach dipped with excitement. I felt his soft breath as our lips almost touched, then the growl of an engine broke the moment, and the Harley quieted beside the curb. I whipped my head around to see Pete in the process of swinging a leg over the bike.

"Pete..." I held my voice to a low screech.

Leaning against the bike with crossed arms, bulging biceps, equally large triceps, Pete struck his usual tough-guy pose. He wore jeans and boots and a black muscle T-shirt. And he was pumped. His shades were pulled up onto his forehead, his longish hair coiled. He looked like one delicious hunk. And he was staring directly at me. Then his stare glided deliberately from face to face, and a smirk plucked at his masculine jaw line.

"What's up?" He focused on me with heavy lids, and performed a head-hitch that could have snapped his neck if not for the straining tendons supporting it.

Indigo drew back, his stare sliding from me to Pete. I could feel his confusion, the tension hanging in the air.

Pete's obnoxious behavior was horrifying. "Just back from the bike-a-thon." I kept my tone even.

Pete rolled his shoulders. "How was it?"

"Terrific," Emma called to him. "What are you up to?"

"Not much. I would've joined you, but ..." He slapped the Harley's leather seat with his palm. I watched his eyes rake over Indigo then trip over Bill before working their way to Em. He shot her his usual disarming grin.

"And how did *you* find today?" As he returned to me, the smirk on his face said he intended to say, what did you *find* today.

I peered up at Indigo, whose face was inflexible. "The wise-guy is Pete." Then I called out in a strong voice, "Peter, this is Indigo."

"Unique name." Pete unfolded from his protective stance and strode toward us.

"Unique bike." Indigo countered, standing his male ego ground.

"Is yours over there?" Pete motioned to the rack Emma and Bill stood beside, as if guarding, or ready to make an escape.

Pete's condescending attitude was pissing me off. I shot him the evil eye, but he ignored me.

"One of my bikes." Indigo's voice dropped an octave.

Pete cocked his head.

"I've got one something like yours out in the Hamptons."

"Oh shit," I mumbled under my breath, wondering, *Does Indigo think–*

Pete's expression broke with a shred of appreciation as his head hitched again, this time his eyes wide, evaluating Indigo from head to toe. "We'll have to ride someday."

My face flamed. I wanted to smack Pete so badly. He was behaving like a jackass.

Disregarding Pete's invitation, Indigo turned to me. He had defended his honor with Pete, but when his eyes searched mine, I had a sickening feeling he was about to bail ... and I'd never see him again. Things were still in the fragile stage. *I* was fragile.

"Guess we should be taking off. Thanks for the company. I had a nice time." Disappointment shadowed Indigo's face before he turned to walk away.

Shit. No exchange of phone numbers, thanks to Pete, no doubt. I shot him a threatening look. My cheeks burned and my eyes were slits. "I'm gonna kill you," I mouthed before my glare deserted Pete's *What's wrong?* shrug and matching mug.

I caught up with Indigo, standing beside him as he unlocked his bike. "Pete's a good friend." I had to control my voice so I didn't sound imploring.

"That's cool." He looked straight ahead.

Pete approached, continuing to size Indigo up like guys do at the gym. What next? I worried, but Pete stuck out a hand. "Good to meet you, man."

"Nice to meet you."

"I'm their bodyguard." Pete grinned, dragging his gaze from me to Emma, but his eyes were serious.

Indigo's stare barreled across mine, then shifted back to Pete.

Breaking the tension, Bill stepped into the circle we formed. "Hey, man. Bill Addison."

"Cool." Pete was like a damn stud horse protecting his mares. I let out a breath when he offered Bill a hand.

After nods and handshakes, the atmosphere warmed. The

guys began talking mountain bikes and motorcycles, comparing *rides* and experiences.

I heaved the biggest sigh of my life as Em and I stood smashed together on the sidelines, watching, listening. We elbowed each other, shooting eye signals, mouthing wow's and oh my God's. The day had been the highlight of the past grungy year, and I didn't want it to end, even if Pete was in the middle of it.

I caught Indigo's glances, questioning at times, then he moved to my side, leaving Pete and Bill in conversation.

"Your friend's a character."

"Tell me about it."

"So ... there's nothing going on between you two?" His eyes tested mine.

"Not in the least." The laugh I let out was more like a thankful burst of air.

Indigo chuckled at my reaction. "Can I snag your number?"

Gracias, Cielo y todos los Santos [Thank you, Heaven and all the saints.] I thought he'd never ask!

"Where's your cell?" I stuck out my hand.

He pulled an iPhone from his pocket and slapped it into my palm. I tapped in my number and saved it to his contacts.

Towering over my five-six height, he leaned in and placed a light kiss on my cheek with the softest lips, whispering, "Thank you for the intriguing day. We should get together and ride sometime. Make a day of it. Bring a picnic lunch, or dine out. Maybe hit the beach."

"Sure. That would be nice. I'd love to." Oh – my – God. It was too good to be true. I almost fainted on the spot. "So, I guess I'll be talking to you then ..." Heart racing, I fought to control my lips.

"Definitely." He nodded, and after the warmest smile, his eyes left mine.

Indigo's tone sharpened when he said to Pete, "See you around, man." Then he mounted his bike and joined Bill, who waited for him on the side of the road. Emma, Pete and I watched in silence until they disappeared around a corner. I already missed Indigo. My heart dove into my stomach.

"Thanks for almost ruining my life." I glared at Pete.

"What?" He stared, clueless.

"Pete." Em tried diplomacy. "You can't keep throwing your weight around like that. Jewel's really into that guy."

"Really?" His mouth slid into a slow smirk I found most annoying.

Men could be so dumb sometimes. I wrapped myself around Emma's arm. "I'm empty," I complained, "how about you?"

She sighed. "Billy's better than I remember. I hope he calls." I'd never seen her eyes so big and bright.

"So, Em." My brows shot up. "That was an impressive game of charades back there in the park. Now that I've got you alone," I shooed Pete away with a flick of my wrist, "what's the story? It's bugging the shit out of me. Why didn't you ever mention him?"

Pete cut into her reply. "When did you meet the stud?" He took me by the shoulders, spinning me around to face him. Staring down at me, he feigned a glare. "Why didn't you tell me about him, Jewel?" Then he confronted Emma. "And you," his eyes narrowed, "I expect more from you."

"Hey. Don't look at me." Emma's serene forehead flexed. "She just met him today."

I jumped in, "If you want the truth. I wouldn't have said anything anyway, because I'm not up to the PEW test."

"After your last boy toy, that's a shocking remark." Crossing his arms, Pete stood his ground, a sour look on his face.

The Peter Edward Williams test was a tough one, and humiliating. The thought of subjecting Indigo, and myself, to the PEW turned my stomach. But Pete was right. Listening to his insight would have spared my suffering during and after the year of Nikos.

My phone chimed. When I checked my inbox, I found his text: *Had a great time. Nice meeting you ... officially. Now you have my number - Indigo.*

Rugged Nuggets: Bring It On Strip Club

I kept checking my cell, but heard nothing from Indigo. I assumed rotation was grueling as hell, and that was my excuse for not hearing from him by mid week.

My saving grace was a classmate, Yvonne, who extended an invitation for me and Emma to accompany her and a few other girls to a male strip joint.

Emma, Yvonne and I nursed a round of drinks while waiting for the other girls to arrive. The club was filling fast, and the first act would start in less than fifteen minutes. I kept an eye on the front door, watching for the trio of lost-looking females.

The crowd was revved and ready to rock. Women of all ages, shapes and skin tones sat at tables, filled the bar, or chatted in empty floor space. Everyone waited to be entertained by some of the most gorgeous males on the planet.

The club was dim, but sapphire blue track lighting showered the walls and occupants with a touch of ecstasy. I checked the time on my cell and yawned as I continued to scan the crowd. Then she hit me like one of the sacks of flour I used to sit on in my parents' bakery. I couldn't believe my eyes, so

I did a double-take, the movement loosening my fake lashes. There she was, the center of attention in a group of females trying to out-dress each other. Champagne bottles littered the table, and a garter hung around the neck of an open bottle positioned before a gorgeous brunette. My detective skills sprang into action. Bridal shower, no doubt.

I elbowed Em. "Pssst. Over there ... in the red strapless ... twelve o'clock high," which meant their tables, lashed together in a horseshoe, were stationed almost dead center in front of the stage and just to the left of the corner where we sat.

"Holy shit." Em's breath puffed into my ear. "That's the blonde from the coffee shop? The one who wedged herself between you and Indigo?"

"Go ahead. Rub it in."

"What are you two whispering about?" Yvonne asked.

I gave Em *the eye*, warning her not to spill the beans about our weekend.

"We're just admiring the dress that girl's wearing."

Yvonne's head immediately twisted in the blonde's direction, then she turned back with a sour look. "Hmm. Miss Whitehall in the flesh. Her and her groupies are slumming it."

"Huh?" I lost control of my mouth.

My anguish must have been evident, because Yvonne pitched me a quizzical look, while Emma's face filled with compassion.

"Do you know her?" Yvonne asked before downing a shot. Beyond beautiful, Yvonne was intuitive ... and thirsty.

"Can't say I've ever had the pleasure." My face almost cracked. I wrapped my palms around my Malibu Bay Breeze. "Looks like a bridal blast. Who's getting married? Any idea?" My heart began to race. I shot Em a look that screamed desperation.

"I doubt Vanessa's gonna be a bride anytime soon." Yvonne drained the last of the three shots lined up in front of her, and motioned to a guy with groomed chest hair and skin tight toreador pants. "The guy'd have to be out of his mind." She laughed. "Another round of drinks, handsome."

"He's not our waiter, Yvonne," I informed. "I think he's the next act." I'd watched him exit the dressing room not five minutes before she flagged him. "Looks like he's on his way to mingle with the bridesmaids."

"Whitehall..." Emma looked thoughtful. "Vanessa Whitehall?"

"Like the designer clothing line?" I chimed in. Great, that's all I needed. Wasn't it enough she was pretty damn striking? Did she have to be rich too? "That would make her a descendent of the billionaire multi-corporate and everything epic mogul ..."

"Nah ah." Yvonne appeared to be in a mood to dish, and I was all ears. "Guess again."

"No way," Emma beat me to the punch. "The condos?"

"The condos, and skyscrapers, and the park, and the biggest shopping malls in the northeast. Should I go on?"

Dear God, what was I up against? Quit now, Jewelia. You're in way over your head.

Yvonne seemed on edge. She kept checking her gold bracelet watch, anxious eyes scanning the room. I couldn't help but stare. With cocoa skin and honey eyes she could take any guy's breath away. Her wavy mane, overflowing her bare shoulders, didn't hurt, either.

"They should be here any minute," I said, offering reassurance.

"Who?" she replied, her gilded eyes taking in my face, then dropping to the cleavage spilling from my plum silk top.

I scrunched my mouth like I always did when confusion clouded my brain. "The other girls." I redirected my gaze to Emma. "Right?"

"Don't ask me. I don't even know who *I* am tonight."

"They're not coming. Didn't I tell you?" Eyes still canvassing the room, Yvonne's comment was casual.

"No and thank you. I've been bending my neck this whole time watching out for no one?"

"I can't wait to see him." Yvonne seemed to be in her own private conversation with her timepiece.

Emma just shook her head.

"I'm lost." Observing the intense look on Yvonne's face, I laughed. "She's this way in school, too. I have no idea who she's waiting for, and she's evidently keeping it to herself." I leaned into Emma, but with the racket, and Yvonne's lack of attention, it wouldn't have mattered if I screamed.

Still, I wondered. If it wasn't the other girls, then who? This was ladies' night ... although a group of guys were gathering on the other side of the club. After our show ended, from what I understood, *drag* would take the stage.

"Who can't you wait to see?" Emma wasn't going to let her slide.

"Ssh." Yvonne's mind and eyes were occupied.

"There's my man," Yvonne announced, the proudest smile spreading across her gorgeous burgundy lips. She sprang from her seat, waving her arms, then tucked in her lower lip and whistled through two fingers, the pitch almost breaking my ear drums.

As the backlit stage turned from blue to gold, techno pulsed, and from behind a shimmering drape, a bronzed warrior appeared. Sauntering out in full battle gear, he paraded around, giving us a taste while the audience almost lost it. The club erupted with screeches, women yelling: *Spartan the Warrior King*.

He looked like he could own a kingdom, and any woman's heart. Beneath the lights his body glistened. So did his eyes: without a problem, they seemed to find Yvonne, for a moment fixing as he thrust his stuff.

He had one of the most ripped bodies I'd ever seen. A studded collar surrounded his thick neck, a wide belt crisscrossing his bulging pecs. Leather wristbands enhanced his bulky arms, and his kilt was so short it didn't leave much to the imagination ... or hide his coordinating black jock strap. He wore the sexiest gladiator boots that hugged the muscles of his legs. No wonder Yvonne went nuts for him. He was the most incredible eye-candy. I could only imagine what he tasted like. I thought I detected a hint of a smile on his handsome face before his features molded into *dramatic* anger.

Ebony braids hung to his shoulders, and topping them off was a gleaming helmet, which he slipped off and extended with those crushing arms, offering it to a damsel in distress seated at Vanessa's table.

Yvonne screamed so much, so loud, her smooth voice turned deep and sexy raw. Her eyes watered, either from screaming, or unabashed love.

I was on my fifth drink when my head started to spin. In my alcohol induced imagination, I envisioned Indigo up on the stage, hips rolling, doctor hands tearing off his green scrubs. Leaving him strutting his stuff wearing nothing but a stethoscope. The thought made me so hot, I needed a cold shower. I could almost feel his arms around me.

"Laters," Yvonne said into my ear after planting a peck on my cheek. "Thanks for coming, sweetie. I'm off to collect my man. See you in class."

She worked her way through the crowd and up to the stage where Spartan lifted her in a bear hug.

By the time the night was over, I was emotionally and physically spent. Even though I'd witnessed a parade of the gods, only one had truly captured my mind, my heart ... please, not my soul.

Party At The Prestige

The Prestige was a West Side club catering to all classes and persuasions. When booze and conversation flowed, legal age was of no consequence. Everyone shared one thing in common: a twenty-dollar cover charge. Hungry for food, drink, and excitement, we were all there to make the most of the night ... and lasting impressions.

Before leaving the apartment, Em and I made sure we'd be two of the hottest imprints, and we shimmered from head to toe. Our makeup and outfits made statements all their own.

We sauntered in shortly after ten, and the club was already in quake mode. Music blasted and people congregated, leaving not a cozy corner anywhere, which was fine with me. I needed some cosmic action to clear my troubled mind. The Prestige was just the place, and I was determined to drink my problems away.

"Did Bill say Indigo's coming?" I dragged Em onto the dance floor. I always lost my mind when I was dancing. Hopefully, I'd forget about Indigo too.

"When we last spoke, he hadn't heard from him." She looked at me with sympathy. "I'm sorry, Jewel."

"Forget dancing. Time for a drink," I screamed into the side of Em's face. When she didn't acknowledge, I danced around her and yanked her arm, hauling her toward the bar that stretched along the entire side wall.

A dusk-like atmosphere engulfed us. The only brightness came from a shower of multicolored track lights strapped to the vaulted ceilings, streaming a multitude of shades across undulating bodies of different shapes and sizes.

Mirrors lined the DJ booth. There was no chance of snagging a seat at the bar, and people lined up three-deep around it. This was where a sturdy frame came in handy, so dragging Em behind me, I elbowed my way forward until I could see my reflection in the bartender's eyes.

A gathering of Wall Street with loosened ties gave us the once-over. A few of the younger guys held up drinks, with head-tugs, attempting to pull us into their crowd, but we didn't bite. Em and I were on our own missions, and knew exactly what we wanted, which didn't include band-less married men out for more than a relaxing evening.

Blowing them off with knowing smirks, drinks in hand, we yielded so others could replace our bodies and try to catch a bartender's attention. My eyes searched every face, stares ricocheting with curiosity. Mine would remain bland until I found him. If I found him at all.

"There's Bill." Emma sounded tense, but her face radiated an indescribable glow. She shoved her glass at me so she could wave him on with both slender arms. He immediately spotted her. Who wouldn't? Thrashing around in a silver dress, she looked like a sleek jet caught in turbulence.

"Go get him, Em." I felt her excitement, and not an ounce of envy. I loved seeing her that way: outgoing, uninhibited, tucking responsibility into the back of her mind.

She turned to me, her eyes shining, then concerned. "Are you gonna be okay?"

I shot her *the eye*. "You're joking, right?"

She laughed and danced straight into Bill's arms. So there

I stood, holding two drinks, wondering if I should slug them both, head into the ladies' room to rearrange my hair, or drop both glasses and aim for one of the exit doors.

The hand on my shoulder startled me. Then I felt the hot breath on my neck. A gasp caught in my throat, as I tried to clear anticipation from my face. I spun to gaze into the drooping eyes of some joker making a clown face he must have thought would turn me on. Instead, I blew out a *pfft* and laughed.

"Seriously?" I shimmied free of his hand. "Hit the road, pal."

"Aw. Come on, beautiful. Dance with me."

From the loosened tie, I assumed one of the Wall Streeters had ignored my earlier scowl and trailed me. With his unsteady gait, one push would have knocked him into a group of biker dudes not more than three feet away. I didn't have the heart to do it to him. The next best thing was to pretend to dump Emma's drink down the front of the white shirt tucked beneath his black suit jacket.

"Get outta my face." My mouth curled in a snarl.

He recoiled and without another word, faded faster than an object undergoing time lapse photography. What pissed me off more than anything was, he wasn't Indigo. But I wasn't about to be heartsick.

I figured I'd hang around until the dance floor thinned, maybe till the room spun, then flag a cab and head home, leaving Emma in Bill's care. We had an agreement. If Em decided to bring her Arkana home, I'd hide out in my room all night, my ears plugged by my iPod.

"I won't be able to function if I know you're in the next room, listening to everything." Emma had looked like a little girl caught checking out her mother's erotic romance magazines.

"I'll stuff my face with cookies and milk. You won't even know I'm here. Hey," I had said, popping my eyes, "maybe I won't be here. Imagine?"

"Be careful tonight, Jewel." Her face had warned more than her words.

"Both of us, sis." We'd hugged, then walked out the door and down to the club, arm in arm.

With Emma's drink finished, I gulped my own, intending to return to the bar to get more shit-faced than I'd ever been.

As I swung my head, he caught my eye. I did an about-face, plunked the empty glasses on the half wall behind me, fluffed my hair, blotted my lips and pulled a one-eighty.

Holy Shit. How long had he been standing there with his arms spread in welcome? Did he expect me to run into them and hug him? Hell yeah! But all I could do was stare.

Dropping his arms, Indigo stood his ground, an adorable interrogating grin sliding across his face.

Just go with the flow, girl, I told myself as I zigzagged, pivoted, and in seconds, waltzed up to him, attempting to appear stunned to see him while remaining casual.

"Indigo." My presence didn't seem to surprise him, but what I said next sure as hell surprised me. "You didn't call." When my ears heard my childlike voice, my stomach fell.

The curl of his lips grew tighter. "You said you like spontaneity ... so here I am, unannounced."

"Nice try." My hands went to my hips.

His face dropped its earlier expression, but his eyes brimmed with atonement. He reached for my hands, gently tugged me toward him, and the next thing I knew we were standing soft breaths away. With an intentional stare, he drew me closer, like I was a long lost love. A chill rippled down the portion of my back exposed by my daring dress. I lost my voice. I mean, I went completely mute, but managed what I hoped was a smile, and not the sick look of stiff lips.

"Hey, you ..." his voice was smooth. "I've been around this club half a dozen times looking for you." His eyes were so intense, I almost froze. His fingers pressed mine with a firm grip, guiding my hands up and onto his shoulders, slowly dancing me backward, all the while staring into my eyes. Still pinning my hands in place, he brought his lips to my ear. "I'm sorry," he whispered. "I really wanted to call, but I wasn't sure when I'd be free ... and I'd never want to break a date with you, Jewel."

My eyes automatically rolled. "You're gonna have to do better than that."

Although I stood my ground, my heart broke loose, pounding like the hooves of a stampeding horse. I prayed he couldn't feel the earthquake inside my chest as his arms slid around my waist. Being a doctor, he'd spot a panic attack in a second. I'd be mortified. My legs grew weak.

His eyes shifted quickly, then landed back on mine. I thought they looked glassy. Yet when he sighed and tensed, I didn't detect alcohol. "I have a lot on my mind. It's been one hell of a week. It won't happen again."

His breath was warm on my cheek and light, lighter than I felt in his arms as we swayed to the sensual pulse throbbing from overhead speakers. The mind-cleansing scent of cool fresh cologne and peppermint gum rushed my senses. I heard no sound. Saw no other faces. Only Indigo's. And right then he was magically mine, about to become the victim of every electric spark coursing through me.

My fingers tightened, found their way to the back of his neck and up into his hair. The way he was holding me, it was like he'd missed me, had longed for me. His lips moved to my neck, softly caressing. My body molded to his in just the right places, my arms urging him closer.

"It's okay." I heard my hoarse whisper. "I know you're busy. I understand." My mind wanted to believe him, my pride wasn't convinced.

"You smell so good. So sweet. Strawberries?" His lips inched up my neck, pausing at the hollow behind my ear where they played, stirring emotions I never knew I had. His hands ran the length of my back, fingers tightening and loosening, as if struggling with intent.

"Mmm. Strawberries." My arms, which had been loosely crossed, locked possessively around his neck. He was warm, gentle, firm, soft; he was every beautiful word I could think of.

"Can I take a bite?" His rich voice teased, so did his hands as they traveled, exploring every inch of my back, then dropped dangerously low. I wondered if he could feel the goose bump skin beneath the delicate fabric that clung to me like a second skin. The slim band of my sheer panties. The panties I prayed would hold up during what I hoped to be the longest night of my life.

"Be my guest." I breathed into his ear.

"You feel so good." His hands on my backside pulled me closer.

"So do you. I didn't think I'd see you tonight." With a mind of its own, my right leg inched around, the inside of my thigh rubbing against the outside of his. I buried my face in his neck, tempted to run my lips the length, then stray to his mouth.

"I wasn't sure you'd be here, either, but I took a chance," he whispered. "I'm happy I did."

"Do you usually work this late?"

"Depends on the shift. I left an hour ago, ran home, hopped out of my scrubs and into the shower. Hopefully I don't smell like a hospital."

"Alcohol doesn't bother me. It's kind of nice ... clean."

"Antiseptic," he corrected. "You don't want to smell what it's mixed with."

"I can only imagine. Must be rough."

"I grew up with it." He held me tighter. "I could stay like this all night." His breath on the side of my face came stronger, faster.

Uh oh. Did he mean? Was he saying he wanted to? An alarm went off in my head. Never go too far on your first date with a guy you cared about. Such a dumb contradiction: enjoy a one-nighter, but never share it with someone special.

Every girl knew the rule. Without exception, curtail the extracurricular activities, keeping the hands in appropriate places, lips only on neck, cheek and mouth. *Mouth.* I so wanted his on mine. I trusted my resolve, knowing I'd hate myself in the morning if I gave into the exploding passion threatening to burst through the seams of my self-control.

"Tell me about it. You're very comfortable."

He chuckled. "Comfortable? You have a delightful way of expressing yourself. But I think I know what you mean. You fit just right in my arms. Not an inch too big ... not an inch too small."

"You know that we're slow dancing to techno, right?" As I lifted my face to stare into his eyes, the scruff of his beard grazed my temple.

"Is there music?" His lips were moist on my ear.

My finger traced his jaw line. "There sure is ... booty music."

He pressed his forehead to mine.

"You don't rock out, do you?"

"I used to."

I pulled my head back. "Not anymore?"

He drew me back in. "Mmm. I like dancing with you. It doesn't matter what kind of music, as long as I can hold you close. Do you come here often?"

"When the spirit moves me."

"I like your spirit ... and your moves. You're a good dancer. Nice and smooth ... and confident. You've got it going on."

"Dancing is the best way to release anxiety, express myself. I guess you could call it a homeopathic remedy."

He tilted his head, gazing directly into my eyes. "Anxiety? What do you have to be anxious about?"

"You'd be surprised." My chin dropped onto his chest.

"We'll have to work on those anxiety issues, but I tell you, I do like your style of expression."

"I can express even better if I'm provoked."

His hands slid softly over my back, while his lips caressed my throat. "So, what does it take to provoke you?"

"It's a secret," I whispered into his ear.

"You're a tease."

"I guess you're just going to have to find out for yourself ... in due time."

"How much time are we talking here?"

"That all depends."

I slid my hands over his shoulders, gripping the muscles beneath my palms, massaging, fingertips drifting up the sides of his neck, aching for another trek through his hair. Then weaving my arms beneath his, I explored the width of his broad back, fingers running across his shoulder blades, sliding down his spine, drawing warm circles, urging him deep into me. Well, in my imagination. I couldn't let the feeling slip away without a taste of what it might be like. It would be good. So good. But I wasn't going there. Not yet.

Still, swaying on tippy toes, I lifted my head which had been pressed against his soft sweater, and let my mouth do its thing, up and down the side of his neck. I knew my lips were plush, and felt them melt into his smooth skin. Desire surging, I began to nibble.

I felt him tense, which made my mouth work harder, wander to his cheek. So in tune, we each drew back, so the only intimacy was in our eyes that locked, and the same magic of our *almost* first kiss slammed me like a ton of bricks. My lids felt so heavy they fell into a slow blink without my approval, creating what had to be a total hop-into-bed-with-me look. His eyes did the same, then clung to mine, so sexy, so determined, reaching for my soul. With his fingertips, he stroked my cheek, positioned my face, and with a dreamy gaze he angled his head, moving in for the kill, his breath on my lips so inviting.

His eyes owned my face, studying, savoring. Telling me everything a girl could ever want to know. His lips dropped onto mine, softly covering the top, then claiming the lower. His lips tasted better than I could have ever imagined. My heart began to hammer. Before I had a chance to slip my tongue over his, the DJ's voice broke our kiss.

Shaking It Up With Indigo

Both of my hands glued to one of Indigo's, I followed him from the dance floor, our steps winding through the club, past the bar. I didn't see Em and Bill anywhere, and wondered if I'd have to lay low when I got home.

We stepped into an alcove where a few others mingled, chatting in low tones, sipping drinks. Indigo chose a corner near the front door where my skin welcomed cool bursts of air as the door opened wide, then with the aid of silent air hinges, closed in slow motion.

A glow from the club's neon sign filtered through the sidelights, washing across our faces. Two girls waltzed through the shadows. They had similar, full lipped smiles. Both had fingers with long, red polished nails, wrapped around half filled glasses of what appeared to be Bloody Marys. My first thought was that they looked like vampires stepping off a movie set. Without batting an eye in our direction, they almost passed, then their pale eyes widened and stalled on Indigo.

"Indigo," the redheaded, poured into a black dress, drawled. "What a pleasant surprise."

The brunette, sexy and throaty, got up in his face, "Never

thought we'd run into *you* here." Her gaze flicked over me, then without expression, flew right back to Indigo. "Buy me a drink later, doc?"

"You look like you've had enough." His tone was smooth and unaffected. "I thought you were heading to the Hamptons this weekend?"

She rolled her bottom lip under. "Our parents are still in Boston. Doing their medical convention thing. So ..."

"So, you're doing the town." Indigo's chuckle held sarcasm.

"Always." The redhead moved closer, taking me in from head to toe. She lifted a brow and shot the brunette a snarky look. "But it looks like you're tied up."

"Give the place a break. Call a cab before you trip over each other," Indigo said, then turned to me and winked.

When their faces fell, mine broke into a smile.

"Catch you later, Indigo." They shared the same raspy voice.

With a sinking heart, I watched them disappear into the crowd. Fuck. Indigo was a player. My distrust of the opposite sex, which had been simmering just below the surface, began to boil. Like an itch that couldn't be scratched, Indigo's excuse for not calling was irritating. Nikos popped into my mind, and I couldn't shake the feeling of dread.

"So, how was your week?" Indigo grinned, then leaned against the wall, a knee bent, the sole of a laced leather shoe propped against the painted molding. Striking an impromptu pose, his arms crossed his chest. It was the first chance I'd had to get a good look at him since he entered the club. He was as gorgeous as ever. His hair was styled off his face and kind of spiky, but one stubborn lock feathered his brow. He appeared as relaxed as his jeans, and his sapphire pullover chiseled blue facets into the gray of his eyes.

"Not very earthshaking." I pruned my face.

"Aw. I figured you'd be out and about burning up gears on your bike."

"I don't ride my bike to work or school." Standing before

him, I smirked.

"Really? I kind of pictured you as one of those cycling commuters, you know, weaving in and out of traffic, throwing hand signals around, playing chicken with taxis." He chuckled, and continued to tease. "Bopping to music with your earbuds ... stopping traffic." He scanned my face. "So, I take it you don't want to ask about my week?" His grin was beginning to shrink.

"How was your week?" My eyes narrowed slightly.

My scowl must have stopped him, because his gaze shifted over my head, to where a *Coors* poster hung on the wall. In a moment his eyes returned to mine, but he had lost his humor, along with his playful tone. "What's wrong? Did I say something to upset you? I was only playing around ..." His brows drew together. "You're so adorable and feisty, I can't help but tease you. I like to get you going. You're fun to be with."

I felt my lids lower, and suddenly, I was staring at the floor. "Something's bothering me."

He brought my chin up with his index finger. "If it's something I've done, tell me what it is, so it doesn't happen again. I don't like making mistakes ... not even once ... no less twice."

"Sounds like you've made some big ones."

His eyes widened. "I don't know what you're implying, and don't believe I want to know, but in my profession, I can't afford to make any."

By the sound of his voice, the look on his face, I knew I was pissing him off.

"You're different tonight." He dropped his arms to his sides, then stuffed his hands into the pockets of his jeans. His back still rested against the wall.

"I guess I feel different."

He pulled his hands from his pockets and palms up, held them out. "You have to tell me Jewel. You can tell me anything, especially if I've done something to hurt you. I'd never want to do that." Once again, his arms crossed his chest in a display of stubbornness that matched his jaw. "If you don't confide in me, how will I know? That's what I say to my patients. If you don't tell me where it hurts, how will I know how to stop the pain?"

"I'm not your patient. And whoever said I was in pain?"

He let out a deep sigh. "Seems we're getting nowhere."

"I guess it wasn't intentional." I scanned the room, focusing on anything other than his face, considering how to phrase the question that had been troubling me all week. "At least I hope it wasn't." Now standing beside him, I rolled my shoulder against the wall. An arm draped behind my pitched hip, I faced his profile. "Did you know Bill was meeting Emma tonight?"

His head turned slowly. "Not until this afternoon." He may have been acting out of indifference, but the movement was sultry, as was his voice.

Holy shit, did he take behavioral sex classes? If this attitude was naturally occurring, and just talking had this effect on internal organs ... Imagine? I couldn't, because if I did, I'd be staring up at him from the floor.

My only alternative was to put my mind elsewhere and harden my shell. "Yeah. So he called her on Wednesday." I thought how Emma and I had bet on who'd be the first one to get a phone call. Of course, I'd lost.

Indigo's eyes were trained on my face. One side of his mouth twitched, but it didn't appear to be the onset of a grin.

"Yeah. She was happy to hear from him. They're having a great time ..." I rolled my cross in my fingers, "... dancing, drinking. Like they really want to be together."

He frowned. "Are you still upset that I didn't call you?"

The fact that exhausted as he was, he had shown up at the club and sought me out, boosted my confidence. "You could have called to say you were busy. You could have texted me," I blurted. I imagined he was with the two girls who'd just all but thrown themselves at him. He seemed to know their business pretty well. Did he know their bodies?

"I shouldn't have asked." His words were tight. "I can see you're upset."

"Kind of." I lifted my chin, ready for our first altercation. "The situation is all too familiar." I wasn't about to go into detail about my rocky past with Nikos, and how when *he* didn't call, he was cheating on me. I wasn't looking for a repeat of history.

For a moment Indigo looked puzzled as he studied me, then his face softened. His arms unlocked and after straightening his stance, he reached for a length of my hair, twirling it around a finger. His gaze moved from the chestnut curl to my expectant face.

"If someone hurt you, Jewel, I'm sorry. But don't compare me to him." His glance shifted to the opening door and returned, accompanied by another cool burst of air. "You should know something about me. When I'm at the hospital, facing those kids, ready to give my life to make them well, I lose all sense of time ... of me."

His face filled with compassion. He was such a humanitarian, reminding me of the sweet guy Emma had dated until he joined the Peace Corps and relocated to the other side of the world. The mere thought of losing Indigo to his dedication shot fear through my limbs. Suppose someday he decided to take off to a distant place where duty called? I was being silly. Stop it, Jewel.

I ran a palm over the side of his face, feeling the bristly brush of sprouting beard. From the circles forming beneath his eyes, I knew he was tired. And here I was, harassing him.

"If you want to call it a night, I'll understand. There'll be other nights ..." After dropping the hint, I vowed to think more about others than myself. I might not become a true humanitarian, but I'd certainly become more accommodating. I'd try, anyway.

He should have left well enough alone, but continued to explain.

"I also had to help my folks move some things to the

Hamptons."

"They're moving?"

"No. Setting up the beach house. They like to spend the holidays there."

The holidays that popped into my head were Christmas and Easter, without sand and bikinis.

"Nice." My voice was flat. I must have been getting to him, because he let out a sigh.

"Would you like to go back inside to find your friend?" Uncoiling the chunk of my hair he was still holding, he smoothed it back into place, brushing it all off my shoulder so it flowed down my back. "I haven't even had a drink yet and you're trying to get rid of me." With his plump, beautiful lips, he faked a pout.

"Never." I hadn't intended for my whisper to sound so husky.

His fingertips swept my cheek, and his placating grin was turning me into putty. "I thought about you a lot this week, and I do want to be with you. If I didn't, I wouldn't be standing here right now."

Without thinking, I threw my arms around his neck and squeezed so tight my breasts sank into his chest. I abruptly let go and took a backward step, mumbling, "I could do another round."

Taking my hand, he chuckled. "Come on, Kit Kat. Hey, where's your bodyguard, anyway? I was looking forward to having it out with him again. How'd he come up with that name for you, anyway?"

He seemed pretty interested in my relationship with Pete. I decided to keep him hanging a while longer. "It's a long story, and it has nothing to do with the candy bar."

"You'll have to share it sometime." His arm went around my waist, guiding me.

We moseyed back into the club, greeted by a thumping beat and a bouncer whose broad shoulder blocked us. "Hey, man. Good to see you." He slung an arm around Indigo.

I paused to watch them share a forearm smash.

"You too, man," Indigo's voice changed pitch when he addressed the other guy, which I thought was humorous. Guys ...

The bar stood before us, available stools inviting. Most of the club's occupants had funneled onto the dance floor, some filling the carpeted area around it. Partiers danced solo, some paired off, making it difficult to distinguish who they were with. A group formed a circle as two dancers tried to show each other up.

Indigo pulled out a stool, waited for me to settle, and pushed me close to the bar. He brought his seat near enough for our arms to merge. The atmosphere at our end of the club was calmer.

After we ordered our drinks, I leaned into him. "You come here often, huh?"

"Not anymore." He rolled his glass in his palms.

"You seem to know the bouncer pretty well," I pulled my drink through my straw, "and the Barbie tag team back there."

"Those two?" He chuckled. "The Stanley twins volunteer at the hospital."

"Stripping for geriatric patients with low heart rates?"

He belted out a laugh. "They read stories to the kids in pediatrics between classes."

"Isn't it past their bedtime?" I scrunched my mouth.

He cocked his head, then a brow. "If I wanted to be here with them, I would be. But I'd rather be with you." His gaze deepened. His fingertips toyed with my drop earring. "I would have introduced you to them, if they mattered." His thumb ran over my bottom lip. "The bouncer is my cousin, whom I rarely see anymore. Funny how you run into relatives in bars, or wherever, and not their houses. Sucks not seeing enough of your own family."

I lifted a strand of hair from his brow, then brought my hand back to my glass, and looked into the mirror behind the bar. "You sound like a loner."

He shrugged and sipped his drink. "Sometimes that's the only way it can be. Sometimes choices are made for you." He slid a finger along the plunging neckline of my dress. "Life isn't perfect. Think of it as a designer dress you pull out of the closet," his fingers caressed the silky fabric, "beautiful, except for that one little wrinkle where it was crushed. When you try to iron it out you end up making more." He brought his lips to the hollow behind my ear and gently sucked, then whispered, "Choices are a bitch. Making the right one takes time, patience." He lifted his head and gazed into my eyes.

You're amazing, and I'm doomed. I swallowed a gulp. "So. My Kit Kat story. Wanna hear it?"

"Sure." Swiveling, he draped his arm over the back of my barstool. I felt his delightful warmth when he leaned into me, pressing his forearm against my back. He brought his face close and watched me.

"Eh. It's no big deal." I felt dumb.

He grinned. "I bet it is. You're just being shy."

"How'd you guess that's how I got the Kit."

He threw his head back and laughed. "Shy, but playful as a kitten. I should have known it was something like that. How about the Kat?"

I held up my hands and arched my fingers; my painted nails like claws, I hissed.

His face filled with amusement ... admiration? He laughed harder. "I was kind of hoping it would be candy though," his face went serious, "nice and sweet on the outside," he sifted a lock of my hair in his fingers, "soft and delicious inside."

"Crunchy." I took a sip of my drink, watching him from the corner of my eye.

His brows rounded.

"Kit Kat's crunchy on the inside ..."

"Kit Kat's cute, but to me, everything about you says Sunshine. Your eyes, your personality. You light up a room, Jewelia Delarosa."

With his chin he nudged my hair from my ear and his lips

made contact. "I bet you're as soft as your beautiful lips," he whispered. "You're really something else, Jewel." His breath was a burst of warm mint lingering from a sip of a Mojito.

"I feel the same about you." I wanted to tell him about my feelings that were growing stronger, but I was afraid to drop my guard completely. Nikos had been a fantastic teacher. "So tell me about your upcoming residency. Gonna be a long haul, huh?"

"Yeah. It's going to take some time to get where I want to be. But I don't mind the hours, or throwing myself into it. Medicine is fulfilling."

"It's nice that you're so devoted." I hoped he'd be so inclined in a personal relationship.

"What's it like in Poughkeepsie?" His arm moved from the chair to my shoulders. His fingers sifted my hair again, then his thumb stroked the side of my face, easing me closer.

"We have a good-sized train station. Awesome shopping malls. Great schools." I swiveled to face him.

"I'm not trying to buy the place." He chuckled softly. "You sound like a real estate agent. And I have to add, you've got a great sales pitch."

He lifted my chin, bringing our lips together, catching me so off guard my eyes remained open. I barely felt the pressure, his touch was that slight. He drew back enough to search my face, then tucked my hair behind an ear.

"So what *is* Pete's story? An unstable ex who can't let go? A hopeful?"

"Not hardly." Somehow my hand had landed on his thigh, and as he stroked circles on my cheek, my fingers drew lines across the fabric of his jeans. "So ... who's the mysterious beauty Bill mentioned at the park?" I had to hear it from his own lips.

"I think you already know the answer to that." His grin was slight, his eyes deep as his voice. "You take my breath away."

"You make mine heavy," I whispered.

His thumb slid across my mouth. "When I close my eyes,

I see your lips."

"Looking at you makes me forget where I am."

"If I could hold you forever, it wouldn't be long enough." He smiled, then chuckled softly. "I know what started with an honest comment, kind of turned into banter, but what's said in jest ..."

The emotion between us had been gaining momentum, the burning attraction impossible to disguise. The stare we held was relentless, refusing to release. The space between us narrowed, our breath soft, blending. I ran my fingers up the side of his face, into his hair. He angled his head. My lips parted ... pursed. I wondered if he could feel the longing in my heart, see the dream in my eyes.

Fighting For Me

*L*aughter erupted behind us, jarring us apart. We spun at the same time to spot a wobbling Emma and Bill, arms binding them together, their free hands holding drinks. They seemed to be about to bail, and I hated the thought. Things were just heating up. I couldn't bear saying goodnight. Not after the most incredible *second almost kiss.* Great timing, guys. From the hint of a scowl, Indigo's annoyance was obvious as well.

Emma looked absolutely wasted. Unwinding from Indigo's arms, I hopped to my feet. "Let's go, girlfriend. You're going home."

"Billy and I worked everything out, Jewel." Her glassy gaze shifted from me to Bill. "I'm so relieved. Did I tell you we loved each other in high school when we lived in Texas? Then I had to move." Tears filled her eyes.

Indigo appeared at my side, draped an arm around my shoulders. "You're hammered, Arkana. Glad you're walking home." He gave me a squeeze and lowered his head, resting his cheek beside mine. "Look at these two. What do you think we should do with them, Jewel? Call them a cab, take them out for food, throw them into cold showers?" He chuckled. "Get them a room?" His words blew into my ear.

"I'll crash at your place if you don't mind." Bill faced Em. "It's closer. Doubt I'd make it back to Texas tonight."

"You'll have to settle for my couch and an afghan, Arkana. I didn't hear the ladies invite you to a sleepover."

I looked at Indigo, who stood shaking his head. We burst out laughing.

By then it was after two in the morning. I didn't care, because we were heading into Sunday, and I could sleep all day if I wanted to. I wondered if Indigo had plans.

Emma's loud yawn broke into my thoughts, and everyone laughed at how her almond eyes looked too tight for normal vision. She leaned most of her weight on Bill.

"Call it a night?" He said to Em, who nodded a yes which included another yawn.

The mass was dwindling. I could look out over the dance floor and focus on the back wall without seeing a conglomeration of bobbing heads and rolling bodies.

I'd barely danced all night, and felt cheated. A great song came on and my glance questioned Indigo.

"You're ready for another dance, aren't you?"

"Sure." How could I resist?

He pulled me close. "I think you could really wear me out." He dropped his lips on my cheek.

I looked up at him, grinning, "Yeah, but you've got the medicine to cure anything."

"And this you know because?"

"I can just tell." I tugged on his hand. "Come on, I'll show you how it's done."

Bill looked at Emma, and she nodded. So I figured the music woke her, or maybe it happened when Bill tried some off-balance moves.

"One dance and we're outta here." My stern voice pointed at Emma, even though I was the one who wanted the night to last forever.

We closed in on the crowd, the four of us mingling with

others. Bill and Emma held onto each other and simply swayed into a corner.

Indigo slung his arm loosely around my shoulders, his sexy voice whispering, "Let's see what you've got, babe ... show me some of that expression."

"Hope you can handle it, baby." I winked and started grooving as we approached the dance floor, but the minute my feet connected with linoleum, I slipped into overdrive. My thoughts cleared, my body turned fluid. Indigo looked as confident as I felt, his body working capably. But this was my place. This was where the real me could surface. I was more comfortable on a dance floor than anywhere else in the world.

We danced solo, then Indigo came up behind me, getting down low to my level. He was in my zone, and I was loving every minute of it. With his hands on my hips, his body matched my rhythm. I felt his hips, loose and rolling.

We were two pieces of the same astral puzzle: perfectly orchestrated, one body, one mind, thrust into another dimension. Although we'd grown close during the evening, with the friction our movements created, excitement struck again. I was lost in the music, the dance, this new side of a guy called Indigo.

His palms ran down my arms, and in an easy maneuver he lifted my hands up and over my head, spun me around, then brought me back in. His arms wrapped around me, palms flat on my tummy, fingers spreading, reaching, gripping. Preoccupied by his touch, I abandoned my deliberate moves and let my body slide into cruise control. I closed my eyes and let him lead me to another place.

When I'd first set eyes on the intellectual looking all-star I'd referred to as college Joe, I had no idea he could be this way. What other surprises were in store for me? His nearness caused a storm, and my stomach, my limbs, every ounce of my being, shuddered.

After a half hour of sliding torsos on the dance floor, Indigo and I gravitated to the bar to wait for Em and Bill who couldn't seem to part. I was hot, both outside and in. Our dance had been sensual, and my insight said we were both feeling the same effect.

Indigo's lips went straight to the base of my neck, kissing their way up to my ear. "You're incredible," he whispered before sliding off the barstool he had pulled close to mine. "I'll be right back. See if you can separate those two so we can get out of here." He laughed softly, but his eyes held the same intensity as when we'd shared the floor, and intimate parts of our bodies.

"I'll grab that fire hose near the door if I have to." My voice faded as he walked toward the men's room.

"Ready to get going?" I gripped Em's shoulders, turning her to face me.

"Not really, but I guess it's time to call it a night." She looked dazed.

I smoothed her messy hair into place. "And you call *me* the partier."

Bill had released her from his embrace, but anchored an arm around her waist.

"I'll call you, honey." The possessiveness of his grip gathered the waistline of her dress. "You can call me too, you know." His lips cruised across her cheek.

"You two danced yourselves sober, I see." My smile was wide. "Glad I don't have to piggyback you home, girlfriend." I laughed.

"I'm starving." Em let out a loud groan and rubbed her tummy.

"I could go for some food," Bill was in agreement, "the diner?"

"Sounds good to ...."

I couldn't finish, because something like a jagged rock slammed into my back, knocking my body forward, and the wind out of me. An elbow? Crap ... Whatever it was, it carved a deep pain in my vertebrae.

My head snapped around in time to catch this guy, about

the size of a small tank, who wasn't looking where he was going. I pushed off Bill's shoulder, caught my balance, then spun and confronted the goon. I felt a menacing glare contort my face.

"Sorry, doll," he said in a sober voice, which left no excuse for him to behave that way. "Ayy ..." He gave me the once-over. "How about a drink, sweet thing?"

"How about taking a hike." My arm was still bent behind me, my balled up fist soothing my throbbing back.

"Aw. Why you gonna act like that?" He proceeded to throw a thick arm around my shoulder, bringing his face in for a ... kiss? What the fuck?

"Not interested." With both hands, I gave him a powerful shove, moving him not more than several inches. His slight ricochet reminded me of a bop bag clown.

I heard Bill say, "Why don't you just take off, buddy?"

But the guy ignored him and zeroed in on me.

Next thing I knew, his fleshy hand reached for me and when I jerked away, his fingers brushed over both of my breasts. In the process, a large ring he wore snagged a delicate fold in my low-cut Grecian dress. I felt the cranberry fabric tear.

Before Bill had a chance to make it to my side, I swung a leg, aiming for the guy's junk, screaming, "Get the hell away from me asshole!"

Unfortunately, my platform sole landed on his thigh, and the three-inch heel on my other shoe didn't help my stability. The impact sent me flying in reverse, almost knocking me off my feet.

Had it not been for the strong arms folding around me from behind, I'd have hit the floor. Still, my short dress rode up with my movements, and there I stood showing off bare thighs and part of my Brazilian.

"All right bod ..." The goon's drawn out sarcasm sounded as nasty as he was.

"You okay?" The rush of Indigo's breath hit the side of my neck.

When I nodded, he set me on my feet and aimed me in the direction of Emma and Bill.

"Oh my God, Jewel." Totally sobered, Emma gasped. "What a pig! Are you okay?"

As I tugged my dress down and repositioned the top, I mumbled every curse I could think of, then turned to watch in horror as Indigo took the guy on.

In seconds, Indigo was in his face. "What the fuck do you think you're doing, asshole?" Indigo sounded rabid. His flat palms came down on the guy's chest, shoving him so hard, he sailed across the floor.

Holy shit. I didn't know Indigo had that kind of temper, or strength.

After a few stumbling steps the guy appeared to recover, but his ego didn't. He lunged for Indigo, who ducked and hopped to the side, dropping into a fighting stance like he'd had boxing lessons, or his share of street altercations.

Had the guy not started mouthing off, it might have ended there.

"Walk away, Indigo." Bill tried to intervene. "He's not worth it."

Indigo ignored him, his focus on the goon who took a wild swing.

I panicked, wondering if drinking all night would put Indigo at a disadvantage. But when he bobbed, avoiding the fist that was aimed for his jaw, I felt relieved. It seemed Indigo wasn't in attack mode, just defending himself. But the guy came at him again.

Then a couple of others, who seemed to be his friends, strode over. Bill stepped up and blocked them. His words were steady when he warned, "Let the two of them work it out."

They shrugged and backed off.

"Give it up, asshole. Apologize to the lady and we'll call it a draw." By the sound of his voice, and the bulging cords in his neck, Indigo seemed to be restraining a massive bout of anger.

Lowering his head, the guy charged, but before he could

connect, Indigo caught him with a smooth upper cut. The guy's head jerked back; his lids twitched. He grabbed his chin, then shook it out.

"Do you want more, or is this over?" Indigo's jaw tightened.

The guy just wouldn't give up, and with hate in his eyes came right back, yelling, "I'm gonna fuck you up."

Indigo was in his zone, this time throwing a precision combo, fists landing powerful blows to the guy's jaw, then his nose which erupted. His head bopped like a punching bag, and he was going down. I figured Indigo lost himself, because he threw another punch that sent the creep tripping across the floor to where he landed with a thud.

What seemed like forever had to be less than a minute. Indigo's cousin and another bouncer appeared and without a word dragged the troublemaker out the door. The cousin did call back to Indigo, telling him to get some ice from behind the bar.

Hands still fisted, Indigo was hyped. He rubbed his knuckles that had turned hot pink.

"Maybe you should ice that hand." My words were cautious as I nodded.

"No, I'm fine." His reply was cropped as he shook out his hand.

Offering comfort, I patted his chest. "What a jerk. I'm sorry ..." I winced. "Thanks for sticking up for me." I felt responsible. Had it not been for me, Indigo probably wouldn't have been at the Prestige. Was I giving myself too much credit?

A vein in his forehead still pulsed. I swept aside the same stubborn lock of hair from his brow. "Do you want to sit down, have another drink, or do you just want to leave?"

Before he could answer, out of nowhere, Vanessa appeared. As if the night hadn't already been shattered. I couldn't believe my eyes when she threw an arm over Indigo's shoulder, and with a nasalized drawl said, "Jim Jim, what in heaven's name are you up to?"

Jim Jim? What the fuck? I wondered how she'd materialized at that precise moment, and why I hadn't seen her all night. Watching her fawn all over him, I did a slow burn.

Indigo shrugged off surprise, and her hands. He ran a palm across his forehead, then finger combed his hair. "What are you doing here, Vanessa?"

"Obviously the same thing you're doing. Well ..." She shot me a distasteful glance. "Not quite. You haven't done nightlife in a while. Your mother would be disappointed if she knew you were here, of all places ... and fist fighting?"

She made everything around us seem coated with muck.

Indigo looked ready to blow. He cut his eyes to me, then back to her. "My whereabouts are not your concern."

Like someone pulled a string in her face, Vanessa cocked a brow and one cheek. I could have sworn her head even wobbled triumphantly when she announced, "I'm coming over tomorrow. Did your mother tell you?" As she spoke, she wound her long blonde hair around a finger, looking straight at me, then moved in on him, close to his ear. "Why are you slumming? It's so unlike you. Nothing's worth the trouble you find in these places."

From the tightening of Indigo's jaw, I knew she was getting under his skin. "Cut the bullshit, Vanessa. I don't need you on top of everything else."

I shot her a stare of contempt, then mumbled, "Slumming? Then why are you here, bitch?"

Her big round eyes sank into mine. I managed to keep a straight face, but my hands curled into fists. I so wanted to deck her on the spot. I knew she was referring to me when she whispered, *slumming*, but I didn't want to make matters worse by kicking her ass. Then I angered at Indigo for not lighting into her more severely. But reason said, why would he? He'd already come to my defense once.

When Vanessa's bottom lip rolled down, Indigo softened. "Look, Vanessa. I know you think you're helping, but ..." his brows leveled, "are you with anyone? How are you getting home?" He took her arm off his shoulder and stood her in front of him.

"I'm with friends." She flicked her head toward a group of people who didn't seem to be looking in any particular direction. "Don't worry about me, sweetie. I'll be fine." She pressed her lips to his cheek, then looking at me, her eyes narrowed. "I'm always fine. I want you to be fine, too."

He rolled his eyes. "I'm fine. You're fine. Everybody's fine. Let's take off. I've had enough for one night." Letting out a breath, he shook his head.

My mind was doing a tug of war, switching gears. *So those are his plans for tomorrow ... a cozy family get-together complete with Vanessa.* Why was he here with me? When she could be a live-in at his house for all I knew ... sticking her pinched nose up his mother's butt.

Rather than throwing a punch, I decided to leave like a lady.

"Come on Emma. Time for us to roll out."

Vanessa's face lit with satisfaction. Indigo frowned.

"Let's walk the ladies home, Bill. I don't trust that asshole." Indigo's words combined irritation with weariness. The base of his neck was still flushed with anger.

It felt odd seeing him standing beside Vanessa, almost as though they were a couple. I found myself envying whatever connection they shared, because it seemed to run deep.

"We'll be fine," I said airily. "I've been through more than one self-defense class," I aimed my words straight for Vanessa's smirking face, "and kicked a few asses."

She lost the smirk and took a step back.

Indigo had to have known I was pissed. He came to my side and ran his hand down my arm, saying, "I'm sorry the night had to end this way. Let's not make it worse." But his words weren't soothing, they were stiff, and I was getting angrier by the minute.

What the hell was he talking about? His gal pal was making it worse. Not me. "Are you insinuating this is all my fault?"

"I'm not insinuating anything. Let's get the hell out of here." He grabbed my hand and practically pulled me off the dance floor, while her words hit us from behind.

"Don't be late for dinner tomorrow." Vanessa's attempt at sounding dove-like bombed. "I'll be over early to help Elizabeth pack more stuff."

"Give it a rest, Vanessa," Indigo said loud enough for heads to turn in our direction. "She's always in my shit," he mumbled, trying to sound humorous, but I knew he felt as uncomfortable as I did.

We left the club immediately. As Indigo towed me into the cool night air, I angled my head, calling over his shoulder, "Elizabeth?"

"My mother." His reply was as stiff as his hand in mine as he pulled me to his side.

"So they're pretty tight. Does she live with you and your mother?" I was such a smartass.

"I don't live with my mother and neither does Vanessa. She just hangs out a lot. With no family of her own, we're all she has." His voice sounded heavier than my heart, which was struggling to digest Vanessa and *Jim Jim*. What had gone on between them? What *was* between them?

We're all she has? He included *himself* in *what she had*. How much of him did she have? The mood of the night had been destroyed thanks to a creep and the bimbo. I shrugged off Indigo's hand. My heels clicked faster, widening the gap between us.

Strolling, Emma and Bill had fallen behind. I heard them chattering.

"She calls you Jim Jim?" I tossed over my shoulder.

"Yeah. Sometimes she does." Catching up, Indigo pulled me to a halt. After gauging my face, he took hold of both of my arms and backed me against the club's brick wall. "Jewelia ..." His voice was ragged. "Don't let anything she said in there get to you. She acts on impulse sometimes ... without thinking. She's got a lot on her plate."

"Don't we all," I flared. "I can't believe you're excusing her bad behavior."

"I'm not excusing anything. I'm just trying to explain."

Before he could say another word, I set him straight. "So listen. Let me know right now. Do you two have a thing going or what?" Struggling for composure, I felt my chin jut out. "Because I don't want to become involved if ..."

"I thought we already were." He stared deep into my eyes then pressed against me, nuzzling the base of my neck. His words were muffled. "I like you, Jewel, a lot. Let's forget the fight ... forget Vanessa ... and start again." He breathed into loose strands of my hair working their way across my cheek with the breeze. "I don't want you to be upset ... or let this ruin anything between us."

I inhaled deeply, trying to unclench my jaw. "What a mess this is turning into."

"Only if we let it." His lips found their way to my ear. "Can I call you during the week?"

I lay my palms on his chest, easing him forward, gazing into his eyes. He must have seen uncertainty on my face because he added, "I'll call this time. And we'll make plans for my next night off – a night we're both free. Are you good with that?"

Nose to nose, he had me pinned, his arms stretched out before him, palms flat against the wall. There I stood, locked between his forearms, and he was closing in. Those eyes ... dark as the night surrounding us ... penetrating ... searching.

"Can I kiss you?" he whispered.

"You already did in the club."

"Not the way I want to kiss you now."

The way he was looking at me, the sound of his voice, weakened everything inside me. "Suppose I said no?"

"Then I'd ask again, and again, until you finally said yes."

My eyes searched his face, landing on his lips, which was a big mistake. At the same time I sighed, my lips parted involuntarily.

"Let me kiss you ..." Without waiting for an answer, he

angled his head, lowered his face, and his mouth was on mine, sliding, tasting, nibbling the top, lingering on the bottom. I let my lips open wider, slipping my tongue over his. I smoothed my palms up his chest, gripped his sweater in my fists, then coiled my arms around his neck. His hands moved from the wall to my back and he spun me, reversing our positions, yanking me into him. He had some smooth moves. I spaced, letting myself sink against him, feeling his passion which skyrocketed mine. When I moaned into his mouth, he seemed to snap out of it and held me at arm's length.

"This isn't right." He was breathless.

"Huh?" I had to shake some sense into my head which was still in the clouds.

He looked desperate, trying to gather his senses, then drew me in, lowered his chin so his head rested on mine. I couldn't see his eyes, but his voice held despair. "I can't be doing this." When his arms tightened around me, I felt him tense.

"Doing what?" Stunned, I didn't move. I couldn't move. I was locked in his embrace.

"Partying. Brawling like I'm back in high school." His lips worked against the side of my face, drifting into my hair. "Making out in alleys."

"You partied a lot? Kicked ass in high school?" I spoke against his chest, and felt the strong beat of his heart. "Made out in alleys?"

"Why do you find that surprising?"

"It's just that you ... you don't seem like ... I mean you're mature ... and you're almost a doctor. I never pictured you as ..."

"As a normal high school kid?"

"As reckless, I guess."

"We all go through stages." His arms loosened, and I drew back to stare at him, but when I saw the hardness in his eyes, I buried my face in his chest, trying to decipher the correlation between his words and the tormented look on his face.

Was I one of his stages? I lifted my eyes, my lashes brushing against the nap of his sweater. "Well excuse me if you're slumming it and I'm not high society like you and your stuck-up friend back there." As I wrenched from his arms, I noticed Vanessa in the process of flagging a cab, watching the entire scene unfold. My stomach twisted into knots.

I wasn't able to move far, because he caught me in his arms again, bringing my face back to his. "You know what I mean, Jewel. I'm supposed to be treating people in a hospital, not sending them to the E.R. I'm disappointed in myself." He seemed to be riding his own wave. "I'm really into you." He pulled me against him, circling my cheek with his. "But I can't get in too deep right now, although it's tempting. I have three long years ahead of me, and I can't have my mind all over the place ... running wild." His lips trailed my cheek, drifted to my neck."I don't want to start something I might not be able to ..."

I rested a finger on his lips. "Listen. I recently got out of a relationship ... a disastrous one. I'm not ready for anything serious." *Liar.* But I was becoming obsessed with him ... what was I supposed to do? I took his face in my hands, then covered his mouth with mine.

My lips swelled beneath his, working as though we'd had months of practice, pursing, sliding. His tongue circled inside my mouth, reached for mine, lingered. Then he captured my top lip, moved to the plush bottom and sucked, gently then stronger, terrifying me with the degree of passion he possessed.

While I blocked out the world, losing myself in Indigo, the headlights of passing cars whitewashed the walls, tearing me from what was escalating into mind-blowing ecstasy from which I would never have escaped had we not been on a public street.

Still, I imagined our bodies sliding down the wall, his hands all over me, massaging my breasts, ripping off my panties, plunging his erection deep into the ache inside me. The sound of traffic, lights piercing the lids of my closed eyes, jolted me to my senses, rendering me exposed, uneasy; along with

Vanessa, could the creep be lurking in the shadows? Driving by in a car? Would he follow me home for retribution? I shivered.

With a groan, Indigo's lips slid off mine. He ran his palms up and down my arms. His breath was hot against my throat. "What's wrong, baby? Are you cold?" His words were thick.

I was still warm from our experience inside the club, and outside with Indigo where he'd heated my body beyond my wildest dreams. I shook my head. My fingers took a sensual walk to his chest where my hands clutched the soft knit covering his pecs. I felt his heartbeat, then realized the wild pulse I felt was my own.

Emma and Bill had given us at least thirty minutes of privacy, but all too soon I heard Em's voice calling from a safe distance. "Jewel. It's after three. We've got to get going."

"Before sunrise." By then, Bill's chuckle was a distinguishable rumble.

"What a strange night, huh?" Indigo pulled back, emitting a breath that reached my face. He quickly drew another. I heard it catch in his throat. "Are you okay?" His deep voice held concern.

Still trembling, I balanced my words. "I ... I guess so," I whispered, practically collapsing against him, then came up for air. "Phew." Coming off my high, I fanned my face and lightened my tone. "I'm okay." I sucked in a breath and forcefully expelled it. "You?"

"I've been better," chuckling, he adjusted his stance, tugged at the legs of his jeans that hugged his thighs. "So ... if you're willing, we'll take it slow then ... so we don't kill each other." He leaned in for a last sweet kiss.

By then I'd recovered, and almost giggled at how he continued to shift from one leg to the other. "Slower ..." My lips crept over his, caressing, teasing, then my teeth gently tugged on his full bottom lip. "See you soon, doc."

I left him standing there and headed for Em. "Come on, girlfriend. Let's hit the trail."

Covering the distance in a few short strides, Indigo caught up to me. "You're not walking."

"We sure are. It's just a few blocks." I pointed to the gleaming Empire State Building, burrowed in the sky a few miles away. "In that direction."

"It's late and it's dark."

"You're exhausted. I'm not having you walk me home," I insisted.

He insisted right back. "Then we'll flag a cab." He faked a stern look, which didn't even come close to the earlier anger that had gripped his face, or the passion that lorded over all of his many expressions.

Attempting to appear intimidating, he looked so cute I had no choice but to cave. I let out an annoyed sigh. "Fine. Find a cab in New York City at this hour and I'll give you a?"

No sooner had I spoken, a yellow pulled up to the curb, hailed by Bill's waving arm.

"Give it to me next time we're together." Indigo winked. Resting a forearm on the open cab door, he was pure sex and seduction. Holy shit. My panties were already soaked. "I'll call you," he whispered, then leaned in and planted a kiss on my forehead.

"Be careful what you request, Jim." I wanted to deepen the intimacy by adding, "Jimmy ..."

His face went so soft, I thought he'd climb into the back seat beside me.

No such luck. He handed something to the driver, then the two guys tucked us in and off we drove.

Phone Sex

On Sunday, Emma and I met Casey, Pete's new crush, a librarian at the New York Public Library.

On the way home, we brought in takeout, and sat in front of the TV. "I can see why Pete fell in love with Casey," I said between bites of Kung Pao chicken.

Em's mouth was filled with a combination of vegetable fried rice and tofu in brown sauce, but she nodded, managing a throaty, "Mmm hmm." After swallowing she asked, "Why did you buy those kids' books? If you're thinking of giving them to Teresa ... isn't your little sister a bit too old for those?"

"You never know when kids books might come in handy." I winked. "If the Stanley twins can do it, so can I."

My cell chimed, and I read the text.

Busy?

It was Indigo. My heart thumped.

Me: Just got in You?

Indigo: Kind of – brb

In less than a second my ringtone exploded with my favorite song and Indigo's number.

"Oh my God. He's calling." My eyes bulged as I stared at

Em. My cheeks felt warm, my fingers tingly.

"Are you going to answer it?" Emma turned down the TV volume, which didn't matter, because I flew into my room and slammed the door.

"Hey." I tried to steady my breathing.

"Hey. What are you up to?" His smooth voice filled my ear.

"Just had dinner. Watching a movie. Did some Sunday stuff. How about you?"

"I just got in."

"You sound kinda beat. Did you have a busy day?"

"The usual. Dinner with the folks. Carted some boxes downstairs for my mom." He stifled a yawn. I visualized him stretched out on his bed, shirtless, and the stir in my tummy was almost unbearable. "How was *your* day?"

"I met Pete's significant other."

"Awesome."

"Yeah it was. We went to a book fair."

"Sounds like an easy way to spend a Sunday."

"Yeah, we had a lot of fun."

After a moment of silence his voice ripened, dropping from business to pleasure. "I had a nice time last night."

"I did too." I took a much needed breath.

"I could be texting you right now."

"Yah ..."

"But I wanted to hear your voice."

Butterflies sprang, along with the memory of how he'd made me feel when he kissed me. I wanted him in my room, in my arms, right now, Kung Pao breath and all. "I thought about you today ... and about last night."

"Did you ... and what did you think about me and last night?"

He was coming on strong, catching me off guard. I wondered if it was intentional, or was he losing himself as I was. "I think you're a really good dancer."

"I try." He chuckled. "No match for you, Jewel."

The way he said my name sounded different than the night

before. More urgent. His voice on the phone was clear, close; it felt as though he was in the room with me. It was as though he was sharing my private space. I ran a hand through my messy hair. "Anyone who can keep up with me has to be good." I sat on the edge of my bed, one leg bent beneath me, plucking my toes.

"Oh, and you're that good?" His teasing voice hit a sexy chord.

"Wouldn't you like to find out ..." And why was I doing this? I twisted a lock of hair around my finger.

"Keep it up and you'll hear a knock at your door." How much deeper could his voice get?

His intensity shot chills down my spine. The thought of him sauntering into the apartment, into my room ...

"That would be nice ..."

"You think?" He sounded mischievous; as much of a flirt as I was.

"I do." I used a *nine-hundred* voice.

"So, what are you doing right now?"

I played dumb. "Talking to you."

"I mean what are you *doing*, like stretched out on the sofa? Curled up on your bed?"

"Are you gonna ask me what I'm wearing next?" I stifled a giggle.

He laughed, then said, "Sure."

Of course I had to lie. If he saw me with a splotch of sticky sauce on my shirt, makeup smudged, baggy sweats. I cringed.

"Let me guess." His words were slow ... deliberate. "Location first. Gotta set the scene. I'm thinking you're in your bedroom. Your bedspread is white satin ... " I heard him draw a breath. "Am I close?"

"How'd you guess?" My heartbeat increased. I imagined his eyes were piercing blue at the moment, lids heavy with desire. This was taking it slow? What a contradiction.

"What's your favorite color, Jewel?"

His questions were odd. Were we having phone sex or talking fashion design and interior decorating? "Um ... I'd have to say purple."

I heard a faint click of his tongue, then his rich voice, "No. I don't think so. Red. With your beautiful dark hair, and sexiest eyes I've ever gazed into, it has to be red." As if deliberating, there was a moment of silence, then he took a breath ... and the plunge. "You're wearing a fiery red babydoll top. It's so silky, so sheer, I can see the outline of your delicious body. Trace every inch of you with the tips of my fingers. The straps are loose ... slipping down your shoulders, almost baring your breasts, which I might decide to uncover right now ... and suck ... one at a time ... nice and slow."

Ignoring the mouthwatering breast comments, I whispered, "Red ... babydoll ... yes ... close ..." I covered the phone with my hand so he wouldn't hear the deep breath I inhaled.

"It's trimmed with lace, and so short ... I can see your thong, Jewelia, and almost everything beneath it." His next breath sounded like it caught. "If I were there ... on the bed with you, what would you be doing?"

My voice was buried beneath a noisy swallow.

"Are you still with me?" He sounded so throaty, I imagined he'd been screaming my name.

"I ... I'm here."

"You're still with me ... good. Do you want to know what I'd be doing?"

My pulse was so erratic, I could barely breathe, no less mumble a response.

"Let me think. Would I be slipping off your top, or diving beneath your thong ..."

"I ... you'd ..." I broke out in a rash of goose bumps.

"I'll lay you down, stretch out beside you, watch the look on your face when my fingers work their way up your arms ... down your neck ... pull you into me ..."

He was killing me. Could he hear the sharp breath catch in my throat? "Keep this up and I'll be showing up on your doorstep."

"You don't know where I live." His voice was devilishly husky.

Mine was faint. "I'll look it up."

"I'm unlisted."

"I'll have Em call Bill and ask him."

"That's cheating."

I could hear every breath he sucked in ... exhaled, imagining the rise and fall of his rippling chest.

"What are *you* wearing?" I whispered.

"Pajama bottoms."

"Bare chested?"

"Yep ... you?"

I couldn't take much more. By the time the call ended I'd be shopping for a vibrator.

"I could be." My fingers traced the length of my neck. "If you were here, maybe I would be." I strangled my phone. "I just got out of the shower. I'm stretched out on my bed wearing nothing but a towel. You tap on my door, and with a sexy voice I tell you to come in."

"Sounds interesting. Keep going."

"You stand at the foot of my bed, staring down at me. My hair's spilling across a pillow, and the towel doesn't even cover my thighs. You like the way I look. I can see it in your eyes. Then you sit down beside me, run your fingers up my leg."

"Where do I stop?" His voice was muffled, as though his mouth suddenly slackened.

"You don't. You say you've never felt anything so smooth. So inviting. Then you part the towel, let it fall, stroke my ... belly."

"Then I part your legs you mean ... and you're squirming as my fingers begin to rub your sensitive clit ..." His voice ran through the phone line like red-hot lava.

I felt electricity shoot through my body. "Yes, I'm throbbing, and you're panting. Dying to feel my hips tucked up against you, but there are so many other things you want to do to me first."

"Like what?" His breath grew labored.

"You want to touch me. Your hands are all over me."

"I'm running my hands ... then my tongue, all over your gorgeous body."

I lost it. Totally lost it. "Indigo, I'm aching." My voice was hoarse.

"Baby ..." He sounded just as hungry. "I wish I could be with you right now."

"I'm so hot, babe. Tell me more. What will you do to me next?" I sank into my mattress, my legs dangling over the side, staring through the blades of the ceiling fan, staring through eyes that suddenly saw nothing but his face ... his hands ... his hardon.

"Snag the cuffs from your nightstand drawer. Pin your arms over your head, cuff your wrists to the headboard. Part your legs wider ... slide my fingers in and out ... and watch your face."

"Kiss me. You have to be kissing me."

"I'll kiss you like you've never been kissed before. Deep ..." He groaned. "Long, slow strokes of my tongue, tasting your lips, slipping in and out of your mouth, down your neck. I'll run my wet tongue across your breasts ... around your nipples."

I ran my fingertips over the front of my shirt. "My nipples are so hard. Will you suck on them? Bite them?" My palms were so moist, my phone almost slipped from my grip.

"No. I won't touch them. I'll make you suffer. Beg me."

"Please ..."

"I slip my tongue between your luscious breasts, drag it across your chest ... licking the soft, sensitive skin around each nipple, but I don't touch them with my tongue, or my fingers. Not just yet. I blow my warm breath all over your body ... followed by a feather."

"I struggle to free my hands, beg you to release me so I could tear your clothes off." A breath caught in my throat. "Take off the cuffs, baby. Please."

"If I remove the cuffs ... what will you do to *me*?"

"We're both naked now. Your body is beautiful. Your cock is smooth and hard. I'm straddling you. Slipping my tongue through your lips, plunging deep inside your mouth. Like I want you ... deep inside me."

The tone of his voice changed from seductive *night caller* to passionate Indigo. "You're driving me crazy, like you did last night. I can't stop thinking about kissing you, Jewel. I want you right now."

I felt the onset of the most intense orgasm which was about to break loose and send rippling shockwaves through my entire body.

"Oh my God, Indigo. I think I might come."

"Then come. I'm right there with you, babe. My hands are yours."

"Are you hard ... ready to come?"

"You wouldn't believe how hard I am. I can't believe how hard I am. But I won't come until I'm inside you, Jewelia, deep inside you ... if that's where you want me to be."

"Oh my God ... Yes ... Yes ... Yes ..."

I had no control over my words. My actions. My own voice echoed in some faraway place, my senses clouded with need, and in my mind, I was actually having sex with Indigo. And I was so ready to let my body flow with a delicious orgasm triggered by my own hands.

"Put your phone on speaker and stretch out on your bed. Take off your panties. Do what I say. It'll feel so good, baby."

About to obey his throaty command, Emma's tap on my door stopped my panting words, my anxious hands. Cleared my fuzzy thoughts. "Jewel, you okay?" She kept her voice low. "You've been locked in your room for over half an hour."

She blew our game to pieces. Although I'd covered the phone with my hand, Indigo must have heard my harsh whisper, "I'm fine, Emma. Go away." I was almost in tears.

"Company?" he asked. By then his breath was even.

"Just Em."

"Phew." His breath through the phone was so raspy, I could almost feel the beads of moisture hit my ear. "I don't know what came over me." I wasn't sure if his voice held more amazement or remorse. Was he upset because he'd just come on like a raving sex maniac with a girl he hardly knew? Or because he was becoming involved ... and wanted to back out. "I'm really sorry, Jewel." He sounded wounded.

I gasped. "Why are you sorry?"

"I lost control. I shouldn't have."

"It's fine, Indigo. I enjoyed it." *I loved it.*

My panties were drenched. I wondered if the erection he'd had to have sprouted was as painful as my aching lower half. Phone sex was fun, but I wouldn't make a habit of it. I wanted the real thing.

Indigo's tone sounded *off*, so I worried. What had made me float on a cloud, had turned into a catastrophe. I felt embarrassed, blushing as much from shame as passion.

"It's not fine. I shouldn't have called– it was a mistake." He dropped from hot-blooded to wistful. "Do you want to see me again?"

"Of course I want to see you again."

"When?" he whispered.

I sighed. "I ... um ... I don't know." How could I know anything? He'd just blown me clear out of my mind.

"I guess I'll let you go, Jewel."

I couldn't believe him. He was behaving like two different people.

"Early morning. Gonna hop in the shower. Hit the sack."

Sure, finish yourself off without me. Thank you very much.

"Are you okay?" He sounded as uncomfortable as I felt.

"I am. But are you?"

"I'll be fine ..." Tense silence, then once again, passion controlled his voice. "I'd like to see you again."

My voice still quivered. "When are you free?"

"How about dinner on Friday evening?"

"Sure." Watching myself in the mirror, I nodded. My heart

refused to slow. My cheeks were red and blotched. I looked like I did after a vigorous workout. And what had just occurred was only an exchange of words. Sexy words. I wondered if we'd lose control when were together. I corrected myself: I *knew* we'd lose control when we were together. Would it be anything like this? Holy shit, if so, there would be an explosion.

"It will have to be late. I'm scheduled until nine. Is that good for you?"

"Nine is perfect. Gives me time to relax, do some studying, shower ..." Thinking about you the entire time I'm smoothing lather over my body that still aches for you. "Where?"

"I'll text you from the hospital."

We were making progress. He'd be thinking about me while he was on duty. A chill shot through me.

"Good night, Jewelia."

"Nite, Indigo."

What the freaking hell just happened? My head swam. I knew I'd be tossing and turning all night trying to figure it out.

Primping For A First Date

As I meandered down 58th Street, facing the morning breeze, I hadn't planned on tackling the monumental future, the risky journey only fate held in its indecisive grasp. Instead, I focused on the deeply buried roots of the past, the point where everything had come together, but now threatened to explode. The pretty girl from Poughkeepsie, outgoing but somewhat aloof, the one who'd hugged a smiling mom goodbye, kissed a proud dad with glistening eyes, promising to always be sensible, careful, always a step ahead ... and above ... seemed to be scraping her way around every twist and turn in the road that was not as smooth as anticipated.

The old Jewelia Delarosa was a droplet of cells bubbling in a Petri dish, and I was the scientist, dissecting, analyzing, taking notes, and I began thumbing through yesterday's pages. My sepia existence had developed into a blooming dahlia, so full, a delectable shade of cherry pink, and there didn't seem time to do anything but breathe the fragrance of promise. A rush of exhaust from the midtown bus caught in my throat just as I approached the entrance to school.

With only two classes to complete, and a job that was

nowhere near demanding, my head still spun, and fitting my life into each twenty-four hour day seemed impossible. Still, time dragged. I could barely wait for my first real date with Indigo.

Monday muddled by uneventfully, with Tuesday rating a two on the Richter Scale, but by Wednesday a cataclysmic event was about to erupt ... inside my stomach, my head. Every nerve in my body coiled into one long circuit of dangerously high voltage. After the intimacy we'd shared on the phone, vivid scenarios that had exposed our inner emotions, how would Indigo and I act? How *could* we act? Like lovers? Be casual? Mortified!

It was a catch twenty-two. How could I face a guy I barely knew after what I'd said to him? How could I have said such personal things to someone I barely knew?

"Oh my God, maybe I'll cancel," I mumbled to my four bedroom walls.

Then my voice rose with panic. "Emma!"

Within seconds my bedroom door flew open and she burst in, eyes bulging, a granola bar in one hand, a mug of tea in the other. "What's wrong?" When she saw the condition of my bed, she gasped. "What the ...? Shit, Jewel. You freaked the hell out of me. I thought someone crawled in through your window and was in the process of murdering you."

"What am I gonna wear Friday night? I can't find anything in this mess."

Emma burst out laughing, set her tea down, and munched on her bar. "This is what turned you psycho?" Her eyes drifted from me, to a dress I'd launched that was making a parachute landing on the floor. "If you don't get a hold of yourself, girl, you'll be a puddle of jello by Friday night. Nothing to wear?" Granola bar braced in her ruby red lips, she rifled through the pile of bold and pastel colored outfits I'd pulled from my closet.

"I see what you mean." She frowned.

"What?"

"Why you're panicking."

I jumped to my feet, let a sparkly gold top slip from my fingers, tossed my head and faced her. "Huh?"

"First of all, calm down. You look like a wild woman."

I checked my reflection in the mirror. My hair was bushy and tangled, my cheeks flushed. I brushed dust bunnies from my arms. "So I was crawling around in the bottom of my closet, looking for shoes to go with this stuff."

"You've got an assortment here ranging from nanny to hooker. Can't you borrow something from the store?"

My lips pursed with annoyance. "Ah ah."

"For just one night?" Her refined brows arched.

"That's so against the rules. I'd lose my job if they found out." Considering the idea, I sucked in my bottom lip.

After stuffing the last of the gooey granola into her mouth with the back of her hand, springing into control mode, she crooked a finger. "Follow me."

"You look like a lopsided chipmunk." I giggled, nudging her arm.

I flopped onto the soft armchair in Emma's room, watching her open and close drawers, slide hangers across the bar of her organized closet. Her hands didn't stop moving until she found the perfect dress. When she turned around, my delight escaped with a breath.

"Holy shit, Em. It's totally gorgeous! How come I've never seen this on you? Why have you been hiding the sexiest dress I've ever laid eyes on?" I hopped off the chair, grabbed a long spandex sleeve, and let the slinky fabric slide across my palm.

"I was saving it for a very special occasion – and right now – you need it more than I do." She shoved the dress at me.

"Oh my God, Emma. No, I couldn't. You should wear this when you go out with Bill. He'd freak."

"It would swim on me since I lost weight, and since I don't plan on gaining fifteen pounds back, it's yours. Knock his eyeballs out, girlfriend. Believe me, Bill's already freaking." She raised a brow and rocked her head in validation.

"If you're sure, well, who am I to argue with a shrink.

You're so amazing, Em." I threw my arms around her neck, then pulled the hanger from her hand. Standing before the full length mirror that hung on the back of her door, I held the dress up against me. "Oh ... my ... God. Wait till Indigo sees me in this." Our phone call whirled through my mind, firing off second thoughts about the jewel-embellished black bandage dress that would cling to every curve of my body.

"Try it on." Emma rubbed her hands together. "It's more your style than mine, anyway."

After slipping into the dress I twirled, inspecting every visible inch of myself in the mirror. "What do you think, Em?"

"I think it's perfect!"

"This neckline is awfully low. I mean, I'm kinda popping out, don't you think?"

"Yeah, maybe ... but the beading might be somewhat of a distraction, you know?"

I scrunched the side of my mouth and shot her a dubious squint. "You really think?"

"No." She giggled. "But the dress was made for you. Take it and scram. I've got reports to write about people with real problems." She propelled me toward the door. "We should all have yours ..."

"You're a lifesaver," I breathed over a shoulder.

I sampled, then re-sampled every bottle of perfume on my tray, even though Indigo had commented favorably on the *Strawberries and Champagne*. I rummaged through two giant jewelry chests, snapping, modeling, unsnapping and carefully placing necklaces and bracelets back into their black velvet compartments. Finally satisfied I was on the right track, I tackled the mess I'd created. It took nearly an hour to clear off my bed, and the floor around it.

Almost ready to dive under the covers and try to relax, I remembered I still had to tangle with my shoe racks. Within moments I spotted them. Heaving a sigh, I grinned with satisfaction.

"I have the perfect shoes," I screamed across the hall, my

voice aiming for Em's closed bedroom door. "Black suede stilettos."

"If they're the ones with the studs, then yes, perfect," she yelled back.

Catastrophe At AMA

I rolled into AMA by one, and after changing clothes wandered through the wide aisles. I took an alternate route, snaking through women's on my way to juniors, stopping long enough to socialize with other staff members. I was careful not to drape myself over counters, or hang out for too long in any one place, or I'd be called into a supervisor's office for a lecture. Electric eyes roamed all over the place, and I wasn't about to be reprimanded for committing unspeakable acts. Although in my case, I was a pretend shopper, so I could dally more than others.

I'd dressed down for the past two days, and my high called for a short leather-like skirt, matching vest and snow white bandeau, and of course, thigh-high black boots. And everything fit like a second skin.

At the makeup counter, I let Brittany give me a ten-minute do-over which enhanced my original application of plum shadow, sooty mascara, and cranberry lip gloss.

"Thanks, gal," I smacked my lips and grinned, "do you make house calls? Cause I've got this hot date tomorrow night," I chirped, repeatedly twisting my fingers until they were red.

"Look like you do right now and you'll knock his eyeballs

out of their sockets." Brittany snapped lids closed, stowing away jars and tubes.

I took one more look in the makeup mirror. "I better get moving."

"They can't complain about you getting a makeover. After all, they want you to look like the clients, two of whom are on their way over as we speak."

"Laters, sweetie." I blew her a kiss and was on my way.

Pausing before a full length mirror, I checked myself. One minor touch and I'd be ready to rock. I swaggered into the hair salon. "Hey Deb. Quiet today, huh?"

"Thursdays usually aren't. Come back tomorrow and you won't find an empty chair, hopefully. With all these new salons popping up all over the place ... one never knows." Debra, the head stylist, twisted the seat on its pedestal. "Hop on. Might as well take advantage of my free time, babe."

I dropped into the chair, balancing my boots on the footrest. She swung me around, pumped up the height and reached for the scissors; all accomplished in a series of swift, smooth movements.

"Whoa, cowgirl. Drop the shears." I pulled my hair into a protective bun at the top of my head. "No cutting."

"May I tease?" Playful sarcasm from the meticulous middle-aged blonde who looked twenty-five.

"Sure, but no rat nests. And above all, no breakage. No frizz. I'm going for the smooth look these days. You know, casual, not like my hot date tomorrow night."

She yanked my hands away, releasing my tresses to flow over the back of the chair. I wondered why I was facing the wall.

"Try this." She handed me a pump bottle. "Smoothing mist. Makes split ends undetectable. So where are you going on your hot date?"

"Not sure yet. Waiting to hear."

"Mystery date, huh? The best kind. I remember my first date with Ray. Now I'm married with two kids." She sighed but her smile was bright.

"Do you miss being single?"

"Sometimes. But the hassle. Is it really worth it?"

"I don't know, Deb, but I'm far from ready to settle down. Especially with kids."

"Yup. You've got to be ready, that's for damn sure. Raising a family is a lot of work. Make sure the future daddy is into it too."

"Into it?"

"That he wants and likes children. Marriage and parenting is a two way street, sugar. Ray and I share everything."

"Now you sound like my mother." I wrinkled my nose.

"Could I be? How old are you, Jewelia?"

"Twenty-two in the fall."

"So what's he like?"

"He's a brilliant med student, and he's out of this world gorgeous."

Debra's eyes widened. "How hot is that," she drawled. "And fruitful. Grab on and don't let go."

The way Debra spoke creeped me out. Marriage, kids, grabbing and holding on. I hadn't been thinking that far in advance, or even in that direction. And since I wasn't needy, like Vanessa appeared to be, the guy would have to do the grabbing and holding. Grabbing ... holding ... Indigo. If any more adrenaline surged through my body, someone would have to call for an ambulance, or at least sedate me.

Debra must have sensed my internal struggle. She patted my shoulder and held up a hand mirror so I could see the back of my hair. "You'll make it, sugar. Life's not easy, but somehow it all works out in the end. And you, my dear, look gorgeous! Your highlights are holding up. Sweet wine is your color."

"Thank my hairdresser."

She grinned. "You're welcome." She began cleaning up her station.

I sucked in a breath. "I look like I'm wearing a wig! You teased the hell out of my hair!"

"Nope." She tossed a plastic bottle into my lap. "Just lift and spray and you've got ten times more volume. Try it tomorrow night."

Before strolling away I studied myself in the mirrored wall. "Between this outfit and my five-foot-high hairdo, I look like I just climbed out of a dungeon." I giggled. "Get me a whip and I'll be all set."

"You look like you stepped off the cover of *Vogue*. Absolutely stunning." Her tongue clicked in agreement.

"Thanks, Deb." My Brittany enhanced lashes fluttered while I held up a hand, signaling my departure.

During a visit to fine jewelry, I did my daily drool over my dream necklace.

"Maybe if you work for another fifty years, you'll be able to afford it," key in hand, Rebecca, the sales associate behind the counter, winked. "Want to try it on?"

I shook my head. "I'd only crave it more."

"Working around this stuff every day you get desensitized. This crap doesn't matter. Love does."

"Having both would be nice." I shot her a toothy grin.

Her hands worked efficiently and the next thing I knew, her arms were extended. She held the necklace out like a peace offering. The gold poured over the edges of her palms, glittering, gleaming, calling out: *Take me, I'm yours.*

"This is beyond magnificent, Rebecca. I'm warning you, if I put this on you might not get it back."

"So I call security." She smirked.

"Yeah, right. And I'll call a cab to rush me to the airport. I carry my passport with me at all times." I patted my rear.

I held the necklace up in front of me, checking my reflection in the oval mirror that rested on the clear glass case.

"Clip it on," Rebecca urged. "See how it looks. Maybe you won't like it. That happens a lot, you know? You drool over something for ages, then when you finally get your hands on it, you realize you don't want it anymore. Kind of like a husband."

"I highly doubt that." After caressing the 18K dazzler, I worked the clasp, heard the snap, then carefully positioned the seventy-five percent pure gold rope around the base of my neck. It was a perfect fit.

"It's breathtaking, and looks kick ass dangling over my cleavage, but doesn't go with this outfit at all. Such a shame." I couldn't take my eyes off the mirror, mesmerized at how the twisted links glistened beneath the powerful overhead lighting.

Then I felt the doom. I sensed curious eyes digging a hole in my back, heating my skin through my clothing. My stomach dipped. I stopped talking and spun, and there she was, Vanessa Whitehall in all her glory, standing not more than five feet away. She was accompanied by another woman who could have passed for her older sister.

When I returned her startled stare, Vanessa's deep-set eyes protruded. After what felt like a minute-long gawking contest, her petal pink lips fell into an odd shape, landing somewhere between a smirk and pasted on smile. She unabashedly nudged her companion, sliding her eyes off mine long enough to whisper something into the older woman's ear. They shared a look of scorn.

"Can I do something for you?" I steadied my voice. This was my job for Pete's sake. I wasn't about to rumble in the aisles, although I felt like tearing Vanessa's head off. A struggle erupted between my loyalty to AMA, my rapidly bruising ego, and Indigo. My mind became cluttered with questions and apprehension.

"What the hell's going on?" Rebecca said, her lips barely moving as she managed a cordial expression. "Why do they look like they want to shoot arrows through your uterus? Do you know them?"

"One of them ... dear God. This I don't need." I was certain my eyes displayed the discomfort of the moment.

As the two approached, Vanessa's voice flowed like a high tide, gobbling up the space between us. "Wow. You never know who you'll run into. Even in a nice place like this." With narrowing eyes, her head twisted in the direction of her companion.

The girl definitely had the ability to transform a fragrant meadow into a sewer. Only a witch could do that.

After our brief but meaningful meeting at the club, I wasn't surprised she'd recognized me, and even if she hadn't, I imagined my outfit would have stood out in any crowd, so either way, I'd just been made.

After once-overs, they both looked like they'd just chewed on lemon rind.

"Elizabeth," Vanessa played it so cool, "this is James's ... friend ... from The Prestige. I ran into him the other night. Did he mention it to you?"

"The Prestige?" Elizabeth paled. "What was James doing there? And what were *you* doing in that place?"

Another one who muddied the waters. I wondered which one of them had rubbed off on the other, because they were a brutal tag team.

"I wasn't *with* James." While her eyes widened, Vanessa's words sweetened. "I had to drop off a contract for the owner, and happened to run into the two of them ... on the dance floor. Apparently right after James had an unfortunate incident with a degenerate." Her face lit with a straight-from-hell grin. "Isn't that right ... Oh, I don't believe I caught your name the other night."

I had to stop the just-slapped-in-the-face look that fought to respond. I so wanted to get up in her face.

"You are?" Elizabeth's eyes traveled from my ten-gallon hairdo to my leg-binding boots, more than likely intentionally dismissing the core of my dominatrix attire.

How much could a mother take? I could almost understand her blatant concern.

"Jewelia. My name is Jewelia Delarosa. I'm Indigo's friend."

Confronting the bimbo seemed much easier. "And you're the old friend, Vanessa, correct?" Honey was no match for me.

Vanessa shot daggers at my breasts, while Elizabeth didn't

even try to hide her suffering.

"Indigo ..." Even her clucking tongue sounded classy. "I detest when people use that tag to reference my son. His name is James."

"You're his mom?" She'd just told me she was, so why did I even ask? And I'd taken her for Vanessa's sister? She was an attractive blonde, well-preserved and dressed to the hilt, in a sophisticated way.

She lifted her chin. I took the action for a definitive, "Yes."

"It's nice to meet you, Mrs. Ballou. I've heard some lovely things about you."

Her lips pruned."Hmm."

"That's some outfit. Is it real leather?" Vanessa hammered.

Recovered from shock, I sharpened my game. I'd be sly, but gracious to the bimbo. "I don't wear animals." I tucked up the corners of my mouth so tightly, I was sure I'd carved new dimples in my cheeks.

Vanessa's face drooped like a pair of stretched out pantyhose. Her cheeks grew pinker than the angora sweater she wore, and her fingers fumbled with the pearl choker that practically strangled her, as I would have loved to be doing with my bare hands. "Unusual costume. It's nice to see they're inventing new fabrics that can stretch endlessly without ripping." Vanessa smirked.

My eyes reached the floor. Vanessa's flats were the identical color of her outfit. Mrs. Ballou's heels looked croc. Real no doubt. Murderer.

Facing Vanessa, I exclaimed, "I adore your pumps. Where did you find a store that carries that style in a men's large?" I'd ride her till she crumbled. "I just love your hair," I ran a finger along the air beside her ponytail, "it's so silky. Is that your real color?"

"Can I help you ladies?" Rebecca to the rescue. "Jewelia doesn't work here. She just stopped by." She gave me the brush off. "But I'd be happy to show you something. We've just added new items to our already stunning collection."

The two converged on the jewelry display like flighty birds, fitting themselves between me and the privacy jog in the wall.

"What are you shopping for, Jewelia?" Mother Ballou inquired, scrutinizing my fingers and wrists. I flipped my rose ring to the inside of my hand, because if either one of them insulted the tiny silver petals and gemstone buds, I'd have to defend my father's honor.

"Gold." My fingers made a beeline for my neck.

"Oh, a necklace. Let me see," said Vanessa, her hands reaching it almost as quick as mine.

Holy shit. I'd almost walked away wearing unpaid for AMA merchandise! And they'd press charges, even if it was accidental.

"I don't think it's for me." I unclipped the rope and handed it back to Rebecca. "Maybe something in *Swarovski*?"

Rebecca shot me a prudent, "Really?" glance, then returned her attention to the two nags and what she must have thought would be a big commission.

Vanessa grabbed the price tag. "It's awfully plain, which is probably why it's so cheap. Perhaps a dangling diamond pendant would add some style." Her bony finger pointed to a tray of heavily guarded sparkling stones.

As we stood side by side, I managed a thorough assessment of their attire. Both wore sweaters and slim-fitting knee-length skirts. Where Vanessa wore pearls, Mrs. Ballou had tied a geometrically patterned scarf around her neck. Was she concealing a bit of crepe? From her smooth-skinned glow, highly unlikely.

My stomach twisted relentlessly. They seemed to share a lot in common. And then there was Indigo, the object of the three of us. Ouch. I questioned my sanity.

"I have to run, ladies. It was a pleasure meeting you." I focused on Indigo's mother, because if I had much more to do with Vanessa, I'd have ended up dragging her out into the alley bordering the building. I stuck my smile in front of Vanessa's face. "If you stop by cosmetics, Brittany will show you a terrific lip plumping gloss. Research has come up with astonishing formulas that work wonders, even on pencil thin lips."

"Is Brittany the one who decorated you?" Vanessa snapped.

Damn. She was quick.

"Laters." When I tossed my head, my hair didn't even move.

Our parting was strained, our goodbyes as phony as the leather I wore. As I walked away I felt my bagel lunch aim for my throat, so I ducked into the ladies room. False alarm. Still, with a racing pulse, I needed a quick calm me down. I checked the time on my cell and pounded a button for Pete.

Me: Break time Need HELP

Pete: Sorry Stuck @ accident scene

Me: Fuck

Pete: Kelly's 15 mins

Thank God for best friends. I punched the time clock and hoofed it down to the café. This was Manhattan. Not a face questioned my appearance. I'd had the presence of mind to grab a handful of toilet tissue to dab at my cheeks, and by the time I walked through the door, my eyes were dry.

I scanned the café, which at midday wasn't jammed as it was during breakfast. No crowds. No Pete. Damn. What next? Then I spotted Pete's boyfriend, flagging me from a corner table right beside the door.

"Hey, Casey."

"Are you okay?" His face held concern. He quickly stood and pulled out a chair. "Sit with me."

I flopped down across from him and stretched my aching legs, making sure my skirt covered every inch of thigh. "Where's Pete?"

"Right after you texted him, Peter called me. He sounded alarmed."

"Pete promised he'd never let me down ... And you came in his place when he couldn't." I felt a rush. Tears gathered. "I feel awful dragging you all the way down here from the library, Casey. It wasn't necessary. I'll be fine. Why don't you get back to work before you're missed? I hope I didn't get you in trouble." My bottled thoughts poured out like my lid had popped.

"Don't worry. I'm a head librarian." He winked a nod. "So what's the emergency? Lover's quarrel? Work related?" He pushed forward the extra coffee resting beside him.

I shook off a *no* followed by a jerking *yes*. "Kind of, both, maybe. Maybe not." I uncoiled my fingers. The moisture evaporated as my palms clamped around the cup.

"So what actually went down?" Casey's gaze was shrewd.

A fine silver chain wrapped his wrist, shooting sparks as he lifted his coffee. With pursed lips, he skimmed the cream from the top. Gosh, he reminded me so much of Pete.

"It was humiliating. Insulting. Degrading." I felt the flush rise.

"I'm still waiting ..." Reaching across the table, he scooped up one of my hands with both of his.

The dam broke. "These two women ... this guy's mother ... this girl ... I don't lack confidence, Casey, but I swear, these two ..."

His face filled with sympathy. "Does the fellow you're in love with know you're being harassed?"

"I doubt it. Vanessa operates undercover." Realizing Casey's inference, I gasped. "In love with him? How could I be in love with him? I just met him."

Casey nodded. "Love at first sight isn't only in theaters."

"You don't think so?" A lump formed in my throat. "It happened to you?"

He smiled.

"Pete?" Who couldn't fall in love with Pete?

"I was in a men's shop, standing behind a sale rack of shirts. These big hands on the other side of the rack seemed insistent upon sliding every hanger I placed my fingers around."

"Pete." I grinned.

Casey's face lit with the memory. "I had no idea who it was, or if he even knew what he was doing, but it was quite frustrating. We eventually started pulling and shoving the hangers back and forth until half the shirts were on the floor."

"Oh, no." I laughed.

"When I tried to snatch one particular shirt I'd been admiring, it wouldn't budge from the rack, because Peter's big hands refused to release it."

"It must have been a riot." Enjoying the warmth of his presence, I leaned forward with interest.

"It almost started one." He sipped his coffee then set his cup down. "So, I decided to be the bigger person and let go of the shirt, then strode around the corner to confront the perpetrator. After a few moments of staring, without a word, Peter threw the shirt at me and stomped off."

"And you knew it then?"

"I did." His hazel eyes glistened. "I bought the shirt, had it gift wrapped and held onto it, because I knew our paths would cross again."

"You did?" I knew I was gaping, but couldn't control my emotions, no less my face.

"Absolutely. And some three weeks later we ran into one another at a coffee shop. The rest is history."

"How sweet." The lump in my throat grew so large I could barely swallow.

"I guess that's kind of how I felt the first time I saw Indigo. Our eyes met and wow, I went reeling. I'm supposed to see him tomorrow, but I just don't know if I should. I mean, how much fighting can you do for someone? Maybe it's more trouble than it's worth. I'm under too much pressure. I have a promising future ahead of me. I don't need this in my life right now."

A breath gushed through Casey's lips. "Sounds painful, and serious. Two bitches ganged up on you and now you're about to fall apart."

"It shows, huh. I can handle myself, but this was at work where I couldn't do a damned thing about it. How can people be so mean?" As I relayed the horror of the encounter, my lips trembled. "Why are people so cruel?"

"I wish I could answer that, hon." Casey's earthy eyes bore into mine. "Refusal to understand. In your case, more than likely envy." While he tilted his head, his lips stretched into a grim line. "I've been there, Jewel. On more than one occasion."

"I wanted to knock her teeth in."

"I have." He grinned. "Not everyone's accepting. We deserve better treatment, but unfortunately, that's the way of our species sometimes. But don't let anyone bully you. Gotta have a strong neck."

"Hold my head high." I smiled. He was compassionate, so much like Pete. I reached across the table, grasping both of his hands. "Thank you, Casey. You've made me feel so much better."

"I'm happy to help. Call me if you need me." He reached into a pocket and slid a business card across the table. "Right now, I have to get back to work."

I checked the clock on the wall. "Holy shit. Me too or I'll be out of a job."

I hugged him and together we exited, each jogging off in our own direction.

Dinner With Indigo

When I noticed the flash, I was dolled up and pacing, my heels embossing dime-sized impressions into my plush bedroom carpet.

"Great timing, thunderstorm. And I spent an hour getting my hair to cooperate."

I kicked off my shoes and padded to the window where I watched a grid work of lightning electrify the distant sky.

"Why am I doing this?" I made sure my voice reached Emma's room. "I have no idea where we're going. If we're even going."

Crap. He's standing me up. My heart sank.

I rummaged through my nightstand, then rearranged everything in my chest of drawers.

"Emma! Have you seen my crystal studded hair clip?"

I'd tossed my cell on my bed an hour prior, and the ringer was maxed, so I'd hear it just about anywhere in the apartment. Not that I planned on leaving the phone unattended. Cradling it in my palm, I flounced into the living room.

"He's not texting ... or calling ..." I stared at the blank face of my phone. "You know. I'm gonna turn this thing off right now and get out of these clothes." I spun, ready to leave the room. "He's gonna flake. I feel it in my gut."

"He'll call." Emma twirled me around. "Jewel. You know what his schedule is like. He made a date with you. Will you chill?" She pulled up the top and sides of my hair, and strategically placed the clip so a thick knot sat on the crown of my head, unveiling my crystal hoop earrings. The rest cascaded down my back in waves.

My fingers checked her accuracy. "He's got one hell of a nerve thinking I'm gonna be sitting here waiting."

Emma took hold of my shoulders, giving me an affectionate shake. "Stop it, Jewel. You're flushing. Next you'll be breaking a sweat. Sit down and relax. Do you want to look like you've just finished ten sets of pushups when you meet up with him?"

"*If* we meet up. I look like a blimp in this dress."

"You look great."

"It's just as well we're not seeing each other tonight. Look at my stomach. I'm getting my period. Crap ... it's protruding like a bowling ball."

"You're beyond anyone's help." She shook her head.

I padded into my room to step back into my heels and do a last-minute check of my reflection, just in case.

"What was that?"

"It's the buzzer, Jewel." Emma annunciated slowly, as if speaking to a child.

"The buzzer? What the ... Who is it, Em?"

Without expectation, I thudded to the window. Pedestrians strolled beneath the flush of street lamps, but no one paused under the building's canvas canopy.

The only other thing I noticed, and not entirely unusual for the area, was the double parked vehicle, three floors below where I stood. Cars edged around it with ease, a few honking out of anger, because an inconsiderate moron had the nerve to block their path. It happened all the time. Around here, nerves ran rampant, and at that moment mine were so tight, with the help of a guitar pick, they could have plucked out jazz.

As I ran into the living room, Emma was in process of

announcing, "It's Indigo ..." She looked as shocked as I felt. "Wow. He's here ..."

She didn't have to tell me who it was. I'd recognize that voice if I wore ear plugs in the middle of Grand Central Station during Black Friday rush hour.

Grinning like an idiot, I restrained a squeal, but managed to mouth an overzealous, "I'm nervous." I shook my hands out in front of me as if flicking off pins and needles, then hit the call button with the pad of my middle finger. "Hey."

"Hey. Come on down ... before I get towed away." His words reverberated through the speaker, followed by a faded chuckle. Simply hearing his voice made me shiver. I almost spaced.

"Be right there." My voice tunneled down on the heels of his.

After cutting our connection I whirled. "What the hell? He said he'd text me." I forced my facial muscles to relax so my foundation didn't settle in the creases Emma swore no one else could see.

Em, arms crossing her chest innocently, shrugged and bobbed her head. "It's nice when a guy's spontaneous."

I rolled my eyes, yanked up my top and pulled down the hem of the dress I wasn't sure had been the best choice. "Wish me luck."

She hugged me. "Depending upon the time, I may not be here when you get back. I'm going out with Billy." Her glowing face floated before me.

"Maybe we should have doubled."

"Don't be such a wuss. I've never seen you this way. He won't bite, Jewel. At least I hope not."

"Mmm. Might be nice." I giggled on the way out the door, but soon grew serious.

The moment the elevator opened, I loosened my hips and swept into the lobby, making as dramatic an entrance as possible in heels that required precision balance. Back to me, Indigo stood gazing out the window, idly whistling something that sounded like a *Maroon 5* song.

"Hey," I called sweetly from a distance, so his first glance would capture the full view. "Here I am." *How ever did I make my voice sing like that? I'd have to remember so I could reproduce the awesome sound for Emma.*

He spun around, all smiles and casual, fidgeting with his keychain. Then his hands dropped to his sides. His handsome features morphed, clouding as though he was struggling with a ten-second decoding of the shocking message his eyes had delivered to his brain. He swallowed hard, looking at me the same way he'd done in the park when I approached.

I should have worn flats. Walking with wobbly legs would have been easier then.

I straightened my smile and cozied up to him, my lips aimed at his cheek, but his mouth caught mine first. "You look beautiful," he said after his lips pressed and released mine.

"Thank you." I softened my voice, then took a step back, hugging the small handbag I carried beneath my arm tighter. "Since you didn't call, yet again, I wasn't sure what time we'd be meeting, or where we'd be going." I concealed the deep breath I required to continue speaking.

His lips puckered just enough to look adorable. "I guess I can't use the same excuse twice, huh?"

My head automatically tilted.

"I'm spontaneous?"

I cocked a brow and smirked, then smiled. "Once a charm, twice won't cut it. I'll let you slide this time, but three strikes and you're out."

His brows lifted dramatically. "I'll have to remember that." He ran his index finger over my cheek. "Phones work both ways, sunshine."

"Sunshine." I smiled up at him. "I like it." No one had ever picked me up wearing a suit before, and for a silly moment I felt like I was on my way to a wedding. That was pushing it. A prom maybe. "You look amazing. I guess I made the right choice." My lashes fluttered above my questioning eyes.

"You're perfect, especially for the place I have in mind." He reached out, placing his hands on my shoulders, with a half smile, deliberately assessing. "You couldn't look any more perfect if I'd dressed you myself." The look on his face sent a chill down my spine. If I'd had to describe his response, it was like a wisp of feathery smoke drifting into an airy sky on a blustery day. And being near him made my head swim.

Even with my stilettos adding three inches to my height, we didn't stand eye to eye. I gazed up at him, murmuring, "Hello."

What? Oh my God. Did I actually double my greeting? *Grandma ... I'm sure you must have been through this ... help!*

I cleared my throat, readying for his chuckle. But he remained silent while his eyes swept my face, roamed my cleavage.

With my index finger, I brought his chin up. "I'm glad you like my dress."

Pleasure danced in his eyes, then his face went soft, his expression anything but amused. "Not just your dress."

I had a feeling our heated phone call was streaming through his head as well as mine. I could tell by the way his fingers gripped my waist, dropped to my hips. Securing my clutch bag beneath an arm, I ran my hands up the inside of his lapels, grazing the charcoal pinstriped fabric. It was silky smooth. I'd never felt anything so expensive other than garments in the clothing departments of AMA – and never on a breathing person. Not like the arrestingly alive, warm, muscular guy who was standing before me, heating in my palms, our lips begging to meet once more.

Our eyes held for so long, it felt like the next day's sun should have already risen. He finally eased me away, gazing at me like an astronomer observing the birth of a new planet.

When a neighbor opened the heavy front door, passing traffic grew closer, the incessant honking of horns urgent. It was the first time my eyes left his since I entered the lobby.

"Impatient drivers. So Annoying." One of my hands

slipped from his jacket onto his soft mint colored shirt, also smooth and silky. I couldn't help but stroke the fabric; beneath it, I felt the warmth of his chest. My fingers stalled, pressed, attempting to trace the beat of his heart.

"Well, I am kind of blocking half the road." Looking down at me, he smiled. His hands touched the part of my back bared by my dress, and after a delectable moment, he said, "We better go ... before I get a parking ticket."

"Sorry we don't have valet, Doctor Ballou."

His chuckle was faded, as through the intercom. I assumed it was his way of breaking the ice, which in my estimation, had already been cracked, chunked, crushed into a snow cone, and liquefied in one-hundred-ten degree body heat ... mine. Then his warm arm folded around my waist as he ushered me to the door, holding it open so I could pass through first. I imagined his eyes assessing me from behind, and took my time exiting.

I angled my head, watching the fall of his steps beside me. "Never worry about parking tickets. Pete would take care of them." I put my arm around him.

"Thank God for Pete." His voice was stiff. He led me to a silver Wrangler and pulled the door open. "Slide in," he said smoothly. "Careful you don't snag your dress on the molding." Like a gentleman, he waited beside me. He closed the door after I settled, strode to the other side and hopped in, like I would have had I been wearing jeans.

He slid the key into the ignition, but before starting the engine, turned to me. "Hope you're hungry."

"As a bear." I grinned, angling to watch him watch me.

"Do you like seafood?" His index finger traced the side of my face, lifting a wisp of hair from my temple.

Light from a street lamp fell across his profile. He was half shadow, half scrumptious male. Although distant sounds of traffic shattered the silence, I was lost in the moment, and it was only him and me, alone on the entire planet.

Nodding, I covered his hand with mine. "Mmm, yes, and I love this car. My parents have always driven Jeeps. But the big ones."

His fingers left mine to grip the wheel. I hated sharing his attention with the road, and imagined us in the back of a darkened limo, hidden behind a privacy shade, sharing more than the planet.

"I like this model because the top comes off. Great for summer nights." As he drove, he stole a glance at me. His voice was light, cheerful. He obviously liked his wheels. I was struck with a sudden image of him as a little boy, rolling a toy car back and forth on the floor. Boyish on top of hot, just what I needed.

"I bet it's great. The doors come off too, huh? How's that work out for you?"

He laughed, looked quickly at me and then back at the road. "Works out just fine. Not on a night like this, though." Stealing another glance, his eyes took in mine, then cut back to the road.

"Huh?"

"It's going to rain tonight."

"And this you know for certain? Because other than a few lightning strikes earlier this evening, the sky looks pretty clear to me." Gazing out the half open window, I watched the blur of neon signs we passed. I slid the window down further, protected my hair from the breeze, and stuck my face nearer the outside. "I don't smell it in the air either, and I have a good nose."

Driving into heavier traffic, he spoke without taking his eyes off the road. "Your nose is lovely, and rain has been forecasted since Monday. Which is why I decided to pick you up at your apartment."

I twisted in the seat to confront his profile. "So you didn't call all week because you knew it was going to rain tonight and that you'd be picking me up?"

"Is that a bad thing?" The side of his cheek crinkled with a grin I only saw part of until he shot another two-second glance my way. "You're not angry with me, are you?" I noticed his brows scrunch together.

"Well, no, but ...You have time to listen to the weather?"

"And news, and catch some sports. Does that surprise you?" His focus swung back to the road and the line of taillights before us.

"Um. I figured since you barely keep in touch ... I kind of thought it was because you're too busy."

"Guess I need practice." When he spoke, I felt a disturbing distance. Had he screwed up with her? And that's why she'd left him? What could he have done?

"So you've never had a serious relationship where you actually called someone when you said you would?"

"I've never called many girls. In high school, maybe. But then, high school guys aren't notoriously thoughtful, or in my case, experienced." His voice didn't waver, didn't change with the subject.

I couldn't believe he was actually telling me he was inexperienced. He hadn't sounded very inexperienced on the phone, hadn't acted it on the dance floor, or on the sidewalk outside the club. But then again, he'd been out of high school long enough to be a pro.

"So, you're telling me you haven't dated much?"

"I dated, but I had other things to do, more important things."

"Sports?"

"Sometimes."

"Work?"

"Let's just say I was a caretaker."

"So ... your father worked in a hospital and you volunteered? Like the Stanley girls?"

He laughed. "You don't give up, do you?"

"Rarely ... and if I have to ... well, I guess you could say not easily."

"That's good to know."

"You're beating around the bush. Are you trying to tell me you're a challenge?"

He laughed again. "You can answer that question after you get to know me better."

"I'm looking forward to it. I give honest opinions on everything. I have to warn you ... I speak my mind."

"I believe I've already picked up on that." With a broad smile, he stole a glimpse at me.

"I bet a lot of girls liked you in school; fell all over you." I watched his profile for a reaction.

"You think so, huh?" His fingers drummed the wheel. "You know what they say ..."

"What do they say?" I smoothed a fold on his jacket sleeve, still watching him intently.

"I'll let you think about it for a while." He moved his left hand to the wheel, and slid his right hand under my hair, his fingers massaging the back of my neck.

I gave his shoulder a playful squeeze. "You know that's not gonna happen. Spill it ... unless you can't pull off philosophical like I can." I laughed, thinking I was totally in control.

The tone of his voice deepened. "One love is worth more than a world of likes."

I swallowed hard. "Yeah ... I guess that's true." I drew a breath. "Profound ... what inspired you to come up with that one?"

"I guess you could say it just hit me." With a tilt of his head, his glance was brief but thoughtful.

He had a way of accomplishing the impossible – rendering me speechless.

Traffic moved smoothly and when we stopped for the first red light, he reached into the back seat, his hand coming up with a beautiful bouquet of wildflowers which he placed on top of my folded hands. "For you." He watched me, smiling until the light changed.

I was stunned. Between monitoring the news, weather, and sports, moving his parents to the Hamptons, and working overtime at the hospital, he'd made it a point to bring me flowers!

"Oh, Indigo. They're absolutely gorgeous. How thoughtful. Thank you." I ran my fingers along his arm, my touch light so I wouldn't disturb his driving.

"I'll have to remember to bring you flowers every time we meet." His voice was tinted with humor. I was certain he was happy he'd made *me* happy.

Bringing the bouquet to my face I inhaled the sweetness. The floral scent and his fresh cologne brewed a sensual blend. As he drove, left elbow jutting out the window, right wrist resting on the wheel, he looked so masculine, so suave ... further from a doctor than I did from a prima ballerina.

We turned onto the expressway, and in no time at all pulled up in front of a fabulous waterfront restaurant I'd only seen in fine dining magazines. Butterflies rose in my tummy. Thank goodness I'd listened to Emma for once, and had worn the dress she'd selected.

A doorman helped me out and a friendly valet parked the car. With his arm locked around my waist, Indigo guided me through the double doors and into a lobby and coat room larger than my entire apartment. I pressed closer than his arm drew me, enjoying the feel of him beside me.

Leaning close to my ear, as if guarding a secret, he asked, "What do you think of this place?"

Grinning up at him, I said, "It looks classy, but I'll reserve my final answer until after dinner."

He laughed. "Okay. You do that." He looked at me as if I was the most adorable thing he'd ever set eyes on. This was shaping up to be a most memorable night. And it was only beginning.

"My parents used to bring me here for birthdays ... special occasions. I have to warn you, they have fantastic desserts. You may want to start with something like a chocolate mousse first, and skip the appetizer." He had a tantalizing way of running his hand up and down my back whenever his arm was around me. I guessed he had no idea of how intimate it felt, or the arousal I experienced at the mere touch of his fingers.

After greeting us, a hostess led us to our table, recited the specials, then set our menus down before two gleaming place settings. She stated our waiter would be with us shortly, then retreated with long, elegant strides.

"Did you reserve this table? It has an amazing view of the harbor."

Indigo pulled out my chair and slid me back in, whispering, "If it wasn't so chilly we'd be dining outside at the water's edge, which would have been even nicer." Before leaving my side, his lips made contact with my ear and lingered. "And to answer your question, yes I did."

I lifted my face, closed my eyes, waiting for his lips to find mine, but of course, only in my imagination, as he'd already taken his seat.

"This is perfect. We can watch the tide, the moon." *I can watch you.* I was heady.

He grinned and reached across the table for my hand. "Don't forget the thunderstorm."

I smirked, then let a slow smile slide across my face. "How was your week?" I sipped my water, my eyes never straying from his face.

"The usual. Saved a few lives. Delivered half a dozen babies." His fingers wound around mine, squeezing gently.

His grin was endless, and his words made me laugh. "I can see it now, you in your scrubs, flying around from room to room, your rubber soles burning tracks in the hallways."

"You paint quite a picture." He laughed and tilted his head."Is that what you think residents do to earn their scrubs and stethoscopes?" Waiting for my reply, he drummed the fingers of his free hand on the table top. "Well?"

"Sure, but you're not a resident yet." I shot him a cutesy smirk.

"You're supposed to say, of course that's what residents do, because you watch those doctor dramas on TV where the hot guy's always the hero."

"Hero, huh?"

"Truth is, we do fly around from room to room." He lifted his water in a toast. "To tonight."

He made everything seem easy, magical, laughable. I clinked my glass against his. "Anything going on other than delivering babies?" I angled my head.

"Not really. And to be honest, this week has been grueling." He freed my hand to open his menu, then studied it.

"I'm sorry ... We could have waited till the weekend." Why was I feeling guilty? Dinner was his idea.

"Actually, tonight's my only free night. I'll be tied up all weekend." After setting down his menu, he captured my hand again. "I don't know why I even read it," he grinned, "I always end up having lobster."

Tied up? Whether or not I retained my high was a coin toss, depending upon his reply to the question teetering on my lips. Withdrawing my hand without jerking it away wasn't easy. "Double shift at the hospital?" I tried to curb the narrowing of my eyes.

"I wish." He grimaced, once again drumming his fingers. "If all goes well, this should be the last weekend of carting stuff to the beach house, for this year, anyway." He emitted a sigh I felt was exaggerated. Of course, he was feigning irritation about moving his family's things, being with Vanessa as she bent over boxes, tempting him with a wiggling butt. And the Hamptons ... I should have had such problems delegating my weekend hours.

"Why don't you hire movers? Isn't that what all rich people do?"

"My mother's possessions are priceless." Shaking his head, he rolled his eyes. "If anything arrived broken she'd blame my dad for not hiring the right moving company."

"Hmm." I drank more water, thinking he had just confirmed, without realizing of course, that his mother was not the most agreeable person. "That urgent to settle in, huh?"

"We go through this every year." His words, and the smile

he produced, appeared charitable. "With Memorial Day almost here, and this year ... graduation ... I guess they want to be prepared. I have a feeling they might be planning something for me."

"Party time, huh?" Wondering if I'd be on the guest list, my stomach balled up like a fist. Somehow, I doubted I'd ever make it to the Hamptons.

"Something like that. More than likely a small gathering of family, a few close friends." He set his water glass aside and reached for my other hand, so that he cradled both. His fingers ran over my glossy nail polish, his eyes examining. "Purple. Your favorite color." As he brought his gaze to mine, he smiled. "I'm good with details." He winked. "Any graduation plans in your forecast?"

Ignoring his charm, I pursed my lips. "Not that I know of ... Gee, it's thoughtful of your parents to throw a bash for you. Parents can be so like that."

"My mother and Vanessa do the planning. My dad's not around long enough to plan anything." He frowned, but I doubted it was due to my sarcasm.

Vanessa. Vanessa. Vanessa. Count to a hundred, Jewelia, before saying something you'll certainly regret.

Retrieving my hands, I sipped more water, then resting my cheek on my palm, I gazed at him. "How'd you know my address?" I fidgeted with my earring, dislodging a strand of hair from the clasp.

"What do you think?" The color of his shirt brought out the blue of his eyes, which took on amusement.

"Duh. Bill."

"Yep, and he's been scarce."

"So has Em."

"I've never seen someone fall so fast." His eyes studied mine.

I watched his fingers lace and unlace, then tilted my head. "You mean ... love?"

"Seems that way. They've been joined at the hip lately –

or he's working a lot of overtime."

"I guess. I don't understand how anyone could fall in love overnight." *Liar.*

"I imagine if you find the right person, you know it immediately." His thumbs drew circles on the backs of my hands. "You grab for it and hold on. Like the golden ring on the carousel ... or so the story goes." I couldn't decide if he was being reflective or sarcastic.

"You sound like Debra." I sat up straight, sliding my hands from his to bring my menu closer.

His fingers laced, and he angled his head, which he seemed to do a lot when we were together. "Excuse me?"

"Just a woman I work with. She said the same thing yesterday about grabbing and holding on." When I felt my brows crunch together, I made a mental note to perform a brisk massage of the surrounding area, in avoidance of dreaded *elevens.* Then I checked Indigo's face, noting his skin looked flawless and smooth, even beneath a light sprinkling of beard.

A waiter appeared and I opened my menu, my eyes glazing over lines of typed words that I couldn't have cared less about. I wasn't here to eat. I had come to be with him.

"Have you decided what you'd like to order?" Indigo faced me, while handing his folded menu to the middle-aged guy who wore the typical black and white uniform, along with an expensive smile.

I'd barely glanced at the entrees, but caught myself before scrunching the side of my mouth. "Um. How about Fettuccini Alfredo." I slid my menu across the table. "That always works."

"I'll have the same." Indigo took on an air of authority. The strength of his voice, and those trained physician hands, made me quiver.

"Wine?" As if I'd had no choice in the matter, the waiter addressed his fellow male.

Indigo turned even more formal, politely including me in the decision. "Is white good with you, Jewelia?"

I'd have been fine with my usual cocktail, even throwing

back shots, but nodded a lazy *yes*.

"Sauvignon." He sounded so cultivated.

"I'll bring a bottle right out, sir." The waiter actually bowed.

Reaching across the table, Indigo took both of my hands in his yet again. He seemed to like touching me. The thought brought with it a chill. "So, how's your week been? Arrest anyone?" His eyes smiled.

"Soon, hopefully. I picked up a schedule of exam dates." I made a swoony face.

His brows arched, his fingers tightened around mine. "That's wonderful. I'm happy things are moving along so nicely for you." He lifted his chin. "I'll personally know someone who'll squash all of the parking tickets I know I'll be getting when valet parking isn't available." He smirked. "You will, won't you?" His sexy smile was now playful.

"I'll reserve that decision too." I chuckled, but deep down inside I meant it. I had no idea how long we'd be seeing each other, or if anything would even come of the night, in which case, I'd probably be the one handing out his parking tickets. "Yeah." I sighed. "So now I wait for a date in June, take the physical, then off to the academy."

"When will that be?" He extended his reach, drawing my hands closer to the floral centerpiece. My breasts hugged the table, but his eyes clung to mine.

"If all goes well, August." I throttled the delight building in my voice box.

"Hey. We're in sync. Graduation is in May. Coordinating training schedules." He looked like he'd just realized we were accidentally sitting on the same flight together.

The way his fingers were massaging my hands made concentration difficult. He certainly was affectionate. "Yup. And we'll be busy ..." I kept my voice lighter than the wings of the butterflies clawing at my insides.

"I hope not too busy." He frowned.

"I guess it depends." Why did I feel the urge to draw away

from this beautiful man who was obviously interested?

"On what?" His brows furrowed deeper.

I almost blurted, "On Vanessa," but I was quickly developing self control. "I don't know. Sometimes things just pop up ... out of the blue."

Breaking the tension, and grip of our hands, the waiter delivered and poured our wine. I was thankful for the grapes and alcohol that made a beeline for my throat, hoping they'd quickly drown those damn butterflies.

"Is everything okay with you?" Indigo, who didn't immediately indulge, shot me a concerned look as he twirled the stem of his goblet between his fingers which always seemed to be busy. "Do you like the wine? Because I can order something else ..."

Thunderstorm In Indigo's Arms

Seated beside a picture window I gazed across the pier, my stare settling beyond the river's sparkling horizon. "The wine's delicious. It's peaceful here. I like this place."

"I'm happy to hear that, but you didn't answer my question." From a side glance, I watched Indigo swish the wine in his goblet before he chugged a mouthful. "Is everything okay?"

"I met your mother ..." I said, noting his difficult swallow, his tightening expression.

He let out a sigh. "And she made you uncomfortable." His eyes told me he knew she could be a bitch, and he was concerned she'd gotten to me before his warning. "So where did this meeting take place?" He couldn't have looked more confused had I lifted my glass and tossed wine in his face. That was certainly something I would have liked to do to Mother and Vanessa sometime. I gulped another mouthful.

"Vanessa didn't tell you?" I hoped my slow blink looked innocent.

"Vanessa told me she saw you in a coffee shop." His face drew into a scowl. "Interesting she never mentioned my mother."

"What?" My head snapped back. Whenever Vanessa became the topic of conversation, I had to intentionally control an instinctive growl. "What exactly did she tell you?"

"That she saw you with Pete, I guess. Holding hands." He forced that faded chuckle again, which was becoming his signature, and slugged more wine.

"Pete? When was this?" I came off as so demanding, I surprised myself. I sounded like a Bronx cop on a street corner, hassling a jaywalker.

"Yesterday." His voice was stiff.

"Did she tell you about our meeting in the jewelry department of AMA?" Mine was stiffer.

"She did not." His fingers left his wine glass and laced, like they were forged iron.

We were so getting off on the wrong foot. A change of conversation was in order, or we'd be better off calling it a night.

"Look at the barges. Do you like boating?" Hard as I tried, my voice simply could not unwind.

"I do. So what did they do to you that you'd rather not discuss with me?" His demand was more amicable.

"It shows?" Recalling the painful encounter, I forced myself to not clench my teeth, ball my fists, pound on the table. Throw my wine at *him*.

"All over your face." Releasing his fingers, he brought a hand to his chin, stroking the bristling beard that spread to his sideburns. "I know what they can be like, Jewel." He smoothed a palm across his forehead, securing that sexy lock of hair that constantly shadowed half of his brow. "I can speak to Vanessa if you'd like. But my mother. She's a different story." He had nursed the remaining wine in his glass, but at the mention of his mother, he swallowed the sauvignon long and hard, down to the last drop.

"That won't be necessary. I can take care of myself ... and Vanessa." I crossed my arms.

"This isn't what I had in mind for tonight." Half lifting

himself from his chair he leaned toward me, straining to reach me from across the table. I stubbornly held my ground, so our lips barely brushed. "This is supposed to be a romantic evening." His eyes saddened.

Romantic? He didn't pull any punches about his intention. I wanted to leap over the table, fall into his arms. He looked so eager to be happy, but there was definitely something holding him back. Through his attempted smile he seemed troubled. He had to be struggling with something bigger than his mother's horrible personality. I was certain his struggle ran deeper.

"Speaking of romance, and hand holding. I need you to be honest with me, Jewel. If there's someone else you're interested in ... it is what it is ... Just let me know. I don't want to be mistaken about anything." His stare drenched mine.

It is what it is? So that's how little I mean to him? I'd have to remind Casey about Cupid's rules of love at first sight.

"Oh my God. I'd never do that." I defended so strongly, Indigo flinched. "I wasn't holding hands with Pete. To be honest, after leaving your mother and Vanessa, I needed a friendly shoulder."

"You could have called me." His mouth set in a stubborn line, so unlike him, I was taken aback. "It did involve me, Jewel, even if indirectly."

I couldn't help but shoot him an are-you-serious look that even sent me reeling. "You hardly ever text me or call me, Indigo. Why would I turn to you? You're so elusive I ..."

He looked stunned that he'd been scolded. "I had no idea you consider me to be so neglectful." His soft voice grew defensive.

"I texted Pete but he was at an accident scene, so Casey showed up instead."

"Pete's Casey?"

"Yes. Casey met me at Kelly's. We had coffee and he made me feel better." I was emphatic, making sure my words inferred I had turned to a stranger who'd made me feel more comfortable than Indigo's mother and his best friend. I knew I shouldn't be taking my anger out on him, but I couldn't help myself.

"Casey's Pete's boyfriend?" The side of Indigo's mouth inched up. "That's really good to hear." He blew out a breath. "Just so we get this straight, once and for all. You're not into Pete, and I'm not into Vanessa." His eyes almost pleaded, knocking the fight out of me. "Settled?"

"As my professor would say, settled like a lawsuit." Drawing a labored breath, I let my eyes do the roll they'd been itching to do each time he'd tried to explain away his mother's and Vanessa's unacceptable behavior. "We've wasted enough time on this subject." Not entirely relieved, I sighed. "Do you believe us?"

"Let's start over." He brought his hands together with a clap, as if sealing the deal.

"Seems like I've heard that before." I raised an intimidating brow.

Easing a finger around the buttoned neck of his shirt, he looked uncomfortable. It appeared all guys weren't made of stone.

Lifting my glass, I toasted: "To starting over."

"Beginning yet again." He shook his head. "How many times can we roll back time?" Appearing worn, he drew in a breath.

The mood lightened, and with the help of the tart wine, my high was back and stronger than ever. While we ate, we watched barges cruise the river, and a three-quarter moon on the rise peeking through wispy clouds.

"Dinner was yummy," I said after draining my fourth glass of wine.

"That it was. Speaking of yummy, how did you make out after our phone call the other night? Were you able to sleep? Because I wasn't." During the evening, he'd made it a point to play with my fingers, plucking the tips whenever they were free.

I knew I blushed, because he let out a soft laugh. I allowed my face to hide beneath my hand, and moaned, "Oh no. Do we really have to go there?" I watched him from between my fanning fingers.

"You didn't like it?" He playfully slapped the tabletop, then palmed his heart.

"I did. Maybe a little too much. That's the problem." Lifting my face, I giggled. "I've never gotten into anything like that before."

"So, you're telling me you're strictly into the real thing?" He angled his head, cocked a brow, and pinned my fidgeting fingers to the table.

My mouth dropped. "I don't sleep around."

"I'm joking. But you did a great job of raising my interest on the phone."

"Was that all I raised?"

I was delirious, disbelieving I was actually saying sexy things to his face.

"Come here and I'll whisper the truth into your ear." With a hitch of his head, he beckoned.

"Don't tempt me." My eyes bore intentionally into his.

He made a move as if to sweep his arm across the table, clearing the space from where the waiter had removed our dinnerware not five minutes before.

"Someone once told me, finding a soul mate isn't easy." My voice sounded surprisingly steady, my stare intense. The wine was doing its job.

"Sometimes, neither is keeping one." He drained his last drop of his wine and reached for the bottle, swirling the last inch around the bottom. "And this conversation is growing serious. Another glass?"

I blinked to focus on the objects around me that had begun to float. Stared out the window, where concrete tables and scroll back chairs took on the color of twinkling lights dangling over the patio. "I think I've had enough."

"Me too, I suppose. I hate to call it a night, but it's like midnight." His eyes searched my face, testing my reaction.

"And we both have early mornings." I so did not want the evening to end. The thought of not seeing him again, perhaps for days, possibly weeks, was distressing. I realized I was in no way on the same level of importance as his mother, maybe even Vanessa, but why couldn't he fit me into his schedule? "I had a wonderful time, Indigo." My voice came so from the heart, had it not been mine, it might have brought me to tears.

He gave my hand one last squeeze. "So did I, Jewel. Do it again sometime?"

What the fuck? If this guy didn't stop flipping from hot to cold, I'd be the one blowing *him* off.

"Sure. I'll check my calendar." My voice chilled, along with my emotions. I had to protect myself. Maybe what I said to Casey *was* right, and this *was* a waste of time.

Things didn't feel right anymore. Indigo was capable of inflicting more agony than a thousand Nikos. And his mother and Vanessa only exacerbated my emotional turmoil.

I slid out my chair and stood, making sure to tug my clinging skirt down to my knees. When I leaned over, Indigo made no attempt to curb his gaze which lingered on my bulging cleavage. The wine had hit him too, loosening his inhibitions. He looked about ready to drool.

"Ready to hit the road, James?" I delivered the shocking blow like a pro.

His head snapped back as if I'd slugged him. He squinted with confusion. "Okay ... Of course. Yes, I'm ready. Let's go."

He ushered me out of the restaurant, into the coat room, without the aid of his hands.

Hugging my sides, I followed him out the door, into the stillness of night, to where the valet waited patiently. Indigo handed him the parking ticket, along with some folded bills.

"It sure has quieted down, huh?" I said, my eyes scanning the empty sidewalk. "Guess we just about closed the place." Attempting to clear my head, I inhaled too much fresh air, which caused even more instability. I did a sidestep.

Indigo caught me in his arms. "Come here. I want to talk to you." It wasn't a request, it was an order.

"We've been talking all night." I shook free.

He reached for my hand. "We need to straighten some things out."

His grip was strong. When he tried to back me into an alcove at the dark side of the building, I once more backed away. His touch made me tingle, and I couldn't bear the inner struggle that was beginning to drive me insane. I just wanted to go home. Fall into my bed, let tears flow, and never think about him again. With the good came the bad, but in my case, I could never accept the obstacles standing in our way.

"Listen. I think I'll find my own way home. This isn't working, Indigo. For either of us. I can sense it. Things are too damned strained ... and complicated." Again I wavered, but managed to catch myself before he reached out to me. I stepped further away.

"What are you talking about? The night may have hit a rough spot, but in my opinion, it turned out terrific." His voice sharpened.

With each advance he made, I retreated, until my feet bordered a garden of shrubbery decorating the side of the building where my heels sunk in pine bark.

Vanessa's face floated across my mind, followed by his mother's, and I couldn't help but take my resentment out on him. "It's never going to work. We both have obligations. In your case, more than ordinary obligations. And it seems to me you're carrying baggage." I reached into my purse for my phone.

"Jewelia ..." He grabbed my wrist.

I jerked away and turned, with every intention of stomping off, calling a taxi. Before I'd moved two feet, he came up from behind, snatched my arm, spun me around and yanked me into him, backing us both into the alcove.

As his back hit the wall, our bodies jarred to a halt. My breath was snatched from my lungs. Infuriated, I stared up at him, too stunned to speak, my free hand hammering his chest. Attempting to shove him away, my out of control palm landed on his cheek. From the sound of the crack, I imagined the sting.

Within moments my hand was captured by his, my arms pinned, so that I stood crushed to his chest, completely helpless.

"Jewelia," his voice was hoarse. "Hear me out, please ..." His face was beside mine, his lips in my hair, against my ear, brushing my cheek, pleading.

Unable to face his words I pressed my nose to his chest, lost in confusion. Did I want to hurt him so badly? As someone else might have done? Could I find that ounce of understanding inside my troubled heart? Or should I bring a knee to his groin ... bite him, headbutt him? Why couldn't I just tell him I'd been falling in love with him since the moment we'd met – and his indifference had hurt me, and now I was spooked.

He drew back, but didn't loosen his hold, repeating my name. "Jewelia, talk to me, baby. Don't shut me out."

We were two silhouettes surrounded by shadows, features barely definable, but his eyes were outstanding, sparkling like jewels as moonlight struck his face. It would have been so easy to let my body melt into his, surrender every emotion that had fought to surface since the first moment my eyes fell upon his. The darkness was a delectable aphrodisiac, but I couldn't let myself crumble. I had to break away.

"What are you doing?" I tried to struggle free, but I was cemented in place. I felt my handbag slip to the ground, where it landed beside my feet. "Let me go!" My body thrashed. This was a side of him I didn't see coming. He could have walked away at that moment, especially after I'd slapped him, but he didn't. His determination to keep us together was stronger than mine that was parting us.

"What's wrong with you, Jewel?" His breath was heavy on my face. He sounded anguished, and absolutely clueless. "Why are you bugging out on me?"

"What's wrong with me? Take a look in the mirror, Jim Jim." My nostrils flared with indignation.

Sheltered from the restaurant's flood lamps, the only light came from the hovering moon. And it dashed across our shadows. For the second time in a single hour, he looked wounded. I wanted to take back everything I'd said. Start the night over. Better yet, not even have gone out with him.

"Let me try it this way, Indigo." I was up in his face. "You confuse the hell out of me. I'd go to battle for you, but I'm not up for fighting with your loved ones ... over you. So let me leave, please, before things get worse."

My heart was breaking. I desperately wanted him, but was I up for all of the unnecessary stress and baggage that came with him? I didn't mean half of what I was saying, but there didn't seem to be an alternative. Being without him was painful, but being with him wasn't much better. I had to escape.

"Fighting for me? Jewel, I think about you almost every minute of every day. Even while I'm at the hospital, trying to concentrate on my work." His breath was short. "You don't have to fight for me ... you have me."

His healing hands were strong, and beneath his touch I was about to break.

"I see your face when I'm not with you, feel the touch of your hands, and I want to ..."

"You want to fuck me." My words tumbled out in a strangled gasp.

"Oh God. I just want to be with you. Can't you get it through your head?"

He watched me with a stare so intense, I felt it deep in my soul. My heart pounded. My chest rose and fell at an almost intolerable rate.

Without warning, he brought his lips down on mine with such force our teeth clashed. His tongue fiercely rounded my mouth, then raked over mine, again and again. He drew in my bottom lip, sucking, caressing, his tongue doing incredible things that made my legs all but cave in.

When I moaned, he released his hold. I recklessly wrapped my arms around his neck, returning his kiss with a passion I never knew existed inside me. My hips tucked against his, rolling like angry waves, while my breasts crushed his chest, our bodies molding together until not even a breeze could slip between us. Then his lips slid from mine, and his breath was hot in my ear. His winded voice sounded desperate. "Baby. Please don't go."

He held me so close I could barely breathe; he was whispering, telling me he was sorry for what they'd done, and he'd never do anything to hurt me.

A flash of lightning lit the sky above us, but it was the Wrangler's headlights that finally broke us apart. "We'll take this up in the car." Indigo sounded like he'd just run a marathon. He picked up my purse, dusted it off, and put it into my hands.

I could barely move, and I knew he felt the same. I watched his fingers fumble with the keys the valet handed him. Even in shadows, the flush of his face was evident. Nervously, I fluffed out my love worn hair, removing the clip, so it hung in unruly waves over my shoulders, down my back.

When Indigo tucked me into the passenger seat my head was spinning, every nerve in my body heightened. The concept of sitting demurely didn't enter my mind, and I surrendered to his hands as he lifted me, rearranging the position of my torso, my legs, the hem of my dress. All the while I felt his breath on my face, fought the urge to pull him down on top of me.

I let my head drift with his movements, craving his body as he rounded the car, the headlights emphasizing his strides, the stillness of his profile. I let my head fall to the side, watched him make his way to the open door across from where I sat shivering, filled with such longing: longing for his hands to tear at my clothing, my skin, my heart, my soul, devouring me until I was no more a part of the universe. Then I would no longer want, or need, or breathe, for life had become far too painful.

My eyes clung desperately as he shrugged out of his jacket and flung it on the back seat. Loosened his tie, rashly stripping it from his neck. Then he was on the seat beside me, and without closing the door, he unbuttoned his shirt midway down his chest, emitting a ragged burst of air as though the clothing had strangled him. But I knew it was desire that had stolen his breath.

He turned to me with a tortured look, as if grappling with the biggest decision of his life, and needed my understanding, my help; his stare intense, as if battling an army of demons.

Concern sprung from my lips, sobering me. "Are you okay to drive? Because we can call for a taxi ..."

"I'm fine." With a firm grip he pulled his door closed with such force it slammed, rattling the windows.

I knew not to question him. He was working through something monumental, no doubt, as I had before, and I would let the decision be his alone. He didn't seem like the same man who'd hours earlier smiled in the lobby of my apartment building.

Lightning struck on the heels of thunder, and the sky turned pitch black, masking the moon, the stars. Isolated raindrops thumped against the windshield, the roof, then the sky unleashed a furious downpour.

Riding in silence built anticipation until I was ready to burst. We seemed to be going in a different direction than the one from which we'd come, and I didn't recognize the route we were taking. "Are we heading home?"

"We were, but with this heavy rain it's difficult to see. Cars seem to be pulling off ... stopping." Obviously concentrating on the road, his words were mechanical, yet urgent. At least the weather wasn't my fault.

I opened my eyes to a blur of headlights jamming the road before us, vehicles gathering on the flooding shoulders. The speed of the Wrangler reduced to almost a crawl. A sign to my right was washed by our headlights, and we took the turn.

"We won't be heading home just yet ... if it's okay with you." His grip on the wheel tightened, as though a conclusion had been reached and he was seeking permission, or forgiveness perhaps for a crime not yet committed.

My silence seemed to be all the absolution he needed. Pressing deep into the seat, I let my head fall upon the cushioned back, while my hands fell limply to my lap, folding in an odd position. I felt my shoes being kicked off, and the wiggle of my toes that had numbed. For more times than I could count, my head rolled to the side and back again, and I watched vehicles transform into residential roadsides.

We coasted onto a tree-lined road where our headlights pointed to gracious homes slipping by either side of the Wrangler. Rain drenched the roof, flooded the windshield, and Indigo turned the wipers to a higher speed.

The rows of trees eventually yielded to a meadow, where our lights grazed a turnaround. Through the heavy downpour I could barely discern the street sign which evaporated when the headlights dimmed.

Rain pounding the roof, keys dangling in the ignition, the relief of thumping wipers, and a clicking under the hood as the engine calmed were the sounds that competed with the rush of blood that drummed in my ears. Inside my chest my heart throbbed, matching the pulse in my head which I managed to lift, although it still felt weighted by a ten pound bag of cement ... as well as the world. I straightened in the seat, searching for my bearings, my eyes halting on Indigo's profile. He was looking straight ahead through what no longer appeared to be a windshield, but rather a sleek ebony ocean.

Lightning continued to bleach the sky, accompanied by rumbling claps of thunder.

"Guess you and the weatherman were right, huh?" I tried for a light tone, but my attempt was pitiful. Suddenly aware of the darkness of night, the isolation, the situation I was about to face, my heart throbbed even faster. "Are the doors locked?"

Indigo snapped a lever on his armrest, and I heard a double click. "Yup. You're safe and sound, in here, with me."

Turning in his seat he faced me, and with each burst of lightning I was able to see the hunger in his eyes. Watch the movement of his hands as they gripped and released the wheel. Before I realized what was happening, I was lifted, pulled across the seat, lowered onto his thighs and wedged between his chest and the steering wheel, defenseless against the strength of his desire ... as well as my own.

He rolled the seat back until it stopped dead on its tracks. For a stunning moment I went limp, then my mind insisted it was okay to feel this way. To go out on a limb, let him know I wanted him desperately. Worry about the consequences in the morning. I burrowed into his lap, wrapped my arms around his neck. And I waited for the sky to fall.

Pulling me close, his hands caressed my back. Then his lips took control, softly at first, running the length of my neck, crossing my cheek, sweeping over my mouth. A stream of warmth flowed into my ear with his whisper, "I don't plan on fucking you. So if you're wondering why I brought you here, I just want to be alone with you, hold you ... kiss you. Is that alright?"

"Yes." My breath blew out an automatic response.

"I've never met anyone like you before. You do things to me. Crazy things I'm still trying to figure out how to deal with."

"I know the feeling." Another breath worked its way through my throat.

"Tell me when to stop." His moist tongue swept my lips.

"I might ... I will ..."

I felt his passion grow beneath me and I shuddered, shifting my body that reacted wildly to his as I unbuttoned his shirt and pulled it open. My fingers explored every inch of his exposed skin, skimming his neck, drifting to his chest where my palms experienced his muscular smoothness, caressing in circles, vertical paths, from his shoulders down to the belt my fingers were longing to unbuckle.

"Can I touch you?" His voice was as persuasive as his hands.

"Yes." My words were becoming so choked, I thought I'd suffocate at any moment.

His lips consumed every inch of my neck, lingering, nibbling. Then his face drifted to my chest where his lips roamed further than I'd expected, caressing the contour of my breasts, the smooth mounds that strained to be freed from the dress that held them tight.

With one arm locked around me, the fingers of his free hand traced the path his lips had taken, slowly sliding down my neck, inching across my chest, dipping beneath the scoop of my neckline. Acknowledging his intention, chills shot up and down my spine. My head filled with recent memories, both torturous and glorious, and realization shattered my senses. The guy whose body was in overdrive beneath me, whose heated breath was on my skin, was the gorgeous man I'd given my heart to in Kelly's, and here I was, in his arms. Should I die on the spot, as my pounding heart threatened to explode? Surrender to that small voice in my head that warned this might be the biggest mistake of my life ... or let myself go ... be swept away by ecstasy.

The windows were fogged, the sound of our breathing so heavy, I wasn't sure if it was his breath, or mine, or the heat of our bodies that clouded the glass. I felt the weight of a single finger as it rounded my breast, lightly skimming the silky fabric, all that stood between his hands and my skin. The stimulating circle grew smaller until my nipple tightened beneath his insistent touch, burning the tingling flesh beneath my dress.

I had no control over my body that strained against his, my hips that rocked with encouragement, overwhelming desire that flooded my senses. I fought the urge to grasp the hardness beneath me, touch him intimately, as he was doing to me.

When I moaned his name, he reacted by cupping my entire breast, his touch growing firmer, lifting, almost ejecting my breast from the garment's hold. Again and again he cupped and released until I thought I would die.

"Indigo ..." I squirmed, feeling him harden even more than I'd imagined possible.

"Baby," he groaned, "you have no idea what you're doing to me. But if you want me to stop, tell me and I will. I'll do whatever you want ... but I'm not going to fuck you ... not here ... not now. You mean more to me than a quickie in my car."

"I don't want you to stop yet ... just a little more ..."

His fingers slipped beneath the beaded neckline, inched to my shoulder, tugging my dress down to my elbow. The spandex bodice sprang from my body, snapping like a rubber band, settling into place where it clung to my ribs, baring an entire breast. An instant rush of cool air, blending with his urgent breath, swept my skin. Goose bumps covered my nakedness.

My fingers threaded through his hair, pulling, tangling. I rocked my hips, sucked on his neck until I almost drew blood, moaning his name, whispering, "Please ..."

He took my breast in his mouth, sucking gently, his tongue circling my throbbing nipple. Feeling the thrill of his lips deep in my belly, I drew his face closer, silently begging for more.

A fierce moan escaped my lips. A voice that could not have been my own whispered, "I thought you weren't going to touch my nipples ... make me suffer." My breath came so fast I could barely speak.

He lifted his face, his hand replacing his mouth. "You drive me crazy ... whether I'm with you ... or without you. I can't stop thinking about you. And that could be dangerous."

"Dangerous?"

"You make me want more than sex ... and I ..."

"Ssh. Just keep kissing me." I moaned into his mouth.

A euphoric throb of pleasure built between my thighs, threatening to explode. Our bodies rocked with a mutual tempo, creating a delicious friction, triggering the reflex of my contracting muscle.

I pulled his face to mine, swept his mouth with my tongue that parted his lips, greedily tasting the sweetness inside. I'd never kissed anyone that way before. I bit his bottom lip, swirled my tongue around his, drawing it deep inside my mouth, kissing him so fiercely, his hips lurched with a force greater than mine.

He peeled down the other side of my dress and slipped my arms through the sleeves, so the spandex rode on my hips ... and then we were skin to skin, my breasts pressed firmly against his bare chest; so firmly I felt his heart, maybe mine. His hands ran up my back, tangled in my hair, rested on my shoulders and massaged, his fingers stroking my neck, circling it from behind, easing my tension. Somehow I moaned, "Mmm, that feels so good."

My breasts slid again and again across his chest, then he murmured something into my ear, a tortured, inaudible whisper, and I was eased away, positioned across his lap, an arm around his neck, my other on the steering wheel.

The sound of his breathing filled my ears. His restless eyes bore into mine, and my heart pounded even harder. While he watched my face melt before him, his palms ran slowly across my breasts, lingering on my nipples. His fingers squeezed; his hands kneaded, driving me to frenzy. Moaning, I brought my lips to his, arching my back, forcing my tingling breasts further into his hands, my rigid nipples deeper into his palms.

Groaning, his lips broke from mine, and he lowered his mouth to suck my breasts until I thought I'd come from the electricity created by his teeth upon my nipples. He repositioned me on his lap, showing my body precisely how he wanted it to rock. His hands were all over me, sliding, searching, caressing, but when his fingers traveled up the inside of my thighs, attempting to satisfy my obvious need, I froze.

I desperately wanted him inside me. The things we'd said to each other on the phone, the emotion between us like a trillion volts of electricity, stunned me, clouding my head, and it would have been so easy to let go.

Should I? Should I not? Being so close to consummation was like craving a five-thousand calorie desert. But then there was the next morning when you stepped onto the scale, finding yourself ten pounds heavier, wishing you'd never taken the first bite. Regretting it. Avoiding the temptation at all costs. Indigo was something, someone I'd never want to avoid.

I may have lost myself in passion, but my inner strength soared higher than delicious desire. I knew right then and there that I had passed the PEW test. At the same time, my decision confirmed Indigo was more than the flavor of the month, and for as much as I wanted him, I was determined to remain in control.

Caught between my thighs, his fingers stiffened. "Do you want me to stop?" His words were barely audible.

My hand slipped down to cover his. "I want you more than anything. I never want you to stop ... but we have to ... I can't ..." Then I spaced, practically fainting in his arms.

His head came to rest on my shoulder. I felt his labored breath against my throat, then his whisper. "We won't go any further. Not until you're ready." His voice shook when he asked, "Can I still kiss you?"

"Yes," I moaned. "Kiss me, please kiss me."

His grip loosened, and he was kissing my lips, then my breasts with such tenderness, as though they were precious. A heartbeat later, he helped me back into my dress. "I don't want you to do anything that makes you feel uncomfortable. I'd never want to do that."

"It's so hard, Indigo. I love how you touch me ... how you make me feel," I groaned with a voice still controlled by his kiss which had ended. "I want you to touch me."

"I guess you could say I lose control when I'm around you ...." As though raking through thoughts, his voice grew guarded.

My lips pressed his chest. "It's a predicament." Still trembling, I let out a burst of air. "I don't know what to do ..." My voice was an odd combination of hoarse, honey and sex.

"I don't want you to think all I want from you is sex. There's something special about you. You're so full of life. So different. When I'm with you, I'm ... you're changing everything inside me. I don't want us to argue anymore ... ever. I just want to be with you, Jewel. Make you happy."

"You make me happier than I ever thought possible, Indigo."

With a finger beneath my chin he lifted my face. "Regardless of how I may react when we're together, don't ever feel pressured." His lips brushed mine. "I can wait."

I buried my face in his neck, my lips caressing the straining tendons as I trembled in his arms, fighting to recover.

"You're the most amazing woman I've ever been with, Jewel." He cradled me, brushing wisps of hair from my forehead, tucking loose strands behind the ear he'd just nuzzled, whispered into. "With or without what just happened. When I look in your eyes, it's like taking a first breath of sweet air on a mountain touching heaven. Like walking through a doorway. I'm on edge, filled with expectation. I'm not sure where I'm going, but I know it's important, beautiful. And I belong there. Wherever you take me, is where I want to be."

Resting my chin on his shoulder, I groaned. No one had ever made me feel this way. Said such beautiful things to me. When I lifted my face, a breath caught in my throat. Tears burned my eyes.

He frowned. "Are you okay?"

"I'm okay. Are you?" I drew back to watch him. "I know stopping like that is hard on a guy. I had no intention of leading you on."

His lips crushed my words and we kissed, halting before passion turned to delirium.

"Believe me," he said softly, "I understand where you're coming from, Sunshine. Getting carried away is so easy. We'll take it slow ... at your pace." His voice was still uneven, as were his fingers when they tweaked my nose. "From now on, we'll make sure our dates stay in public places." His bottom lip quivered, then stretched into a smile.

I gazed up at him, my eyes half closed. "You're sure ...?"

"Don't ever worry about me. I'm fine. As long as I'm with you. You make me forget the world."

Making Plans

Morning cut a blistering swathe through the slats of the blinds shielding my double windows. With closed eyes I stirred, stretched, luxuriating beneath my warm and cozy and very fuchsia percale sheets. Lazing beneath the covers, enjoying the relaxation rarely afforded to me, I let my mind, my entire body, drift into the night before. Just as I was reliving the part where I'd almost surrendered to my inner craving, my cell chimed, jarring me from my sexy dream world where instead of bedding, I was draped by Indigo's body, hard and demanding.

"Shit," I mumbled. Rolling onto an elbow, I slapped my mattress a few times, my hand reaching beneath the covers, searching for the phone I was never without. I found it under my pillow and opened my inbox, thrilled to see Indigo's name staring up at me.

Indigo: Hey beautiful. Am I waking you?

I ran my fingers through my hair, brushing strands from my face, then fluffed my pillow and lay back down, holding the phone above me.

Indigo: U up yet?

Me: Yup U? *Duh, do you think he's texting you in his sleep?*

Indigo: Just rolling around in bed ... thinking about you

Eeeek. Had he read my thoughts?

Me: Really? No work?

Indigo: Joking Been up since 5

Me: God U must be exhausted

Indigo: Had a fantastic time last night

Me: So did I!

Indigo: Get enough sleep?

Me: Yes U?

Indigo: I'm used to 3 hr naps What's it like out?

Me: The weather?

Indigo: Yeah Locked in lab No windows

Me: Sunny

Indigo: Like my face right now :-)

Me: Aw U @ hosp?

Indigo: Yep You're amazing, Jewel

Me: So are U Indigo Miss u

Indigo: Miss you more Gotta run, babe

Me: Laters :o)

Indigo: Sooner xoxo

I stared at his text, almost melting, then hugged my phone, wishing it was Indigo sharing my pillow instead of an electronic gadget. Ugh. I hated how I missed him. But loved how he made me hate to miss him.

The ringtone jarred me, and my phone almost flew to the floor.

"Jewelia?"

"It's me, Ma." *You're calling my number. Who else did you think I'd be?* "Is everything okay?"

"Daddy hurt his back."

"Oh no." I panicked. I loved my family dearly, and being away was hard enough without having to worry about them getting sick or suffering accidents.

"He'll be fine. We could use you here."

My heart flipped inside my chest. "Is he in the hospital again?"

"He was, but they sent him home with medication and a

wrap after they took x-rays. It's the same two discs that always give him a problem."

"I'm sorry I can't be there."

"We miss you. How have things been, Jewelia? We don't hear from you often enough."

"Things are fine. I'm just busy, and I miss you guys too." Without me there to help organize things, I worried. "Can Tony help out at the bakery? Maybe Teresa can come in after school without eating all the cookies?" I chuckled.

"Your brother and sister have been helping, and Teresa's been dieting, so all cookies stay on the shelves till sold." She returned my chuckle.

"Really? Why's she dieting?" We'd all been chubby kids who'd slimmed out in high school, so I didn't see why Teresa was concerned. I hoped she wasn't idolizing Tony's girlfriends, trying to grow up too fast.

"You'll see when you come up. She wants to surprise you, so I can't say."

"Soon Mom. May's almost over. I'll have free time soon." Then I thought of my obligations at work. My loyalty was to my family, but I had to finish school, and keep my job.

"I took on more hours, Mom."

"Don't jeopardize your studies, Jewelia. You've worked too hard for this."

"I'm doing fine." I couldn't wait to show my parents my final grades. My 3.8 would be almost as good as my older sister's 4.0 GPA. "How about I come up on Sunday? Early and I'll stay till the last train. Maybe Dad will be better by then and we can go to the park like the old days. We'll have a nice time."

While growing up, besides picnics and planned outings, we'd have family basketball days as often as possible. I missed those times.

Then it hit me. Why not ask Indigo to come to Poughkeepsie? I'd met his mother, he could meet mine. I was proud of my family and dying to share them, not to mention, show Indigo off to them.

"I may bring a friend, Mom. Would that be okay?"

"You don't even have to ask. Emma's always welcome. I'll make a big pot of that chili and rice that she loves. Tacos too."

"I wasn't talking about Emma."

Silence then Mom's giggle. "Is there a man in your life?"

The sound in her voice set me off and everything gushed out – well, almost everything – with me telling her how handsome and sweet Indigo was. She almost fainted when I told her he was going to be a doctor.

"We'll have everyone over to meet him."

"No, please don't, Mom." I could see it all. The fiasco of the entire Delarosa clan in action. "I don't want to overwhelm him."

"Oh, Jewelia. Angelina will kill us if she finds out we didn't invite her."

"Whatever." I'd have to tell Indigo to sedate himself before leaving the city.

After hanging up, a wave of nostalgia washed over me, and I worried. My parents weren't getting any younger, and had always been strong. I didn't want things to change. And the thought of losing them some day was incomprehensible.

Then my thoughts shifted to Indigo, wondering how he'd react being bombarded by my overzealous family. Although he was down to earth, his mother was uppity. I had no idea what his father was like, and hoped for Indigo's sake, he was warmer than she appeared. If not, he must have had a lonely time growing up. I wanted to hug him, right then, right on the spot. But my only option was to text him, hoping he wasn't on rounds or in a patient's room.

Me: Taking temps, doc?

It was a half hour before he got back to me. By then I was at the gym, ready for my workout.

Indigo: Hey you

Me: How's it going?

Indigo: Good U?

Me: Great U working Sunday?
Indigo: Nope
In moments, my phone rang.

A breath caught in my throat when I heard his voice on the other end. "Texting's okay, but I'd much rather hear your voice."

"Oh, so would I ... Your voice, I mean." I giggled. "Are you on a break?"

"I have a few minutes and couldn't think of a better way of spending them than talking to my Sunshine."

"You're so sweet." I clasped my phone tighter and settled on a bench.

"But I'd much rather be right there with you. Where are you, by the way?"

"At the gym."

"So that's the secret to those killer curves."

I giggled.

"What's going on Sunday?"

"Poughkeepsie. Wanna come?"

"Meet the folks, huh?"

"You wouldn't be nervous, would you?" The thought he might be was astonishing.

"All guys are." He chuckled. "Does your dad – maybe your mom – keep a bat behind any of the doors? Under beds?"

"Funny you should mention bats." I laughed.

"Uh oh. I might be busy on Sunday, after all."

"They may jump you, but in a good way."

"I'll wear my football padding."

"And helmet. My little sister likes to roll around on the floor."

Playfulness left his voice. "Sounds like a lot of fun. Of course I want to come. Gotta run. I'll call you tonight to firm up the details. It may be late, though. Is that okay?"

"Any time, any place, baby." With my sexiest voice I teased.

"I'll make sure to take you up on that." His chuckle was teasingly sarcastic, and very sexy. "Later then."

"Sooner ..." I spoke too late, because he'd already disconnected.

Wheelin' To Poughkeepsie

Indigo and I decided to rendezvous at Grand Central Station at eight a.m. I arrived at seven-forty-five and waited in front of one of my favorite breakfast stands.

I'd told Indigo to dress very casual, as I wasn't sure of what we'd be doing. Watching him stride into the terminal, I almost fell over with desire. Apparently, so did a few other females whose eyes tracked his every move. He wore relaxed jeans that still hugged his thighs, a pale blue tee covered by a long-sleeved plaid shirt that lay open, exposing the contours of his muscular chest. The flaps of the shirt rippled as he moved, showing off his toned abs.

At my request, he'd been letting his hair grow, and it curled over the collar. A hint of shadow highlighted the area of his face where a man's beard usually grew.

I hurried toward him, my lips spreading into a slow smile. "You made it on time," I breathed.

Our eyes had a way of transmitting this amazing electricity. From the look on his face, I knew he could read my every emotion. "Of course I'm here on time, babe. I wouldn't miss this for anything. In fact, I've been gearing up for this visit since you invited me." He winked, then his lips touched my forehead. "Didn't have a chance to grab my morning coffee, though."

"No problem." I swept an arm across the front of a glass case overloaded with mini pies and pastries. "Pumpkin? Apple? Cherry?" I stared up at him with concern. "I hope you're not counting calories today. These are nothing like you'd find in my dad's bakery, but like they say, make do with what you have and don't bitch 'cos things could be worse."

He chuckled. "You can take the girl out of the bakery, but not the bakery out of the girl." He slipped an arm around my waist and squeezed. "You're the expert. You make the selection." He had the sexiest habit of burying his cheek against my hair, the way a snuggling kitten would when it purred and burrowed against its human's chest.

"One pumpkin and one apple mini, please, and throw a plastic knife in the bag. And a lot of napkins, and two mocha lattes, extra foam. Not in the bag." I joked with the guy behind the counter. Deepening my dimples, I faced Indigo. "I can never make up my mind. We'll share." I ran my tongue over my top lip.

His eyes were as soft as the touch of his fingers as he stroked the side of my face and lifted my chin. "Does that statement apply to everything?"

"That's something you'll have to keep guessing about, smarty pants." Staring up at him, I crinkled my nose.

He kept outdoing himself, making my legs go weak, my stomach drop. Would the way he made me feel ever stop? I didn't want to know the answer. A voice brought the flow of blood back into my limbs as it shot through the PA system, announcing the number of our train and its departure time.

"Ooh." My shoulders jerked with excitement. "Train's almost ready to pull out. Let's hoof it." I grabbed the bag off the counter, and Indigo snatched the lattes. We fell into a perfectly timed trot.

Mounting the steps, I noticed a rolled up magazine sticking

out of his back pocket, not quite hooded by his shirttail.

"What's this?" Standing in the aisle I pulled it out and let the glossy pages unravel. I arched my brows. "Cycling?"

"I thought I might read it on the train." He grinned. "I don't get all that much down time."

"Down time? Is that what I am?" I took a swat and the magazine connected with the wallet in his other back pocket, resounding with a loud crack. "No way. You've got me to keep you occupied for an entire hour and forty minutes." I pouted. "No reading."

"Yes, ma'am. Now can we take a seat? Unless you want to lap your latte off this disgustingly dirty floor." He faked a scowl. "Because this train's about to pull out of the station."

"You silly." I bumped his hip with mine. "You ride the subway, don't you?"

"Actually, I don't ride the subway."

"Oh ... just climb in, will you?" I shot him another jolt of my hip, but when the train took off I boomeranged against him, laughing.

We chose seats in the rear of one of the last cars where we could face one another. As soon as the conductor clipped our round trip tickets, I tore into the bag.

"I'm starving." I handed Indigo a fork and napkins.

"So am I. These pies look delicious. Here you go." He held out my latte.

We sipped our drinks and dug into spicy pumpkin and juicy apples, stuffing our mouths as if we hadn't eaten in a week. Between bites we chatted, laughing as we wiped pie from each other's lips.

I kicked off my flats, ran a foot up and down his calf. "I see you came prepared. I like your hiking boots." I stuck a toe through the loop of one brown boot, playing with the lace until it loosened and uncoiled.

"You're a little brat." He snatched my toes, tugging on my foot, pulling me to the edge of the seat. "As soon as we finish eating, you can come over here and give me a real massage."

He fluttered his brows.

"Hey," I yelped when my butt all but slid off the slippery vinyl. "Is physical contact all you ever think about?" I shook my head, disguising my delight.

"Look who's talking." He laughed. "I had a hard week. I could use a nice massage ... good company ... relaxation."

"I'm afraid all you'll be getting today is the second of your three desires."

"We'll see about that." He winked.

The train picked up speed and we left behind urban areas, some isolated, some with graffiti decorated buildings. Then the ride smoothed out, along with the scenery. We followed the Hudson River most of the way, now and then the car jostling on the track.

"It's beautiful, isn't it?" I said, gazing out the side windows, watching blossoming foliage slide past my left, the peaceful river on my right.

"Sure is. Next time we'll take my boat." Indigo smiled. "We can go tubing. Get all nice and sludgy together."

"Let me guess, and a nice warm shower afterward?" When my eyes bulged, he laughed.

"I'm joking about the tubing, but the shower would be nice." He sipped, then licked latte foam from his lips.

"Do you own a yacht?" My question was spoken with innocence. "I'd choose a smooth sail over a noisy train ride any day."

"I'm afraid not, babe." He almost choked on his last mouthful of latte. "I'm more the speed boat type."

Just what I'd figured all along. Smug, I curled my lips. "Fourth of July on the Sound, right?"

"Yes, and it's spectacular. So what am I in for during today's visit?" We sat knee to knee, near enough for him to reach me with his fork and shove pumpkin pie into my mouth, laughing when it smeared across my cheek. "You've got to help me with this. You stuffed me so full of apples ..." He flopped back against his seat, sliding the fork over his lips and tongue, then patted his flat stomach.

"Umm." I put a hand over my bulging lips. "You wait." I giggled, attempting to swallow without choking. "Payback in Poughkeepsie. And you may have to come over here and give me CPR if you keep trying to block my airway with pie." I snorted and he let out a burst of laughter.

"How big is your family, anyway?" He compressed our cups and containers into the bag and folded it neatly.

"Two sisters, one brother in law, a younger brother, and a soup de jour girlfriend might be there. One never knows when dealing with Antonio."

"Your brother's Antonio?"

"And my father, but in this case, I'm talking about Tony."

"I'll have to remember that." Reaching across the seat he grabbed my hand, pulled me over his legs, and plopped me down beside him.

I snuggled under his arm, buried my lips in his neck. Coming up for air, I threw an arm around his chest, a leg over his, and squeezed. "You're so nice and cuddly."

"And you are irresistibly huggable." Wrapping me in his arms he kissed me, his tongue gently parting my lips, but not entirely entering. When he drew back his eyes were heavy. "And you taste so much better than pie and latte." He gave me a big hug, then ruffled my hair, easing me back onto the seat. "Maybe you should give me a crash course on your family before we get there."

I slung my leg back over his, snuggling as close to him as possible. "Yeah. I guess it's time to warn you."

"You're starting to make me worry." He squeezed my kneecap and I let out a scream.

"Don't worry, they'll love you. Hopefully the feeling will be mutual." I slapped my palms on my thighs. "My family is wonderful. But kinda like acquiring a taste for scotch, they take some getting used to ... and can be somewhat overwhelming."

"Like you?" He kissed the tip of my nose.

I giggled, then ran my fingers through his hair. "I like playing with your waves."

He shot me a funny look, then tugged my ponytail loose, completely ransacking my hair. I pulled my brush from my purse and slapped it into his palm. "Here. Let's see if you can fix what you just destroyed. I feel like a mangy poodle."

He brushed my hair smooth, then swooped it off my shoulders, securing it back into a fluffy ponytail.

"Wow ... you do have the touch. As good as any hairdresser, I might add." I took his hand, inspecting its perfect proportions. "These fingers are very talented. You'll be a great surgeon someday."

"More than that, I hope." He tweaked my chin, then stared out the window for a moment.

"I'm sure you'll be everything you want to be." Gazing up at him, I twisted the silver rose ring I always wore on my right ring finger. "Let's just say, I'm positive."

"I'm glad you're positive. Let me see," he snatched my hand and examined it, "you've got such delicate fingers. It's hard to think of you wrestling guys twice your size to the ground when you're a cop. Cuffing them. Dragging them into the station." There was an odd sound in voice, something like protectiveness. "Let me see your ring." His finger skimmed mine. "I've noticed you wear it all the time. Just partial to it? Or is there a story behind it." He ran a fingertip over the rose in full bloom, then touched the amethyst buds on either side.

I sighed. Blinking away tears pooling in my eyes, I angled my face toward the window. "I almost wasn't born. My mother had to stay in bed for the last five months of pregnancy. Something to do with blood pressure and proteins."

"Preeclampsia?"

"Yes. That's it. They strongly advised her to abort. She was that close to ..."

"Oh, I'm sorry." Indigo drew me close, stroked my hair. "At least you're here and your mom is fine."

"Yup. She's fine. And my dad was so scared, and so happy

we were both okay, that every year on my birthday I got a cake and my mom got pink roses – a symbol for joy. When I turned sixteen, he gave me this ring."

"That's a beautiful story, Jewel."

"That's when I got this." I leaned forward, yanking the collar of my knit shirt off one shoulder.

"Awesome ink." I felt a tingle as his fingers ran over my rose tattoo. "Mi Rosa Mi Joya?"

"My mother's name is Maria Rosa, and I guess I was his joy. So ..."

"So, you're not only beautiful, you're sentimental." He tugged me close.

With my head on his shoulder, I snuggled beside him for the remainder of the ride. We didn't talk much after that. We didn't have to.

The Delarosa Clan

By the time we pulled into the Poughkeepsie train station, I had that morning after hangover headache from the long ride and sugar high.

"We'll hike it, okay? It's just a few blocks," I said casually to Indigo whose head rotated every which way like a drifter would do when he blew into town after being gone for months. "I need the exercise. Have to get into shape for the Police Agility Test."

"From my point of view," Indigo gave me an intentional once-over with mischievous eyes, "everything looks perfect to me. Although, without giving you a physical, I can't say for sure."

My hand flew to my mouth to keep my bubble gum from ejecting with a burst of laughter. I swatted his arm playfully, but shivered at the thought of his touch, remembering how hot he'd made me feel in the Wrangler.

Imagining women lying half-naked on his exam table, my hand tightened around his. Professions like that had to be hard on any relationship, regardless of the physical and emotional shape of any spouse.

Then the thought of him specializing in pediatrics brought sudden relief. Had he been an OB/GYN, I don't think I could have taken it. The thought of him anywhere near another woman's private body parts, professional setting or not, would have taunted me to tears. Women ogling him, coming on to him. How many doctors fell in love with nurses, anyway? With patients?

After my reverie I took his hand, squeezing as if the pressure would keep him at my side forever.

"Hey. There's our bakery," I said, pointing to the glass front building with wedding cakes and other goodies decorating the window.

"Oh nice. It looks like a cool place."

"Yeah, it is," I giggled, "I worked there till I finished high school. I liked to help out ... and organize."

"Are you a little neat freak?"

"Hardly. But I was great at keeping track of stock and ordering. I hated the idea of waste, and since throwing food away wasn't an option, we'd give away fresh baked leftovers to neighbors and our best customers – and brought far too many home." I patted my tummy. "Sometimes we'd deliver dozens of boxes of yummy donuts someone had ordered and never picked up to a local shelter."

His face went all soft. "The first time I saw you, I knew there was something I liked about you."

"And what was that?" I stared up at the sky, then shifted my wistful gaze to him, wondering if I could stand it if he started getting all sappy with me in broad daylight.

"Donuts!" He tickled me.

I squealed and pulled away from his fingers that dug mercilessly into my ribcage.

"You're not going anywhere." He laughed, capturing me in a bear hug. "I know all the right spots."

"Yes you do." I giggled, wrenched free and started running.

"I've got all the right moves, too." I laughed, but before I could move a muscle, he swung me in front of him, wrapped me in his arms, and walked me backward, very deliberately, one step at a time. And there it was yet again, that stunning look on his face. Sleepy and sexy. Grandma would have called it *bedroom eyes.*

"I like your moves." As if dancing in reverse, I locked my arms around his neck and let him lead.

"I know you do." He brought us nose to nose.

"Show me some more." My pursed lips reached for his.

"Later ..." At the same time he swept me into the air, his lips came down on mine.

I was spinning, losing track of where I was, who I was, locked in the wonderland of his arms, when the sound of a honking horn startled me back to reality.

"What the hell?" I said, twisting my head toward the irritating sound.

Indigo set me down, and we both spun. His arm remained snug around my waist.

I stared at my little brother's primed Camaro idling at the curb. The passenger window was rolled down, and he hunkered between the steering wheel and a blonde girl who sat in the bucket seat beside him. She had that deer in the headlights expression.

"Tony," I yelled, hunching down to see inside the car, "what the hell are you doing? You want to give me a heart attack?"

He chuckled. "Come on, hop in." His coal black hair was pulled severely to the nape of his neck. His green eyes were smiling and filled with mischief. He was simply dashing. He so reminded me of Antonio Banderas.

The Camaro's back seat was not only small, but it was loaded with boxes of car parts and blankets. Tony threw an arm over the seat and started shoving things to the side.

"Don't bother. I'm not riding with junk."

"It's not junk. It's part of a delivery I have to make."

"Doesn't look bakery to me."

"I work for a car dealer after school." He grinned up

at me.

Tony started sizing up Indigo, kind of like brothers had a habit of doing. I noticed the blonde's eyes had been roaming over both of us during the entire conversation. She didn't even smile.

"Antonio," I said, "This is Indigo."

Indigo reached into the car and they clasped hands. I heard their muffled voices overlap a deep, "Hey, man." Then Indigo moved back to my side.

In Spanish, I called out to Tony, "What are you doing with a crabby twelve year old? You better be careful you don't get arrested, jerk."

He made a thumbs up behind the girl's head, then shot me the *A-ok* with his thumb and forefinger, returning my Spanish. "She's almost your age, sista." His smile was so broad, I could almost count his straight white teeth.

"No way," I said, the side of my mouth curling dubiously. "You better check her I.D."

He nudged her arm. "Shannon, that's my sister, Jewelia. Tell her how old you are."

"I'm twenty years old," she replied in a flat voice.

"Oh my God," I whispered to Indigo. "With a ten year old brain ... if that. Leave it to my brother."

Indigo smiled and shook his head. "Gotta love youth. The world has an entirely different face."

"Tony, you're blocking traffic. Get home. We'll walk," I ordered.

The Camaro roared off, with Tony's arm hanging out his window, flipping me off.

"The Delarosas are certainly lively." Indigo chuckled.

"I wish I could say the same about his girlfriend." I shook my head.

"Yeah, she was kinda solemn. Cute though."

"So you like blondes better than brunettes? Is that what you're telling me?"

He twirled me around, rested both hands on my shoulders

and said, "That's a loaded question. If I say brunette and you go blonde next week, I'll be in trouble, right?"

"Maybe." I stared up at him with my tough broad expression, nodding defensively.

He pinched my nose. "See, a guy just can't win." He slung an arm around my waist and squeezed so tight I lost my breath. Then he whispered in my ear. "I'd like you if you had a purple mohawk." After kissing my forehead, he said, "Your brother seems like a nice kid. Good taste runs in the family."

"Very funny." I jabbed his ribcage with my elbow, then unwrapped his arm and grabbed his hand, pulling him up the walkway. "Here we are. This is my parents' two-story which doesn't seem like the largest colonial anymore."

His brows scrunched together. "How long since you've been home?"

"Not that long. Guess I never noticed." I cringed, knowing nothing on my street could compare to the houses in the Ballou neighborhood.

He surprised me by saying, "I like the area. Seems comfortable, friendly."

"Jewel!" Teresa stood at the doorway, the first to greet us. She flung the door open wide, holding it for us to walk in ahead of her. Then she threw her arms around me like I was a birthday gift she'd longed for and was finally delivered.

"Tessie. I missed you, squirt." I kissed the top of her jasmine scented hair and gave her a huge squeeze. "You smell as delish as whatever Mom's cooking." The house was still but the aroma of spices and tortillas filled the air. "Where is everybody?"

Teresa looked up at me with brown eyes almost too large for her pixie face. "Daddy's in the garage working on the Jeep. That's why he didn't pick you up."

When her stare shifted, I said, "Teresa, say hi to Indigo."

"He's hot." Her voice was flat, but her dark eyes drank in every inch of him.

"Chill out, squirt," I said with affection.

Indigo looked about to roll with laughter. He leaned down

and gently shook her hand. "Nice to meet you, Teresa. What grade are you in?"

She stuck her hands in her jeans pockets and squared her shoulders. "Just finishing fourth."

"Jewel!" My mother called from the kitchen doorway. Her palms slid over her apron which covered part of her slim figure. After untying it, she brought her hands to her mouth and stared, in her native tongue gasping, "Oh, my." Her eyes were stuck on Indigo as she addressed both of us. "How was the train ride? I'm sorry we couldn't be there to meet you, but I've been in the kitchen since seven –"

"I figured. And Dad's out in the garage." I threw my arms around her and planted a kiss on her warm cheek. "I take it his back is better?"

She patted her French braid into place. "He's a fast healer. Speaking of which, you're on your way to becoming a doctor?" She stared at Indigo, unable to suppress her pleasure at the mere thought her daughter was dating a professional. I could see it in her eyes; she was already planning the wedding. "How wonderful."

"Yes, I am." Indigo strode to her side and held out a hand. "*Hola. Es bien en conocer te la Sra. Delarosa.*" [*Hello. It's good to meet you, Mrs. Delarosa.*] Then he leaned in and planted a quick kiss on her cheek.

"*Y tu tambien. Tu hablas español?*" [*And you too. You speak Spanish?*]

"*¿Hace no todo el mundo?*" [*Doesn't everyone?*] He winked at me.

She brought a hand to her heart and turned to me. "He smells like fresh air, with eyes like the sky. He's gorgeous ... and multilingual. You said on the phone, his name is Indigo? An unusual name," my mother commented, the subtle accent she placed on each word making her Latina heritage even more alluring. "But who are we to talk, right? Jewelia Rosa de la Corte Delarosa." She chuckled. "Go and relax in the living room. I'll bring in coffee."

Mom disappeared back into the kitchen, dragging Teresa with her.

I looked at Indigo and lifted a brow. "Wanna see my room?"

"Of course I do." He winked, and followed me up the stairs, pinching my butt as I double-timed the steps, swatting his hand away.

When we reached the landing, I put my arm around his waist, guiding him down the hall and to my room. Once inside, he took me in his arms and began kissing me. I kicked the door closed, reached behind me and locked it.

When we came up for air, Indigo make a quick survey of my room, grinning, saying, "So this is the place, huh?" He walked around, dragging me behind him as he picked up odds and ends, examining books, figurines, even a doll which he held out before me. "You played with dolls?"

"It must be Teresa's. I played with balls."

He laughed. "Now you tell me."

I giggled, "Baseballs, basketballs, you know, those kind of balls."

He stood before my dresser, fumbling with some empty perfume bottles, bringing one to his nose. "Strawberries." I watched his reflection in the mirror drop from a smile to a frown.

"What's wrong?" I asked, pulling him around to face me.

"I have a problem." Looking anguished, he ran his hands through his hair, then backed me into the wall.

My eyes were wide. "What kind of problem?"

His palm came down heavily beside my head, and his face was inches from mine. "You." His lips broke into a grin, and his free hand ran across the front of my shirt.

A tingle raced through me. "I might be able to solve that problem ..." I backed him into my bed, pushed him down, and fell on top of him. He pulled my shirt over my head, ran his hands over the silky cups of my bra and began kissing me with passion. "How much time do we have," he whispered as he unhooked my bra.

He rolled me on my side, and when he pressed his erection against my ass I gasped. "All the time in the world."

"Baby." His breath hit the side of my face. "I really want you." One of his hands brushed my bare nipples, while the other lodged between my thighs. "Right here. Right now."

I felt his body tremble and tense. He flipped me on my back, and rested on an elbow, and while he gazed down at me, I felt the zipper of my jeans being tugged.

My voice came out in a low growl. "Do you have a condom?"

"Of course."

Warnings shot though my brain, but desire won the battle. I turned to face him, slid a hand under his shirt, then my fingers found his fly. His cock was so hard, so hot, I wanted to wrap my lips around it. Before I could, his mouth captured mine, and my jeans were yanked to my knees. His hand swept the inside of my thighs, then his fingers teased their way up to my panties, massaging my clit through the dampened silk.

His cock pulsed in my palm, the rhythm much like the rapid beat of my heart. I slid my fingers loosely up and down his twitching shaft, then increased the pressure. His tongue darted between my lips as he moaned in my mouth. "Are you sure about this, Jewelia?"

Then I heard my name being called.

"I guess it doesn't matter now." My laugh came out as a groan.

Indigo exhaled a long breath. "It's okay. We came to spend time with the family."

Before heading downstairs, I pushed him into the adjoining powder room, where I splashed water on his face, dabbed him dry, then went to work on my own complexion.

We paused in the hallway, flushed and trembling. "I'm sorry," Indigo's voice was gruff.

"About what?"

"What almost just happened."

"Why do you always apologize when we get carried away?" I shot him a puzzled look. "Don't you find me desirable enough?"

"Desirable enough? Christ, I fight a hardon every time I look at you."

"So why are you sorry?"

"I just feel we should keep things light. At least for now."

"Nice way to end a beautiful moment," I mumbled, heading for the stairs.

He caught up to me and spun me around, bringing his lips to my ear. "I'm doing this for you."

I stared up at him, question clouding my eyes.

He kissed the tip of my nose. "I want us to wait until you're ready."

"Are you sure your concern is for me?" I wiggled free and skipped down the stairs.

When we entered the living room, all eyes gravitated to us, leftover heat radiated from my chest to my cheeks. Mom broke the awkwardness by calling everyone to the table. I took Indigo's arm and led him into the dining room.

Dad stood at the doorway, a stern look on his face. "I'm Jewelia's father, as I'm sure you guessed." His gaze went from my pensive expression to Indigo's widening eyes. "I want you to know my children are half of my heart," he thumped his chest, "and this one," he yanked me over for a quick cheek-to-cheek hug, "this one is special."

"She's special to me too." Indigo squeezed my shoulder. "My intentions are honorable, Mr. Delarosa. You don't have to worry about Jewelia when she's with me."

Dad's expression softened and he stuck out a hand. "If I can call you Indigo, you can call me Antonio. And with my speech out of the way," he winked at my mother who looked frozen across the room, "welcome to the family."

As my father's voice boomed, my cheeks burned. I shot Indigo an apologetic look and rolled my eyes. Indigo grinned and squeezed my hand, giving me the impression he'd been in this position before.

Teresa stood beside us, craning her neck. She couldn't seem to take her eyes off Indigo. She chirped in, "His name is Jimmy."

I scrunched my mouth. "Everyone calls him Indigo, Tessie."

She shrugged. "I like Jimmy."

"That's cool." Indigo tugged her hair, which was now in a ponytail like mine.

During casual conversation, we both tried for cool, but the tension between us was explosive. I wanted him so bad, my body still throbbed. We'd come so close. I wondered what would have happened if my mother hadn't called me when she did, and how the hell Indigo could stop so easily after being so damn hard.

"Dinner was fantastic, Mom," I said, but all I could focus on was Indigo's passion. His lips. His cock. I'd catch him looking at me with a heated stare, and wondered what the hell he was waiting for. I thought I had already let him know I was ready.

The photo albums came out, and I held my breath. Indigo seemed amused, but now and then his eyes shadowed with a brooding look that had almost become his signature. The side of him I couldn't see through was troubling.

The chandelier glistened above the table, and I realized it was lighting the room more than the sun, which was setting in brilliant reds and violet blues behind the treed backyard. I checked my watch. "It's been a wonderful day," I said, "but we better get going or we'll miss the last train."

"Good. You and Jimmy can stay over then," said Teresa, who bounced up and down, clapping her hands.

Teresa sat between Indigo and me in the back of the Jeep as Dad drove us to the train station with Mom seated beside him, rambling on about it being the best day in a long time, welcoming Indigo back anytime. Teresa kept cutting in, "Can you come back next week, Jimmy?"

Wheels On A Hot Track

Our visit to Poughkeepsie must have been overwhelming for Indigo, because it had been borderline nerve-wracking for me. The moment the train left the station, he pulled me into his arms with an urgent kiss. "I needed that," he whispered the moment our lips unlocked.

I stroked the shadow of beard spreading from his sideburn to his chin. "It was that bad, huh?"

He chuckled. "No. It was great. I like your family, Jewelia. They're generous, warmhearted folks. Now I know why you're you."

For a breath-stealing moment, I thought he was about to say, "Now I know why I love you." But of course, he didn't. I had to remind myself we were taking things slow.

My lips swept his cheek and I whispered, "They *are* the best. I'm happy you enjoyed yourself. I know they like you too ... especially Teresa." I giggled. "She came on pretty strong."

"Like her sis."

Brows lifted, I stared. "Do I?"

"Without even realizing, which is even more disarming." I wasn't sure which was stronger, the softness or desire in his eyes.

Wrapping my arm around his, I let my head sink onto his shoulder. "Teresa kept calling you Jimmy. She must be into some dude with that name."

"Runs in the family, I guess." He squeezed my thigh.

I peered up at him. "No one calls you Jimmy?"

"Not anymore." His gaze made an uneasy shift to the window. With falling darkness outside, I watched his sober reflection in the glass.

I wondered if the name had been reserved for someone else, and by calling him Jimmy I'd be inching closer, or poaching. My stomach dipped. "Should I call you Jimmy?" I angled my head and studied him.

When he turned, he was himself again. "Coming from your lips, it sounds good."

I lifted my chin. "Okay. I might."

He chuckled. "I especially liked the photo of you under the Christmas tree, wearing your flannel pajamas with the sheriff's badge pinned to your lapel. So, you always liked guns, huh? Remind me not to look at you the wrong way when you're on the force. Maybe I should start now." He shielded his face with his arms, then peeked through his fingers. "And handcuffs from what I understand. You really handcuffed your little sister to the playpen?"

I tugged him free, then pressed my elbow into his hard abs. "Hey. When am I gonna get to see *your* baby pictures?" I lifted a brow.

"In due time, tamale." Knowing it was one of my weak spots, he squeezed my kneecap. I screamed.

"Hey. I didn't know you speak Spanish. How come you never told me?" I gave his abs another nudge.

"Why didn't you tell me *you* speak Spanish?" Eyes innocent, he grinned, pushing my elbow away, pinning my hand to my thigh. "Keep your paws to yourself. My ribs are getting sore."

"I'll have to start telling *you* that." I shot him a sarcastic look. "And who could feel a rib through that muscle?" When I tried to pinch his side, he grabbed my hand.

"Since we've been speaking fluent English, I guess I didn't find the need to mention I speak one or two other languages." His tickling fingers tortured my sensitive ribcage.

I screeched, hopping around in the seat, panting, "What other languages?"

"Russian. Learning Chinese."

"What are you gonna do? Work for the United Nations?"

He turned serious. "Jewel. I'll be practicing ..." he hesitated.

I angled my head. "Yes, I know you'll be practicing ... go on."

"I'll be working with children from a variety of countries. I plan on learning the languages, backgrounds, traits, histories, likes and dislikes of each and every child who walks, or is wheeled through the doors of the hospital."

I'd never witnessed such a degree of dedication. All I could say was a breathless, "Oh."

"No child is going to slip between the cracks if I have anything to say about it."

"Oh." Again, I felt the need for an extra gulp of air.

"There's a lot of work to be done."

"You're such a humanitarian." I threw my arms around his neck, and a leg over his thigh, and started kissing him, compassionately at first, then something deep inside me snapped like a fragile spring stretched beyond its capacity.

We'd left sunset behind in Poughkeepsie, and dusk was settling over the river, colliding with mist. A moon on the rise projected a glow on our surroundings, but it was far too subtle to invade the dimness that had befallen the interior of our car.

When I straddled him, I knew I was asking for trouble. I was mindless. I was floating. I was trembling with passion. Nothing could have torn me away from Indigo's arms other than a train crash, perhaps.

I felt as if the car we were on unlatched and barreled on its own track, swaying, tumbling, and I was thrust headfirst into a tunnel from which I never wanted to emerge. Life was Indigo and me. There was no such thing as tomorrow, because if I had my way we'd be locked in that moment, in each other's arms forever.

My hips were rolling faster than Metro North's wheels. My hands roamed his chest, rounded his pecs, traced his abs. My fingertips swept his neck, stroked his cheeks, tousled his hair, while my mouth occupied his. It didn't matter if I could barely breathe, because I never wanted to come up for air. As my fingers dug into his flesh, the grip of my lips grew firmer. I heard Indigo gasp, felt him stiffen, then he seemed to be carried away with the tide. His arms tightened around me so fiercely, the air in our lungs was shared.

"Jewel ... people will ..." he managed to free his lips, but only for a moment.

"The car is empty. There's no one here but us," my whisper assured.

From our position, we were shielded by the opposing seat, encased in a cubicle of privacy. I felt his craving and longed for him to find the button on my jeans again, confess that he loved me, smother me until our final breaths were drawn as one.

His hands slipped under my sweater, hungrily running the length of my back, the soft pads of his fingers unclasping my bra, drifting up and down my sides.

Moaning, I locked my fingers around his neck, pulling his lips to mine, unable to bring myself close enough to the man who was driving me insane.

Indigo's cologne smelled masculine, his warm lips sweetened by mints. His hair feathered through my fingers, and as thoughts of tomorrow swirled through my mind, everything inside me began to explode. I angled my head every which way, teasing his lips, then sucked in his tongue until it almost touched the back of my throat.

His palms grazed the side mounds of my breasts, each scathing caress capturing more of me. He pinched my nipples between his thumbs and forefingers, twisting until the sensation lit up my insides. I squirmed in his lap, moaning. He drew in a heavy breath, ragged and indecisive, as if struggling with something so much stronger than he was capable of handling.

Suddenly his hands were beneath me, pressing, urging, until the only thing between us were my breasts and his hardness. My body climbed his, rocked without mercy, then slowed, eased, again and again, the friction heating the clothing we wore.

My hips danced, rolling faster than the wheels that carried us home, until I was brought to a screeching halt by my panting partner, who gently pried my fingers from their death grip on the back of his neck, peeled my undulating body off his, and set me onto the seat beside him, his hoarse voice whispering, "If we don't stop now ... I can't be held accountable." His chest rose and fell as if recovering from a five mile run. His face was flushed, his hairline dotted with perspiration.

He shocked me to my senses. I struggled to catch my breath, to throttle my emotions: my racing heart, the tingling ache inside that solicited more and more from me ... from Indigo.

My head rolling in my hands, I groaned. "Oh, God."

He pulled me close, but didn't kiss me. He just held me. I felt him tremble. "Oh, babe. I don't know. I just don't know." His words were choked. "It's getting harder and harder."

"It sure is." I attempted a laugh.

Guilt replaced the butterflies that chewed holes in my stomach when I was with him. Attempting to lighten the mood, I casually said, "Are you okay?"

"Not really." His words were tight.

"Is there anything I can do?"

He stared at me in disbelief. "Seriously?" He heaved one of the biggest sighs I'd ever heard slip through anyone's lips. "Haven't you done enough?" He tried to laugh, but only his shoulders moved.

"If it's any consolation, it's not easy for me either. Women get blue balls too. Even though we don't really have balls, you know the blood collects, and we feel like we're gonna freak if we don't ..."

He looked at me as if I'd just confessed to murder. "Jewel," his voice was flat, "I have extensive knowledge of the human anatomy. I know the physiology of an orgasm, and the effects on a body when it's denied release." His eyes bore into mine. "I know what to do to a woman ... how to bring her to a screaming climax." He ran a finger over my lower lip, a thumb across my cheek.

"You'll have to show me your skills sometime soon, doc." At the thought, my stomach clenched, and my panties drenched.

The train pulled into Grand Central Station shortly after we'd composed ourselves. I cradled the containers of rice and chili Mom had packed for Emma. We hailed a cab and headed for my apartment.

The streets were dim and relatively empty, the pavement glossy with a light drizzle that had begun to fall. Indigo's arm was around my shoulders as we sat in the back of the cab. I put my hand on his knee, once more desperate to know. "Are you sure you're okay?"

In the dimness his pale eyes were crystalline. His thumb strummed my chin, brought my lips to his for a sweet kiss. "Don't worry about anything. I'm fine." He drew back and smiled. "I should be off duty by six on Friday evening. How about I pick you up on the way home? We'll get dinner, take in a movie. Sound good?"

"Sounds amazing." I heaved a sigh and plastered myself against his side, confident everything would be just fine.

Relationship Counseling

𝓕riday couldn't arrive fast enough. I spent the week wallowing in a dream. Indigo was like a drug, and I was addicted. I'd become such a clock-watcher, I felt like a player at crunch time.

After pulling up the zipper of my jeans, I made sure the embroidered seams were smooth and straight.

"Emma! Which sweater goes best with my studded jeans?"

In less than a minute, she appeared in my bedroom doorway, granola bar in hand.

"I keep forgetting to call and thank your mom for the chili and rice she sent home with you," she said as she munched.

"I already told her you ate it almost every night this week for dinner, which says it all."

She laughed. "The only reason I'm not having it tonight is it's finished." She chomped her last piece of granola, crumbled the wrapper, and tossed it into the vanity wastebasket beside the door.

Standing in front of my closet, I pulled out several hangers. "What do you think of this?" I held up a white linen shirt.

"Nah. Looks too western for those jeans."

I wedged it back between others on the rack. "Okay then.

How about this?" I presented a yellow tube top and somewhat matching striped shirt.

Emma laughed. "No way. He'll try to pick you because you'll look like a daffodil in bloom."

I shot her a smirk. "This is the last of my wardrobe." I yanked a purple v-neck angora sweater off the end of the rack.

"Perfection. Purple's your best color." She pulled her cell phone out of her trouser pocket, flopped on my bed, and proceeded to check her messages while I slipped the sweater over my head.

"There goes the hair," I complained. "Nice and staticy." I grabbed my brush and the bottle of static relief Brittany had given me, and went to work on the tangles. After a few minutes, my hair was sleek and shiny, my frizzy head no longer transmitting signals to outer space.

"When's he picking you up?"

"Sixish. How do I look?"

"Splendid."

I plopped down beside Emma. "I have a few minutes." I swept my hand over the smooth satin spread. "You know, something's been bugging me."

She swung her head in my direction. "As usual, I'm all ears."

"I've been really losing control lately. It's like, when I'm around Indigo, I want to be a total slut."

Emma burst out laughing. "I've never known anyone who'd admitted to wanting to be a slut."

"We're getting closer and closer. It's like we're nearing a cliff, but neither of us wants to fall off ... I guess for our own reasons."

"What's yours?"

I curled my bottom lip down. "I'm twenty-one, Emma, and old enough to get laid physically, but psychologically, I have to hold back. I don't want to completely lose it over him. I don't think I could take another Nikos. And Indigo is so much more than Nikos ever was. But there's something about him that's so secretive. He's like a thermometer registering so many different temperatures. That's what's got me going in circles."

"What do you mean? Like he's lying to you? Seeing someone else? Married? Oh my God." She covered her mouth with a hand. "That fuckstick."

"Nooo. I know he's not married. He barely has time for me. I doubt he's hiding a wife and kids anywhere." Suddenly, I felt childish. I leaned to check my reflection in the dresser mirror. "From the boobs up, I guess I look okay," I said offhandedly, carefully lifting the crown of my hair with my fingertips. "He gets distant sometimes, moody, like something's bothering him, but never admits to anything when I ask him. And I know he's holding back."

I stepped in front of my full length mirror, swiveling so I could check my shape in the new jeans that had cost half of my paycheck. "I'm hot, Em. Why can't he lose control with me? I mean, I was like so all over him on the train on Sunday. My boobs in his face, my crotch on his, and he was able to stop on a dime. If I'd had my way, other passengers would have gotten a free show they'd never forget. Thank God no one else was around, because at that point, I didn't care. I was practically unconscious with desire. Had we not been speeding to Manhattan, maybe we wouldn't have stopped. Who knows."

"So, you want him to jump you?"

"No ... yes. I just want to know why he's not. We get almost there, and he stops, like it's as easy as closing a book. I've never known another guy who could do that without coming in his pants."

"So the guy's got great self control. Can't fault him for that. Besides," she giggled, "you wouldn't want a guy who lost his load in his jeans, would you?"

A hand over my mouth, I burst out laughing, then with a tissue, blotted the lipstick I knew would have to be reapplied after my session with Em.

After we finished clowning, Emma straightened her back

and slipped into analyst mode. "It's one of two things. He's not ready to settle down, obviously, since he's got years of training ahead of him, and if you two consummate the relationship now, it could be the nail in his coffin, leading to marriage, or at least a binding commitment while he's still a resident, which I doubt he'd want to do. He seems level headed and secure in how he sees his future."

"Not a bad concept. What's the other option?"

"He's into Vanessa, and for some reason can't be with her, but he doesn't want to hurt you. Maybe he can't decide what he wants, if he even wants anything."

My eyes bulged. "What do you mean?"

"Maybe he doesn't see you as a long termer, you know?"

"Oh my God, you're harsh! And to bring Vanessa into this? Are you serious?"

She sighed. "Just being realistic, Jewel. I don't want to see you get hurt. You're an adult for Pete's sake. Why wouldn't you have sex with a guy you're dating? Why would he be treating you like a virgin?"

"I told you. I don't want to fall off the cliff and hopelessly in love with him, and he respects me." I closed my eyes for a long blink. "Maybe you're right. He's not ready for commitment. He's honorable, so screwing me would mean he'd be tied to me."

Emma shook her head. "Something else to consider, Jewel."

"Haven't you already ruined my night?"

"I don't know if this is such a good idea, anyway. If your relationship does work out, you'll be in your thirties, and he'll be in his forties someday."

"Holy shit, Em. What's the difference? So he's like six or seven years older than me? That's shit in a bucket."

"It may not matter now, but as the years pile up, it could become a problem. Like when you're in your sixties and he's in his seventies. Make sure he stays in good shape and brings home plenty of Viagra."

I threw one of my bed pillows at her head. "You're kidding,

I hope."

"I am. I don't want to send you off in a bad mood. Figured I'd lighten the moment."

"Lighten the moment? You just painted a horrendous picture in my head. I don't want to be old! My life hasn't even started yet. Now I'm gonna be giggling to myself all night, visualizing Indigo as a cranky old man with a drooping dick ... oh my God, ever wonder what we'll be like? All wrinkly and saggy?" I cupped my breasts, testing their bounce.

"That'll never happen. We do Yoga." Emma pruned her face and held up a hand. "I shouldn't talk about patients, but since you don't know any of mine, listen to this." Emma pulled me down beside her. "This guy was falling apart for similar reasons as what you're describing."

"Oh great. A reverse situation? So what happened?"

"This girl seemed to like him a lot but wouldn't commit. And there was someone like a male Vanessa in their history. It turned out, not only did the bitch break his heart but, ohhh, she broke it bad. She left him at the altar and took off with the other guy."

"The male Vanessa?"

"Ah ha." Emma's nod was virtuous.

"Thank you very much. You should write a self help column in the daily paper. Dear Emma. Want to go off the deep end? Contact Emma Kim. She'll walk you to the edge and even give you a push." I grabbed my satchel and checked inside for all my necessities, then spread on another coat of glossy plum lipstick and smacked my lips. "Speaking of the edge. What's up with you and Arkana?"

A dreamy look controlled Em's face. She rolled her eyes and smiled so Cheshire, I almost reached out to pet her.

"RSVP not needed. I can see by the look on your mug. You're desperately in love, happy, and secure." I drew a dramatic breath and blew it out.

"Billy's everything I've always wanted in a man." The yowl she emitted made me jump off the bed. My heart actually tripped. "I'm going to Texas to meet his family soon."

I threw my arms around her. "Oooh. I'm so happy for you!"

My cell chimed.

Indigo: I'm downstairs

Me: Be right down

I headed to the closet.

"Wishful thinking," Emma laughed, "but you're going the wrong way."

"When I take him to bed, it won't be here." I smirked. "I almost forgot the children's books I bought at Casey's library sale. I can't wait to show them to Indigo."

"You waited long enough to give them to him."

"I had to read them first." I laughed. "Gotta run, Em. Don't wait up for me." On the way out the door, I winked.

Indigo's Apartment

I flew down the stairs to meet Indigo, bypassing the elevator, as my stomach was already in my throat. The Wrangler was double parked, with a grinning Indigo inside, dressed in green scrubs, forearms resting on the steering wheel. His face was framed by the open passenger window. I felt his stare follow as I neared. Mindful to not overwork my moves, my hips swayed just enough to entice.

Reaching across the seat he swung the door open, looking so cute, so sexy, so happy to see me. "Hey, Sunshine," his voice was effortless.

A day at the hospital had done nothing to subdue his charm. *Dear Lord, he's gorgeous*, everything inside me screamed. Then my stomach spazzed. With the way he made me feel, how was I going to keep my hands off him? Easy ... I wasn't. My emotions were in turmoil. This guy was turning me into a drooling contradiction.

I poked my head in and flashed an adorable smile. I tossed the shopping bag into the back of the car, then my body slithered gracefully onto the seat. "Hi, babe," I said, running my hand along the side of his bristly cheek, up into his tousled hair, my gaze glued to his.

"Hey, baby." With the interior lights still on, his eyes flicked over me before our bodies touched. His lips were soft, his kiss minty. "You look terrific, as always. What's in the bag? You plan on staying over?" He grinned.

"That's an invitation I might take you up on sometime, but not tonight." I smiled. "I picked up some books at Casey's library sale a while back. I thought you might use them in your office."

He reached over the seat and rummaged through the bag, bringing up a glossy book covered with bunny rabbits and bright green clover. "These are great, babe." He pulled me in for a kiss. "How thoughtful of you." His eyes shined. "Not sure when I'll have an office, but I bet the kids in the hospital would love these. Mind if I take them there?"

"Sure. Kids are kids, regardless of where they are. I hope they like them."

"They'll love them." His brows rounded. "So will the volunteers who read them."

"The Stanleys? Over my dead body. Give them back. I'll come and read to the kids." I felt my cheeks flame.

Chuckling, he dropped the book back into the bag. "Okay, Sunshine. I won't let the Stanley sisters anywhere near them."

I squeezed his biceps. "Or you."

He rolled his eyes. "Why don't you just march into the hospital and mark your territory."

I clicked my tongue. "Just drive."

"Yes, ma'am. Are you hungry?"

"For you." My voice was seductive when I squeezed his thigh.

His laugh sounded apprehensive. "What would you like to eat? Other than my lap."

"Italian okay with you? I could be coerced into Penne A La Vodka." My smile was bright. I had to push the earlier conversation with Emma out of my head. "How was your day, sweetie?" I sat angled in the seat so I could watch his every expression. As he drove, my eyes dragged over him. "Slow day? I don't see any blood on your scrubs."

"You're insane, you know that?" He shook his head. "I spent the entire day in geriatrics, reading charts and diagnosing."

I imagined his job wasn't the easiest. Watching the sick recover would be exhilarating, but watching people die had to be horrendous. How did one leave *that* kind of work at the office? I was happy I could make him laugh.

"Hey. I finally get to see where you live," I chirped.

"It's comfortable," he said as he turned into the entrance to the parking garage, "and convenient."

"You have parking?" I was astounded. Only high class buildings had ground level parking.

"Yep. And a storage locker where I keep my bikes."

"As in bicycles?"

"Yes, and Triumph."

"Ritzy, huh?"

"A place to call home." He edged into a numbered space and cut the engine. Leaving the keys dangling, he reached across the seat and pulled me over the console for a kiss that made me quiver. "I've been waiting for that all week." His fingers ran through the side of my hair, tucked a lock behind my ear.

"You have, have you?" I ran my tongue around his lips, teasing, then drew back and gazed at him. "Is this up to your expectations?"

"Absolutely ... and yes, I've been dying to kiss you, my little tamale." He ran his hand down my arm, straight to my thigh which he caressed. "I enjoyed the entire day in Poughkeepsie, especially the train ride home." He tweaked the tip of my nose.

I was speechless. He had a way about him. Regardless of the subject matter, his words sounded hot as hell.

"Let's get going so I can get out of these clothes and take you out for a fantastic Italian meal." He blew a kiss into my ear.

We walked hand in hand to the elevator, kissed after the

door closed, our lips parting only when the door slid open on the fifth floor. Stopping at apartment number five-ten, Indigo unlocked the door and pushed it open. The hardwood foyer gleamed. To the right was a wall rack where a lightweight jacket and hooded sweatshirt hung on pegs beneath a polished shelf. On the floor below it was a shoe rack, clutching a pair of running shoes and the hiking boots he'd worn on Sunday. He obviously didn't walk on his white carpet with shoes, so I kicked off my heeled boots before entering.

Indigo emptied his pockets and set his wallet and keys onto a sofa table backed against a sprawling sectional, careful to protect the finish on the shining cherry wood.

"Ready for the grand tour?" He took my arm.

"I've been dying to see your apartment." Excited, I squeezed his hand and stretched my neck to peek down the hall.

His fingertips brushed my cheek, then he grabbed my hand. "Come on, beautiful." He tugged and I followed.

We bypassed the kitchen, walking directly down the hallway. I noticed a telephone receiver fastened near a doorframe. "Odd place for a phone," I commented.

"That's the intercom. They put it there so you can hear it from any room " supposedly." He rolled his eyes. "Not always true. I've slept through it."

"Mine's just a speaker mounted inside the wall." I scrunched my bottom lip.

"Come on, silly." He drew both of my arms around his waist, towing me close behind him, the tips of my toes stubbing the heels of his feet.

To the left was a spacious bathroom, and on the right a huge bedroom. The walls were all white, the furniture finished in black lacquer.

"It's stunning, Indigo. Talk about clean freak. It's spotless."

He sighed. "The maid comes twice a week."

I stared up at him, eyebrows raised, mouth slack.

He chuckled and pulled me into his arms. "Kidding, babe. I make the mess. I clean it. But I'm here mainly to sleep."

"Nice." I motioned to his king sized bed, covered by a blue tailored spread and matching shams. "Even a sliding glass door to a terrace," I said appreciatively.

"Yeah, it's great in the summer, even if our city air's not entirely pulmonarily friendly."

"Is that a real word?" I squinted.

"I think I just made up the usage." He laughed, and pulled me back down the hallway. "And here is my rarely functioning kitchen."

The appliances were gleaming stainless steel. Even the sink. There was no table, but a half wall served as an island, dividing the spacious room into dining and living room.

"It's enormous," I said, marveling. "And luxurious. I had no idea you could get an apartment like this in our area." Struck with the sudden concept of expense, my eyes widened. "No less afford it."

"Yeah. The rent's not too bad, though. How about a glass of wine ... or a mixed drink?"

What he considered not too bad would have been a year's salary for me.

"Ah ah. I'm fine." I reached up and locked my fingers around his neck, covering his lips with mine. After breaking for air, I murmured, "Now that's a proper hello kiss."

With a mind of their own, my hips tucked into his, moving as if on the dance floor, rocking with a deliberate rhythm.

His hands tightened around my waist. I brought my face up, gazed into his gray eyes that looked like the sky on a cloudy day. A low groan that sounded more like a growl erupted deep in his throat. He wrapped his arms around me and lifted me onto the counter. I slung my legs around his hips and squeezed.

"What you do to me should be illegal." His breath hit my ear. "At this rate, I'll never get into the shower. And you won't have your Penne A La Vodka."

"Who needs food. You taste better than anything I've ever had the pleasure of ..."

"Baby," he whispered. "Be careful. We're alone up here

on the almost deserted fifth floor."

He sounded different, ultra confident, bolder. Had he been planning this? Would tonight be a continuation of Sunday in my room? The thought was staggering.

This was it. The time had come. It felt so good, so right; I knew what I wanted to do.

His hands were beneath me, fingertips digging into the cushiony flesh of my ass. My legs tightened around his hips, my heels pressing into his lower back, urging him closer. I took his hands in mine and brought them to my face, sucking on his index finger. I felt his cock harden against me when I stared in his eyes and ran my tongue up and down his finger. I brought the palm of his other hand down my throat and pressed it against my breast.

"How about that shower?" My voice was not my own.

"Baby, are you sure?" His brows tugged together. "This isn't why I brought you here."

For a split second I focused across the room, at a porcelain vase wrapped with long tangled stems, a disarray of petals running up, down and around, like my emotions. Then my eyes returned to his.

"I've never been so sure about anything in my life ... Indigo. I've never felt this way before."

I rested my forehead against his chest, my head sliding back and forth, praying I was making the right decision. I was entering another dimension, and there was no turning back. The muscles in my stomach tightened, struggling with an onslaught of frenzy.

His chin brushed my hair, rested lightly on the top of my head, then his moist lips moved to my ear. He pulled me to my feet, and I stood before him, swallowing hard, closing my eyes, waiting.

I felt my sweater being lifted up and over my head; my electrified hair smoothed back into place. His palms skimmed the cups of my bra, then his hands slipped behind me and unhooked the band, peeling down the straps. His breath increased, and I imagined his surging heart rate, which couldn't have possibly exceeded mine. He whispered, "Tell me now if you want me to stop."

"No ... don't stop."

His touch was gentle, but determined. His lips kept brushing my face, my mouth, my neck. "Are you sure?"

"Yes."

My back hit the edge of the center island at the same time my elbows landed on the polished surface, bracing my buckling legs. He lifted my face, his thumb sliding across my trembling bottom lip, which he kissed until the warmth of his mouth calmed my shudder.

I watched his eyes glaze, then focus on my breasts, scorching my skin without even so much as a touch. My heart hammered inside my chest, which rose and fell as I fought for air. Each moment I stood before him was like an eternity filled with thousands of electrifying fingertips sweeping across my bare skin.

"God, you're beautiful," he murmured when his gaze reached my face – gauging my reaction as the tips of his fingers strummed my swollen nipples, torturing me with the lightest touch, until every muscle in my body went limp, and I could handle no more. Fighting for consciousness, I lowered my lids, threw back my head and gasped as the air around me thinned.

When his hands clasped my breasts, the room began to spin. I sank against his chest, felt my body being lifted, laid out on the countertop. For a moment I held my breath, then let my limbs relax, my head fall to the side. His touch was easy, yet assertive ... and very persuasive.

I clung to him, my fingers threading through his hair. Dragging his face against mine, I whispered nonsense into his ear. Heard the unzipping of my jeans, felt the softness of his hands as his fingers dribbled like melted butter down my belly. Finally reaching the ache between my thighs, his hand cupped my drenched pussy. He knew exactly where to touch, and how to touch, bringing my moisture with the tips of his fingers that rhythmically brushed my clit. I was in another dimension, floating in a semiconscious state, where all my body felt were frenzied fingertips ... hungry lips, and the rush of blood exploding in my head.

As I squirmed, my breasts slid across the fabric of his shirt, exciting my tingling nipples beyond comprehension. I spaced – my body reacting on its own, rearing up, never settling.

My jeans were pulled to my ankles. His fingers circled my clit, while his palm coasted teasingly. The throbbing sensation almost unbearable, I strained against him, longing to bury him inside me.

"Oh God," arching my back, I screamed, "Indigo ..."

"Ssh," he whispered. "Someone will think you're being attacked." He pressed my right palm over my lips, the left across my breasts. The heat in his eyes was so intense, I thought he'd mount me. But instead, he kissed his way down my body, lifted my hips, and lowered his head. His moist lips nibbled, while his tongue flicked, sending jolts of agonizing pleasure through my insides, manic signals to my brain. He took my clit into his mouth and sucked, letting his wet tongue swirl around it. I arched my back and bucked, gripping my swollen nipples, unable to control the savagery of my moans. He rubbed my clit with his thumb, spread my folds, and slipped his tongue inside. I lifted my knees, draped a leg over his shoulder, and pressed his face so fiercely, he might have smothered had my hips not braced for the onset of an explosive climax.

Then I shrieked, or was it another sound that hit my ears, something as desperate as my cry, but distant. I wasn't sure of the origin ... I just wanted the irritating noise to cease. Wanted only to hear our whispers, restless breathing, rustling of clothing I intended to remove. My hand slid under his shirt, ran up and down clawing the smoothness of his back, drifting down his spine, when he tensed.

I opened my eyes to watch his head lift, his chest heave. I heard his throaty whisper, "Shit," escape the grim fold of his lips, followed by a distracted, "Fuck, it's the intercom."

"Let it ring," I panted, gripping his hand firmly, my hips still writhing. "Please baby," I begged, "don't stop." My ragged words echoed from a far off place from which I did not want to return.

His lips crashed into mine, his fingers pleasingly manipulative, but the hideous shrill endured. It tore at my nerves, angered my mind, pulling me back to painful reality.

When his lips left mine, I covered my face with my hands, literally moaning with agony as I pulled my legs up, curled up on my side.

"I'm sorry baby," he rasped, and I was lifted to my feet, steadied, handed my sweater and bra. Had his lips not been pressed to my ear, I wouldn't have heard his words through the onslaught of blood coursing through my veins. "You better get dressed."

My mind spun, trying to comprehend, to recover. The walls were glazed with swirling gray specks, the room itself cloudy. In my dazed state, I saw the pain on his face. The moment I wavered, he reached for me, and as I caught my balance, my body skimmed his and I instantly realized why he looked the way he did. His erection was enormous. I imagined the pulsation inside his pants, and had to hold my hand in place. I so wanted to relieve him, but was forced to watch the ripple of his roomy scrubs as he headed down the hallway.

Pathetically posed – topless, jeans around my ankles – defenseless I stood, a quivering mess in the middle of the kitchen floor, while he answered the intercom.

I hiked up my jeans, covered my breasts with my clothes and hesitated, but when I heard the tone of his voice, I had a feeling our evening would be ending abruptly.

Barely able to walk, I slowly made my way to the bathroom, listening to his end of the conversation: "Hey." His voice, no longer muffled by passion, was kept low. "Are you okay? No ... it's alright. Come on up."

Before I had a chance to close the bathroom door, he shot me a sheepish glance. "It's Vanessa." He sounded helpless, pleading for my mercy.

I glared. "You have to be fucking kidding me."

"She's pretty upset." He ran a hand through his hair, repeating, "I'm so sorry, babe."

"Now I know how you must feel," I muttered, before slamming the door in his face.

Easy Come Easy Go

I stood in the spacious bathroom, on a cold floor tiled with marble, shaking from head to toe. Shaking with the hunger he'd aroused, and anger. Anger at Vanessa for destroying our interlude, anger with Indigo for ever having known such a witch.

It was the third time she'd invaded my privacy, and her presence, even the mere mention of her name, was getting under my skin. I wanted to pull her into a boxing ring, pound the hell out of her, because that's what she represented: pure hell. I was certain she wasn't the most honest person, and had ulterior motives where Indigo was concerned. I'd known her kind before. And they almost always ended up with either a big payday, or searching for another victim. I hoped Indigo wouldn't be her victim ... or her payday. Could one ever trust another person one hundred percent?

I stared into the mirror hanging over the double sink. My face was so flushed my cheeks looked like beets that had been sitting in the sun too long. I slipped my bra on, my nipples so sensitive from Indigo's mouth, at the mere touch of the fabric, I felt a stir. My chest was mottled, but had quieted. I heaved a sigh, pulled my sweater over my head, and was horrified at the girl staring back at me. My hair was a mess. I'd left my handbag in the entry foyer, and without a hair brush, I faced embarrassment, doom. I would have to exit the bathroom eventually.

My first order of business was to dab wet tissues around my already damp hairline, beneath my chin, down my neck, between my cleavage. Indigo had done a job on me, that was for sure. My body still pulsed, furious the hunger hadn't been entirely satiated.

I sat on the oval lid of the toilet, head in my hands, ready to break down. This was the rockiest non-relationship I'd ever encountered. Between struggling with celibacy, Vanessa's interference, and concentrating on finals, I was filled with agitation deadlier than the worst bout of PMS I'd ever experienced. Still, I couldn't cry. No ... I wouldn't cry. I was not about to let the likes of Vanessa Whitehall crush me.

I bowed my head, allowing my hair to fall almost to the floor. With dampened fingers I raked through my tresses, releasing every knotted strand, calming the ends that had been charged with passion and angora knit. When I faced the mirror, my hair fell past my shoulders in voluminous waves, surpassing any lion's mane.

Before leaving the bathroom, I refreshed every part of my body, and the ache had abated. I zipped my jeans, tugged my sweater to my waist, pasted on a smile, and opened the door.

Before I even left the room, I heard their muffled voices. "What the hell?" I mumbled. "Why are they talking so secretively?" When I rounded the corner, they were embracing. "What the fuck?"

I heard Indigo say, "I know how difficult it's been, Ness. It's something you never get over." His voice was hushed. Not seductively hushed. A weird hushed.

Vanessa said, "I know you do, Jim. Of all people, you know best how I feel, which is why I came here tonight ... to be with you."

My feet froze to the floor. "Ness??? To be with you? How *what* feels?" I wanted to scream, but casually said, "Am I interrupting something?" as I strode into the living room wearing a broad smile that strained my cheeks.

Indigo, whose palms had been warming Vanessa's shoulder blades, instantly let his hands fall to her hips to separate their bodies. But Vanessa stood her ground. Her arms were locked around his neck, her body pressed closer to his than I would have done to any friend, including Pete.

At the sound of my voice, she turned, hurling a lopsided smirk over Indigo's shoulder. Her green eyes were wide, her brows arched.

Indigo peeled her arms away, taking several steps back. He shot me a distressed look, as though to say, "Don't get mad. I'm guilty of nothing!" My eyes replied, "Maybe you just haven't been caught ... yet."

Fool. I was a freaking fool. Jewel, when will you learn? I longed to call Pete, have things return to normal where loneliness was bearable. Pete was an antidepressant. His pep talks always made me laugh. I was no longer lighthearted. I felt like a slug dragged through the mud, sprinkled with salt. I felt emotions I'd never believed I'd be capable of feeling. I'd never *had* to feel before meeting Indigo. I wouldn't scratch her eyes out, or land one on her jaw. I'd promptly leave his apartment, my head held high.

"Jewel," Indigo's voice strained as he watched me in the doorway, "You know Vanessa."

Of course I knew Vanessa, and he damn well *knew* I knew Vanessa. "I sure do. Hey," I said as though her presence meant nothing to me. As though Indigo meant nothing to me.

"Jim Jim and I were just talking personal stuff." She fired a sour expression over his shoulder, still hanging on greedily. It wasn't difficult to figure out what she was thinking: "I knew him first and will know him long after you're gone, bitch, so back off."

If holding my breath was guaranteed to prevent an

outburst, then I would have suffocated on the spot, rather than display an ounce of insecurity or jealousy.

"Yeah, and we have dinner plans. So make it quick." My voice was casual, yet full of intent.

"Let me guess, Mexican?" She pitched me a sappy grin.

Ignoring her, I scooped up my bag and slung it over my shoulder. Indigo's eyes bulged. His brows furrowed. "Where are you going?" He moved in my direction.

Vanessa glowed, apparently convinced I was about to concede. Her expression turned from sugar to smug.

I don't think so ... The fight was on.

"I'm not going anywhere, babe." I sidled up to Indigo, ran my fingers through his hair and kissed his cheek. "Just came out for my hairbrush." I clutched his arm, grinning at Vanessa. "You did a number on my hair." I rubbed my head against his shoulder. Gazed up at him adoringly.

Indigo let out a breath, his troubled expression turning dubious. He drew back, his eyes asking: "So, you're really okay with what you just saw?"

"Your hair looks fine," he said. His voice was tighter than my throat. "Maybe I'll just go and take a quick shower, so we can get to dinner. Will you two be okay?" He shot me a look of concern.

"Of course, Jimmy. I'll entertain your friend." I smiled sweetly. "I'll be right here when you get out." I sent him off with a pat on his butt.

"Jimmy?" Vanessa flared. "Calling you Jimmy almost got me a black eye."

He turned in the doorway, and hissed, "Shut up, Ness."

"What's she talking about?" I demanded

"Just kid stuff." His face tightened before he disappeared down the hall.

Vanessa looked like she wanted to strangle me.

We faced off in the entry to the living room, where I did a preliminary check of her attire.

Her blonde hair was sleek and impeccable, knotted at the

nape of her neck. Her cream colored ankle boots were the exact shade of her spandex breeches. She wore a white linen shirt, and a cocoa blazer.

"Would you like a drink before you leave?" I said, sauntering toward the kitchen.

"Why not ... I have all night."

"Jimmy and I don't." From a side glance, I watched her check me out from head to toe.

"Nice jeans ... and are those your muddy boots in the foyer?" Her voice was a phony as her smile. "Are they pleather like that skirt you were stuffed into?"

"You betcha."

I heard Indigo slamming around in his room, preparing for one of the quickest showers of his life, no doubt. No problem. Five minutes was all I needed to get rid of her.

Since I acted like I owned the place, I had to think fast. Where would Indigo keep the booze? In the glass cabinet of course, next to the half dozen bottles of pricey wine. Very perceptive, Jewel.

I opened the fridge, which was spotless and neatly stocked, and pulled out a container of orange juice. I filled two glasses with ice, grabbed an open bottle of vodka, and in less than a minute we were sitting in the living room, sipping screwdrivers, chatting like enemies.

"Where's your sidekick tonight?" I asked. I couldn't help but glare.

"If you're referring to Elizabeth, she's at home, finishing the guest list for Indigo's grad party. We're so proud of him."

"We are too." I wanted to grit my teeth but flashed them instead.

Seated at the edge of the sofa, she reached down to free the buckle of her boot from a stitch in her hem. Her feet were firmly planted in white plush. Apparently, her soles never touched any dirt.

My eyes swept over her. "Nice outfit. Did you just leave the stable? Where'd you park your horse?" I asked innocuously.

"Out in the alley, beside your tent." She didn't bat a bright green eye.

Only one side of my mouth moved with sarcasm. "Oh, I didn't realize we were neighbors when I squatted there." My bopping head was fluid.

Her pink cheeks clashed with her tangerine lipstick, which she began chewing off.

"They sell marvelous cover up at AMA. Won't show a line or a blemish. You should try it."

Her complexion turned entirely ruddy.

"Indigo says you're going to be a cop? Seems like a perfect choice. You do have the masculine build for it." Her voice pitched.

Mine deepened. "Anytime you want to step outside, let me know. I'll show you how close to a guy I can be."

Her neck snapped, but she made a quick recovery. "So, where are you from, Jewel? Some upstate farm?"

"I've never lived on a farm, but last time I passed one, I thought I saw you grazing with the cows."

Her mouth tightened so drastically, she looked lipless. "Speaking of cows, do you shop at a feed store? Is that where you found jeans with an all elastic seat?"

I angled my head. "Speaking of elastic. Are you wearing one of those binding bras for added support, or are you intentionally trying to look like a boy?" Waiting for her comeback, I stared.

Her face pruned, and she started to stutter. "I ... you ... Did you pull that sweater out of a dumpster? Because it's pilling."

"Is that the nose you were born with, Vanessa? Or did you have it surgically extended so you could crawl further up Elizabeth's ass?"

She stiffened and moved so close to the edge of the cushion, she almost fell off the sofa. "I hope you pass the police exam, Jewelia. I've heard applicants need to know the alphabet."

"Was that slobbering goon in The Prestige your ex, or are

you still dating him? Wasn't that you over in the corner, hanging all over him?" I winked. "Hold onto him. You make a stunning couple."

The look on her face turned to shock, and her mouth went pencil thin again. Had I hit a nerve? Was there really something between them? I burst out laughing at the thought, then wondered if she'd had him deliberately bump into me to start a fight.

"You should medicate whatever it is that's spreading across your chin, Jewelia, or is it razor burn?" Crossing her arms, she relaxed into the sofa, her face smug, as though she'd landed the best punch.

"Brunettes don't tend to bald so easily ... or young." I strained to see the crown of her head.

She huffed and pulled away, then slugged her drink.

"Well, would you look at that?" I said with amazement as I reached for her chin. "What do you know? A silky goatee! And you *are* a natural blonde!"

I heard the bathroom door open, and caught a whiff of fruity steam. I had to taunt her one last time before Indigo entered the room. One way or another, she was going to pay for what she'd done to me ... including any future transgressions.

I extended my neck, my head inching toward her, and whispered behind my hand. "Did you step in something hidden in the hay," my secretive tone was virtuous, "or are you wearing an experimental deodorant?"

With slanted eyes she scowled. I was ready to throw up a hand to protect my face.

"I'm a pro, Ness. You'll never outrank me." I showed her my dimples.

Before she could open her mouth, Indigo strode into the center of the living room, pausing before the three ceiling-to-floor windows. "You found your way around the kitchen, I see."

With his hands on his hips, Indigo appeared relaxed, and entirely refreshed. His hair was still damp and curling at the ends. His shirt wasn't completely buttoned, and his jeans fit just right. God, he looked amazing. I noticed Vanessa's eyes trail him from head to toe, then she bristled. Ha. She blew her game.

"Jewelia seems like the perfect little housekeeper, Jim Jim. Your mother tells me she's looking for help." She arched her brows and smiled, acting so serious and accommodating. "Why don't you give her Jewelia's work number?"

Indigo's head angled. Did he seriously think she was trying to be helpful?

"Jewel's working on a promising career, Ness." He winked at me. "You'd better stay on her good side. She might help keep you out of the slammer some day." He chuckled. "Remember when we were kids?"

She glared at him. "That was an initiation."

"I don't care what it was, you've got a record." He attempted to chuck her under the chin, but she jerked away, repositioning at the far end of the sofa.

"You have a record deal? You can sing?" My eyes widened more than the stretch of my lips.

Indigo burst out laughing, almost doubling over.

"My record's sealed. And it was kid stuff. Could've happened to anyone." Her glare turned on me. "What sorority were *you* in, Jewelia?" Her eyes narrowed.

"I hate to break this up, ladies. But it's getting late." Indigo pulled me to my feet and rested an arm around my shoulders. "If we're going to have dinner, we should get a move on." He shot me a questioning look, and shrugged his eyes toward Vanessa.

"We're having Italian food. Would you like to join us, Nessic?" I hoped my contorted face looked angelic.

Her body lifted stiffly. She gathered her purse and her lips, ignoring my sarcasm, which went right over Indigo's head. He stood beside me, grinning at my courtesy.

"Pasta might put some meat on those bones." I reached to swipe her arm, pretending to be playful, but she jerked away.

"Not for me, thank you." She walked toward the door. "Eat an extra Cannoli for me, will you, Jewelia?"

"What was that all about?" asked Indigo after Vanessa closed the door. He looked me square in the eye, lifting a brow. Then a smile slid across his face. "Did you two actually hit it off?"

I choked back a laugh. "Eh. We just shared girl talk." Reaching up, I kissed his cheek.

"I'm happy you made her comfortable. This is the anniversary of her parents' deaths. She gets pretty upset this time of year." He frowned.

"I can imagine." I shook my head, then squeezed his arm. "She's lucky she has you and your family to lean on." Beneath my smile, I boiled. She had Indigo - probably everyone - snowed.

Then and there I knew Vanessa would always be like a glob of chewing gum that stuck deep inside the grooved soles of running shoes. Sticky, annoying, and never completely gone.

Graduation Surprise

Some of the best restaurants were a stone's throw from Indigo's apartment, so we walked in the chilly night air, which was delightful, cooling my emotions, my anger. We strolled, fingers locked, hands swinging in an arc, now and then pausing to kiss. By the time we reached the restaurant, it was almost closing time.

We sat side by side in a very private corner booth. A Tiffany chandelier colored one side of Indigo's face pale blue, the same color his glistening eyes appeared beneath the spray of artificial light.

Over glasses of wine, Indigo took one of my hands in his, kissing the back, nibbling each finger, burying his lips in my palm.

"It's so good being with you, Jewel," he said in a soulful tone, which made me worry. Although his words were soft, honest, I felt no closer to the secret place inside him. Why did I always feel that cliff's edge ... impending doom? "You lighten the weight of the world." There it was again, the brooding look I'd first witnessed at Kelly's.

I smoothed his cheek, gazing deep into South Seas blue.

But his eyes weren't cool or calm. They were turbulent. His stare burned into mine.

"What's on your mind, baby?" I asked, bringing him close for a kiss. "If something's bothering you, tell me."

"It's nothing, honey. I've got a hectic scheduled for the next few weeks, and won't be able to see you as much as I'd like."

My heart sank, but I understood where he was coming from. We both had crazy workloads and had to focus on finals, careers, family.

"We can meet for lunch. And text, and phone ..." I laced my arms around his neck, holding on for dear life. My chin was buried in his shoulder, my words falling lightly into the air beside his cheek. "And we'll have free time in June, and part of July to be together, right?"

"I'm looking forward to a break ... and being with you." His lips brushed my cheek, nibbled on the lobe of my ear. "I'm sorry about tonight, baby. Thank you for understanding ... and for being kind to Vanessa. I know she's not the easiest person to be with at times."

Duh. Didn't I already know that, firsthand? I tried to smile, but my lips felt like they'd coil into a spasm at any moment. I hated being dishonest with him, but would he be acting as such if he'd heard us ragging on each other as we squared off in his living room? I highly doubted it. He was elevating me onto a pedestal. I loved the height, but I didn't belong there. I'd have to be kinder to Vanessa. Earn my place.

"I don't have a problem with Vanessa." Wide-eyed, I lied.

"Of course you wouldn't." He curled a shaft of my hair around a finger, freeing my diamond cut silver hoop earring, tapping it gently with his fingertip. "You're one of the kindest people I've ever known. And you're very special to me. You've become a big part of my life, and I hope the feeling is mutual."

Uh oh. My heart thumped. Here it comes. I braced for his confession of love.

He was so sweet, it almost tore my heart out. Sweet and

sensitive was the best kind of sexy in my book. Although he had everything else to go along with it. And was he about to tell me he would always be mine?

"You're important to me too, Indigo," I said, my words featherlike. "Very important."

His eyes searched my face and his lips closed over mine, but all too soon his mouth slid free. "I'm happy we had this conversation. And we know where we stand."

We do? My neck almost snapped back with surprise. My willpower had almost evaporated, and he was – happy we knew where we stood? Was I missing something? The only thing I knew was that I was special, which I'd picked up on, anyway. Men ...

When we left the restaurant, we made out in an alcove beside the building. It was a lot like the first night we kissed outside The Prestige, minus the arguing. Indigo's lips were so soft and plush against mine, my body ached for more of the thrilling experience they had offered in his apartment. How would I ever overcome the appetite he'd created?

While we waited for an empty cab, he made a promise.

"I'll keep in touch with you, text you every day, okay? And make sure you call me, maybe we'll even have phone sex," he teased, tweaking my nose. "Once the heat is off and finals are over, I hope to be seeing a lot more of you."

"After tonight in your apartment, I'm not sure what you mean by seeing a lot more of me, because you pretty much saw it all." I giggled.

He pulled me close, burying his lips in my hair. "I can't believe Vanessa's timing."

"I can," I mumbled. "It sucks, but for now, phone sex will have to suffice."

"Oh, so now you like it?" he breathed the words into my ear.

"I've got a good teacher," I nibbled his neck, "and feel I could become an expert."

"You'll have to show me ... soon ... because after tonight,

I tell you, Jewel, you're killing me."

"We'll see if I can drive you as crazy as you drive me." My whisper was so hoarse, my throat burned.

Just before a cab pulled to the curb, he let out a load groan.

* * *

As the days dragged by, I moped around the apartment, missing him like mad, complained of boredom to Emma, and wondered how I'd feel with my handful of close friends stuck in our apartment while Indigo partied hardy at the Hamptons after graduation, with Vanessa, no less. Each time I thought of it, I grit my teeth. I should be there with him! It was so unfair!

My only salvation was that I had a date for my computerized police exam. As I studied, I could barely wait for the arrival of summer, free time, and Indigo.

Indigo texted as often as he could, which could never replace being with him. Still, I knew he was thinking of me. We held hands during stolen lunch dates, and even managed to fit in a movie. We sat in the back row of the dimmed theater, his arm around my shoulders the entire time, whispering, unable to concentrate on the flick. Our kisses grew so demanding, he tried to remove the barrier between us – the armrest – but it wouldn't budge. I strained so close, my hip was imprinted with a red welt when I returned home.

Pete and Casey visited often, and on the Saturday after graduation, they loaded the apartment with cases of beer and bottles of booze. Emma and I had shopped for snacks, and had brought home tons of drink mixes as well. We piled bagged ice in the shower, stocked up on paper goods, and were set to give it hell for at least twenty-four hours straight ... or so I was led to believe.

Rocking out on the coffee table, I fanned my diploma with one hand. In my other hand, I gripped a bottle of beer, the liquid sloshing each time I toasted.

"To Jewelia," Pete's voice rang out, "Manhattan's next meter maid."

Everyone laughed.

The doorbell rang. I was so hyped, I sprang off the table to buzz in Yvonne and Derek, aka Spartan the Warrior King. Before I could slug down my remaining beer, they burst through the door, rowdy and ready to riot.

I grabbed Yvonne and started dancing around the room yelling, "We made it, baby! We're gonna get soooo shit faced!"

"You're already there, sweetie," she said, and threw her arms around me. We swayed to hip hop. "Congratulations to us. I wasn't sure I'd make it. How'd you do?" Her lips caught in my hair.

"Better than I expected, and the best part is, we are done!" I swung her out and she revolved like a wobbling top. "We'll be wagging our asses in blues pretty soon, baby girl."

Lifting her arms, she snapped her fingers, rolled her hips, then started dancing around Derek. "Not me, baby. I'm gonna be a paralegal."

"That's my courthouse doll," said Derek with a thousand watt smile. "Defend and protect; is that what they say about cops, Jewelia?"

"To protect and to serve more drinks," Pete yelled from across the room as he passed out ice-cold bottles of beer.

"Emma. Where's Emma?" I called to Pete.

He shrugged, then Casey pointed to the bedroom.

I burst through her door. "What are you doing in here? Where's Bill? He's coming, isn't he? You didn't break up, did you?" I felt my face tense at the thought.

She put a hand over her phone and pointed to the door. "I'll be right out," she said, her voice uncharacteristically firm as she shook her head and grimaced at me.

"What's up with you?" I muttered on my way out the door, hoping she and Bill weren't having problems. I had to know. I burst back into her room and landed on her bed on all fours. "Are you okay?" I knew my words were slurred.

She laughed. "Jewel. It's barely two in the afternoon. I thought this party was supposed to last for twenty-four hours? At this rate, you'll be sleeping by your usual bedtime. Or throwing up in the bathroom."

"I miss Indigo." I pouted. "I so want to see him. Why did I fold so easily, Em? Tell me. Come on, shrink me."

"Oh God," she whispered something and closed her phone. "Will you pull yourself together? Crap. I didn't want to tell you."

"Tell me what?" I felt my eyes bulge.

"You're being an enormous pain in the butt." She sighed. "Bill's on his way over now. He's got a surprise for you."

"Unless it's Indigo, I don't want it." My bottom lip rolled into my chin.

"That's all I can say. Now, out of my room. I need to get dressed." She shoved me out the door.

Running through the living room, I yelled, "Bill's bringing me a surprise. And it better have arms and legs and be wearing scrubs."

Pete and Casey had settled in front of the TV, and were watching sports. They nursed bottles of beer. But Yvonne and Derek were slugging shots, dancing like strippers in the middle of the living room. I had no alternative but to join them. And that's what we did until Bill arrived: we threw back shots and grooved until our bodies glistened.

When Bill walked through the door, I threw my arms around him, screaming, "Arkana," straining to look over his shoulder . "Crap. You're alone."

"Thanks for the warm welcome." He laughed. "Sorry to disappoint you, but it's only me."

"Where's your guitar? Let's liven up this party." I pulled him to the center of the room. "Everybody, meet Billy Arkana. He's a rock star."

Emma came out of her room, shaking her head. "This is what we're taking to the Hamptons?"

"The Hamptons?" I almost fainted. "We should stop at Indigo's house while we're there." I felt my eyes bulge at the thought and twirled around the room until I got so dizzy, I fell onto Pete's lap.

"That's your surprise." Bill pulled me to my feet, hugging

me like a sister. "Congratulations, Jewel. Indigo wanted to surprise you, so he asked me to bring you – and I suppose everyone else –" he looked around the room and rolled his eyes, "to his grad party. For obvious reasons, he's not driving, or he would've picked you up himself."

I almost freaked, screaming, "*Madre de Dios.*"

Bill addressed everyone in the room. "Get yourselves together people – we're partying in the Hamptons – for the weekend."

Watching him, Emma wrung her hands, then pulled me aside. "Jewelia. You're about to meet Indigo's family. Sober up, for Godssake."

She turned to Bill. "I'm not sure about this, Billy. A bunch of drunken party crashers? How do you think that's going to go over with the Ballous? You know them, what do you think?"

"It's Indigo's gift to Jewel. I'm following orders. I've got a van outside to drive us to the charter. Let's rock."

"You're not driving us to the Hamptons?" I asked.

"Hell no. With all you loons? We're taking a party bus."

"Let's rock!" The chorus erupted, rounding the room.

"Oh my God." I pulled Em aside. "What should I wear? What will I say? Oh my God. I'm actually going to meet Indigo's family? I'll faint. I'll convulse. I can't do it. I think I'm gonna throw up."

"You can do it," Emma assured. "We'll sober you up on the bus. They've got snacks, even movies."

"Drinks?"

"Water for you, love," Pete said, slinging an arm around me, pointing me in the direction of the bathroom. "And I think you better hop into the shower before we leave."

Emma and I opened our closets to Yvonne, and we stuffed our backpacks and were out the door in less than an hour, all showered and ready to party.

I was in heaven. I was with Pete and Emma, and on my way to see the guy I had fallen in love with.

The Hamptons

We traveled to the Hamptons in less than three hours, raging on the bus as we would in any bar. Music flowed, along with drinks, but at Emma's insistence, I abstained from hard liquor. I wasn't even permitted to nurse a beer.

After policing me for thirty minutes, Emma hunkered down beside Bill, and they spent the balance of the trip chatting and making out ... making out and chatting.

Resigned to the fact that I was about to face Elizabeth and Vanessa, on their own turf, cold turkey sober, I sank into my plush fabric seat and divided my attention between the fringe of the city, its colorful lights flashing beyond the window, and Yvonne and Derek, who shared bottles of booze and bopped in their seats across the aisle. They were a riot, laughing, kissing, hanging all over each other. I guessed they were in love. My mind fixed on Indigo, his face, his neck, his hard inviting body. The way his lips felt on mine, how his hands heated every part of me.

I had to cool my thoughts, so my head rotated often, my eyes scanned. Pete and Casey had been designated the guardians of the group, although I thought Pete started slurring three-quarters of the way to my graduation gift.

I so wanted to sleep, but the noise level was bordering deafening. I let my head roll back and forth on the seat, gazing out the window, daydreaming.

The sun dipped into the Atlantic, feathering the horizon with brilliance, the sky fleecy, like one of Teresa's stuffed bears, striated with pastel pinks, blues, and purples. As we neared our destination, whitecaps closed in on both sides of the highway, mesmerizing, dizzying. I could even smell the salty air through the slightly open windows. The Hamptons appeared to be amazing! And the best was yet to come.

I was sober enough to know what I was doing, but still somewhat anesthetized, feeling pretty confident about making a positive impression in my proper attire: cream colored Capris, a cranberry tank top, and Grecian sandals. I wasn't smokin', but was very much presentable in my family oriented apparel.

My hair was swept up in a ponytail and clipped with a jewel studded band that matched my top. My gemstone earrings and rose ring were perfect accessories. I also wore a sterling charm bracelet my parents had given to me for Christmas. Of course, my cross hung above my neckline, which showed only a minimal slice of cleavage.

The bus finally pulled to the curb and the doors burst open. Packs strapped to our backs, yawning and stretching, we streamed out looking like weary hikers. My head felt fuzzy and my legs were stiff as walking sticks, which might have come in handy for all of us. A line of taxis idled in front of the train station, our drop off location. All seven of us jammed our bags, and our bodies, into two cabs.

Bill instructed the drivers, and the area we headed into was absolutely breathtaking. The homes were prestigious and gigantic. Manicured lawns ambled on either side of the road, subduing masses of exotic looking plants and trees ... exotic for New York.

When we arrived, Indigo was waiting for us, dressed casually in khakis and sport shirt. I thought he looked intense, expectant perhaps, but he was smiling. At the sight of him, my heart started doing flip flops, and goose bumps rippled across my skin. I couldn't wait to leap into his arms, cover his lips with mine. We'd been apart for too long. My only consolation was that the separation might bring us closer together. It had on my end; I hoped he felt the same. Arms crossed, he leaned leisurely against a stone wall that curved with the driveway, leading to what looked like a granite palace.

In my peripheral were colorful plants and shrubbery, but my immediate focus was on Indigo as he made his way toward us, covering the distance with long, agile strides. As he walked, he brushed back both sides of his hair, and stared at me with lazy gray eyes. Tongue tied and slackened jaw, I gazed up at him. Before uttering a sound, he pulled me into a bear hug and squeezed so tight, air rushed from my lungs.

"That's the welcome I was hoping for," I said as he released me. I drew a breath. My hands roamed his face, his hair, stalling on his chest. "Did you miss me?" I grinned up at him.

"Like crazy," he whispered, then his lips swept over every part of my face, my neck, settling on my mouth.

I sucked in his breath, his bottom lip, his tongue, then realized we were standing in the middle of his driveway. Grudgingly, I pried my mouth off his, but my hands refused to let him go.

"It's so good to see you. Were you surprised?" He eased our embrace, drawing back to watch my expression.

I was heady, practically speechless. All I could do was roll my eyes toward heaven and sigh. I forced my dimples to deepen. "Surprised?" My eyes opened so wide they burned. "I almost fainted when Bill told me we were coming here."

He chuckled, scooped me up and whirled me in the air. "I've missed that enchanting smile. Not to mention those tantalizing lips."

"I can't describe how much I've missed you, Indigo," I breathed, my chin nested on his shoulder. "We're gonna have an awesome summer. We have a lot of catching up to do."

Grinning, he kissed the tip of my nose. "And you're making plans." He lifted a brow.

"You better know it, baby." I slipped my fingers through his hair, ruffling its softness. "Thank you for the charter. It was like a vacation cruise! And here we are in the Hamptons, instead of the Bahamas," I teased, then hoped my remark hadn't come off as ungrateful. "So, what kind of party do you have going on here? Family, friends, both ... everyone?" My stomach twisted into knots and my legs felt wobbly as my heels hit the ground.

"No big deal. Just a few of us. Come and see for yourself," he said, wrapping an arm around my shoulders, leading me toward one of the most fantastic houses I'd ever seen. The others grouped behind us, chattering enthusiastically. I heard Pete grumble about the zigzagging creases in the back of his woven cotton trousers, and Casey laughingly console him, joking about a travel iron.

Surrounded by stately homes, expensive cars, I naturally made a quick comparison with Poughkeepsie. Even though Indigo welcomed us with open arms, I felt like an intruder. This was definitely more Vanessa's territory.

"How was graduation?" Indigo asked as we walked. He kept leaning into me, kissing my cheek.

"It was awesome. The ceremony was so moving, I almost cried." I buried my face against his arm, then surfaced with a smile. "My family was there, of course, and afterwards we went out to dinner and they stopped back at the apartment for a while. It was really great. You were the only thing missing." I skipped ahead and walking backward, blocked his steps.

"Sorry I couldn't be there." He yanked me close, his lips working from my cheek to my neck. "I'm happy you had a great time. You deserve the very best."

"So do you. How was *your* big day?" I was caught by the intensity of his gaze, wondering what could be brewing behind those stunning smoky eyes. To ask: "What are you thinking?" seemed so cheesy - words that were spoken in fluffy romance movies. I guessed time would tell all.

"Not half as good as yours, I'm sure ... and don't forget. I'm nowhere near finished like you are." His sigh was so heavy, it could have torn a heart. "I've just completed Step 2. I've got a long way to go. Sometimes I feel like I'll never be done." He focused into the distance.

I patted his arm and grinned. "Like they say, doctors are always practicing."

He turned to me and chuckled. "So true. How did you ever get so damn smart ... and beautiful?"

I tilted my head, scrunched my mouth, and shrugged, which made him kiss me more.

We walked to the back of the house, where a solarium-like addition was edged by a wide patio extending far beyond the main structure. As we rounded the corner, music filled the ocean air, colliding with boisterous voices. When we entered what looked like a huge barroom, I almost dropped with astonishment. It was definitely a multi-million-dollar mansion, inside and out.

Indigo escorted me through a door, and the moment my feet hit the wood planked floor, I did a three-sixty, awed by the wall to wall windows inviting in the Atlantic, which was practically in the backyard. I stared up at vaulted ceilings that were so high, the room could have housed another floor. By then, everyone had drifted inside, and we began ooohing and ahhhing like we'd just been transported to another universe.

"Come on, babe," Indigo's arm slipped to my waist. "Let me show you around, and introduce you."

We circled the solarium, with tall doors leading to less significant rooms. When I peered through an opening, I lost my breath to a weight room and spa. Another room looked like a small movie theater.

The barn, as Indigo referred to the humongous rambling structure we'd first entered, held a pool table, and bar that looked almost the size of the one at The Prestige: mirrored, and fully stocked. A chess table was tucked into a corner surrounded by windows. Sofas and easy chairs were scattered about, many occupied. Someone was handing out drinks, but even sober, I was certain I could hold my own with the crowd. Why had I even worried? I felt I handled the luxury rather well.

Two guys mixing drinks rocked out behind the bar, and a few others stood alongside girls who lounged on tufted stools. High society celebrated more fashionably. The party was lively, but appeared contained, and not half as wild as the one we'd left behind in my apartment. Still, everyone I met was friendly, flashing smiles, slugging drinks, swapping fist bumps and small talk about school and future plans.

When we stepped through a wall of sliding glass doors, I couldn't help but scream. "Oh my God. Your swimming pool looks Olympic ... and it's sitting right beside the ocean! How cool is that?"

Indigo watched my enthusiasm with delight, doubling up with laughter. "Have I ever told you how adorable you are ... especially when you're not mad at me?" He tweaked my nose, a sign of affection that seemed to bring him pleasure.

My next outburst was, "Holy shit. A dock. It's way out past the waves! Is that the boat you told me about? Bobbing way out there? And a private beach. Geeze. This is paradise." With everything hitting my brain all at once, my mouth froze, along with my feet. How much extravagance could I handle in one freaking day?

"Yup. We can take her out later for a ride if you'd like." He snatched me from behind, backing me against him, his arms folding around my waist. I covered his hands with mine and we swayed, gazing out over the ocean. Lights dotted the coastline. I watched flickering windows of houses that followed the curve of the beach. Their outlines were nothing more than a distant, untouchable photograph, and I was secured in the pocket of Indigo's embrace. I felt his breath on my neck, exciting the fine fibers of my hair, then his warms lips trailed to my jaw line.

I turned in his arms. "I'd love to go out on your boat, if it means we'll be alone." When I ran my lips up and down his throat I could feel him swallow hard.

Someone started a fire in a huge outdoor kettle. I felt the waves of heat rush over my body, which Indigo had already warmed. A fieldstone barbecue pit was flaming away, and whatever the group of guests was cooking smelled outrageously delish. My tummy growled.

It turned out the cooks weren't guests, but caterers. They had strategically positioned rows of banquet tables covered with white linen cloths and bowls and platters of every type of delicacy one could desire, including fruits, vegetables, salads, and roasted meats that were of no interest to me. I headed for the chips and dips, reserving the dessert table for later.

"This is amazing, Indigo. I feel like I'm in one of Manhattan's finest hotels." I dragged a sesame cracker across smooth ranch dressing, and munched.

He shrugged. "Once you get used to it, it's like our apartments."

I was sure he was being gratuitous. "Yeah, right." I laughed and squeezed his arm. "I'm waiting to see a carousel next. Where are your parents? Is Vanessa here?"

"They were here earlier, but disappeared upstairs before you arrived." He shook his head. "They're working on a project, or whatever it is they do when they lock themselves away."

I'd never figured Vanessa for a wallflower. She had to be brownnosing.

"We'll meet them later. I want to show you the grounds."

In the distance were sand bars and jetties, dunes and tall grass, and miles and miles of endless beach. The houses were far apart, with each property separated by weathered fences.

"The gardens are gorgeous," I said as we headed down the beach.

"One of my mother's pastimes." He spoke into the sky.

I couldn't imagine Elizabeth crawling around in dirt to

plant and nurture the stone encased beds filled with colorful flowers and foliage. My expression must have reflected my thoughts.

Indigo chuckled. "My mother orders the gardeners around. That's the extent of her horticultural skills." He guided me to the water's edge, where we kicked off our shoes and traipsed through the tide. "She does do one thing by herself though."

I angled my head. And what could that be, besides throwing her weight around, flashed through my mind.

"She designs clothing. Even sews. She's getting ready for a summer fashion show of her line." As he swept a lock of hair behind my ear, I noticed his eyes wanted to feel admiration for his mother's achievements, but fell short of the glint.

"She has a clothing line?" Duh, of course she would have.

Like the fading sky, he lacked enthusiasm. "Before marrying my father, she was a model."

She still looked like one. "Impressive ... and Vanessa's one of *her* models ..." That would account for the nose extension.

"She'd like to be, but my mother's very picky about her work ... and her models. They're usually men," he said dryly.

When I recoiled, Indigo laughed. "Come on, let's go inside." He squeezed my shoulders, then looked across the horizon. "The gulls have packed it in for the day. Guess it's time for the formal introduction." His face tightened, along with his grip on my hand.

We washed sand from our feet, tiptoeing barefoot during the rest of the tour. The interior of the house was even more amazing than the barn, the backyard, the pool, the multiple patios, the five car garage.

The hallways and staircases were so wide, I could have stretched my body across and still left walk room. We passed through the huge kitchen which had its own flight of stairs. I followed Indigo from room to room, one more impressive than the next. The course was ever changing: my feet sank deep into smoky gray carpeting, then padded across gleaming hardwood floors, only to be cradled again by the plush of blood red oriental rugs.

"Does every room have a fireplace?" I asked.

"Not the kitchen or bathrooms." Indigo sounded serious, then added, "I take that back. The master bathroom suite has a gas fireplace."

"I see." I gulped, then my stomach did a flip as we climbed a circular staircase and I stood before the door of an angled room.

Indigo took my hand and led me inside. "This is the sewing room, and my mother, Elizabeth." He waltzed me across the crimson carpet, to the woman who barely turned her head in our direction. Chandeliers lighted the room, highlighting champagne streaks in her already light blonde hair that curled beneath her chin.

"We've met," she was brisk, focusing on Vanessa, who stood like a princess on a round pedestal rising from the center of the room. She looked like a plastic figure on a birthday cake. I assumed it was the platform where Elizabeth measured bodies and hemmed legs.

Vanessa simply nodded when we entered the room. Then a haughty grin broke over her sharp features when her eyes flicked over me. What was that all about, I wondered? Was I not dressed appropriately for the occasion? My face heated, but I willed my cheeks to hide the flush.

"This is Jewelia Delarosa." Indigo seemed to be attempting his *formal* introduction, but his mother couldn't have been more disinterested, which was fine with me.

Her sharp eyes turned thoughtful, raking over me as if I were merchandise hanging on a rack. "I don't suppose you know of a bronze god." Her words were as sour as her ageless face.

I almost emitted my classic "Huh?" accompanied by my all too common scrunched up mouth which personified my curiosity. But in the presence of royalty, I caught myself. *Thank you, Grandma ... I owe you so much.*

I must have looked either stupid or stunned, because I was

suddenly able to glimpse Elizabeth's top row of perfect white teeth. "I've designed an ensemble, and the model I had in mind has gone missing ... from the country, or so I've been informed." She looked like her nose had just come in contact with the spray of a skunk.

No wonder her model left the country. I held back a belly laugh. Her indignation diminished her presence, but I knew I could never be *me* with a woman like *her*.

She was dressed like a model, in a trim, peach colored skirt and ivory top, with a paisley scarf wrapped twice around her neck, the fringed edges sweeping her square shoulders.

Some women were known for their perfume, some for their designer handbags and footwear. I decided scarves were her personal fashion statement.

"What sort of model are you looking for, Mrs. Ballou?" My head still tilted, my words were sincere.

"I told you. A bronze god." She was huffy, and so miserable for a woman who seemed to have so much.

"As in a warrior?" Pursing my lips I lifted a brow, restraining the smart ass tone that was raring to be unleashed.

She hiked her chin, studying me with narrowing eyes. Indigo had taken their color, but nothing else.

"A dark-skinned king? Something like a Spartan?" I smiled.

Her brilliantly blue eyes sparkled with interest. "And ... you know such a person?" Her gaze swung to Indigo, as if seeking affirmation.

He shrugged, the humor in his voice not visible on his face. "I think there's one downstairs, Mother." He aimed a thumb at the door.

"What?" Her exclamation was grandiose. I expected her to start air-kissing.

When Elizabeth's eyes widened, Vanessa's almost squeezed shut, and she couldn't seem to hide a scowl as she stepped down from her podium, crossed her arms over her chest and sulked. I figured she was pissed off because she wouldn't be saving the day after all.

"My friend, Derek Thomas, aka the Spartan King." I smiled with pride that crushed my dimples. "We brought him with us. He may be just what you're looking for. He's built like a ..." When I caught a glimpse of Indigo's face, I stopped describing Yvonne's hunk of a boyfriend, and said, "you can see for yourself ... I can go get him."

"Vanessa," Elizabeth ordered, "run downstairs and find this Derek fellow. If he's everything she says," her gaze cut to me, "I'm sure he'll stand out. Bring him up here, stat." Elizabeth was great at barking out orders. No wonder her gardens were so splendid.

"Look for the handsome guy with the braids," I tried to be helpful.

Before Vanessa left the room, she swung a dramatic half turn. I could feel Indigo's eyes on me, and Elizabeth's were on him. Mine flicked over Vanessa, of course, and I watched a look of hatred color her features before she did an about face and disappeared.

Elizabeth was out of her mind thrilled with Derek, who was equally elated to be chosen as the highlight of her Manhattan fashion show. However, it would have taken a stick of dynamite to permanently loosen Elizabeth's jaw line. What was the woman's problem?

After introductions, Indigo and I left his mother, whose eyes and hands worked Derek over like a pastry chef baking for celebrities. I inquired where his father was, surprised we hadn't yet run into the man who'd provided the striking home and amenities. Indigo's face was strained when he nodded toward the far end of the very long hallway. "In his study, I would imagine." He grunted. "Having his own party, more than likely." I'd never heard his voice drop into such a demeaning tone.

Derek later told us Elizabeth had indicated appearing in her show could very well be the stepping stone toward the modeling career he'd been striving for. He'd even confessed he was a stripper, which hadn't seemed to trouble her any more than she already seemed to be. He also said he'd give up his Information Technology Computer career in a heartbeat, if the *amazing woman* could make his dream come true.

I wanted to gag.

Derek laughed when confiding, "Elizabeth measured absolutely every part of me that could be measured, while my sugar babe inspected the lady's every move. And she *is* da lady."

By the look on Yvonne's face, I could tell she didn't care for the svelte designer who had her hands on her boyfriend's body parts, but she was willing to make exceptions.

We hung around the barn for a while, then were lured outdoors by blaring music which could never be considered disorderly conduct, as the faraway rooftops of the nearest neighbors pointed to the distant, star studded sky.

The patio lights glared. Emma and Bill shared a lounge chair, food, drinks and lips, while Pete and Casey played endless games of pool. And with Yvonne and Derek involved in a game of beer pong, Indigo and I were on our own.

Comfortably barefoot, we trudged through sand until we reached the shoreline. The lapping waves tickled my toes, gripped my ankles. In daylight, I'd have taken the plunge, but in darkness, the menacing body of water felt like the creeping unknown as the tide rolled in with a roar.

The interior lights brightened the rear section of the house that glowed like a Times Square Christmas tree, its brilliance dwarfing the patio torches. Leaving the party behind, hand in hand we strolled, retreating from breakers, splashing through ebbing waves, feet sinking into drenched sand. We strolled along the beach, with Indigo pointing out lighthouses and other landmarks. I held onto his arm, and his every word. The ocean smelled delicious, and now and then my breath was stolen by gusts of damp air, and Indigo's lips. We passed a jetty, climbed a sandy knoll, and paused in seclusion where Indigo settled on a stout tie wall.

The sky was a sailor's paradise, with a bright chunk of moon gliding through starlight, now and then crossed by wispy clouds.

Separated only by a fragile curtain of night, I watched Indigo's perfect silhouette, my gaze tracing his features, the solace on his face. "Finally alone," I said, attempting to sit beside him.

"Ah ah," he said. Grasping my wrists, he extended me before him. "Let me look at you." His gaze slid from my face to my feet. "It feels so good to be together," he said, his voice seductively rich.

"And so hard to be apart ..." My throat felt so narrow, I could hardly swallow.

"I missed you, Sunshine." He pulled me so close, I had no choice other than to part my legs and straddle his thigh.

Sinking against him, I sighed. "I missed you too, so much." Our foreheads pressed, our whispering lips barely touched.

His hands ran up and down my back, coming to rest beneath me. "It's been too long. I missed looking at you ... being with you ... touching you."

"I couldn't stop thinking about you, wondering when I'd see you again." I squeezed his biceps, buried my face in his chest. "I missed these arms ... these lips ..." my fingertip traced his mouth.

I couldn't see the waves, but heard each thundering breaker crash onto the beach behind us; the only sound other than our breathing was my pulse in my ears. We clung to each other as though our arms could stop time.

"There's a guest cottage ..."

"Don't tempt me." My breathing grew more shallow.

"I mean," Indigo chuckled, "not that I wouldn't love to share it with you ... there's a guest cottage for your friends. You're sleeping in the main house, right down the hall from my room." His arms tightened around me. "Although I'd rather have you in my bed, beside me, doing all kinds of naughty things to you ..."

The tone of his voice, and electrifying suggestion, sent chilling excitement through every part of my body. He'd obviously been thinking about going further than we'd ever ventured.

"Naughty things, huh?" I breathed into his ear. "Like what?" My lips slid across his neck, and I couldn't help but suck his smooth skin.

"Why don't I show you ..." His hands slipped beneath my top, ran the length of my spine, then dipped beneath my pants, reaching as deep as possible, settling on my buttocks. He squeezed my ass, pulling me so close, I could barely breathe. "Mmm, baby, you feel so good," he groaned against my throat, leaving me breathless.

I sucked his neck harder, nibbled his jaw line, then swept my lips across his, moaning his name. My hips rocked, my fingers worked through his hair, along the side of his face, tracing the outline of our lips as they pressed. "Show me what feels good ..." I pulled my lips away just enough to murmur, but my tongue continued to work slowly around his.

"Closer," he whispered, "turn around."

"Like this?" I began to slide off his thigh.

"Like this." He lifted me, spun me around, and drove my ass into his lap. His hands on my hips urged me into a rhythmic grind. I felt his hard cock as he strained against me, and reached behind his neck, pulling his face close to mine. His breath came fast. His fingers grazed my skin, reached under my shirt, clutched my breasts, then slid beneath my bra. My back pressed against his chest, I arched, bringing my aching nipples closer to his palms.

When I groaned, "Yeah ... like that," his hands kneaded vigorously, fingers plucking my nipples sore. His hands left my breasts to dive beneath the waistband of my pants. Delirious, my feet planted firmly in sand, I let my ass sink deeper into his lap. He was so hard, I could feel his heated erection poke my ass through our clothing. Hips rolling, my body strummed his. I felt the vibration of his chest as he moaned, heard a mouthful of air catch before it left his throat, listened to a desperate groan escape from his lips. "I need you,

Jewel. You make me want things I've never wanted before."

The next thing I knew, we were sinking to the sand. Indigo was kissing me fiercely, and I was being tossed about. Everything hit me at once: the cast of silver moonlight, waves crashing against the shore, his breath on my neck, his hands running the length of my body.

I was a figurine made of clay, turned and twisted, undressed and stretched across his lap. A damp breeze grazed my bare breasts; I shuddered, not from the chill, but from the ecstasy of it all. My Capris hugged my ankles and my thighs were urged apart. "I want to taste you again," he whispered. "Then I want to be inside you."

My voice was so fragile, I never thought he would hear my body's response when I uttered, "I want you to fuck me."

"I want to fuck you so bad," he gritted.

I was cradled and kissed and backed against his chest where my head came to rest on his shoulder. My eyelids involuntarily fluttered, and when I gazed up stars spiraled through the sky in glittering whirlwinds, or was it my head that was spinning like a cyclone?

Indigo's arms were around me, the fingers of his one hand circling my aching breasts, teasing my rigid nipples, while his other hand slid down my belly. His fingers raked the inside of my thighs, working their way up to my clit. He circled the throb with his thumb, then plunged a finger deep inside me.

All the while, his breath blew over my face, his mouth trailed my neck, nibbled my ear, as he whispered, "I want to do so many things to you ... make you scream all night."

Coiling and twisting, his fingers felt urgent. My head rolled from side to side. Again and again I screamed his name. With the pressure of his hands, my body jerked. Bracing for an orgasm, I covered his hand with mine, doubling the pleasure. "Oh ... oh ... oh my God." Sucking in a breath, limply I fell against him, groaning, drawing out the sensation for as long as humanly possible. "Holy shit. It feels so good. Don't stop. Don't stop."

"I won't stop. I'll never stop." His words were fierce. "Tell me what you want. I'll give you anything, anything you want."

"You ... I just want you. I want to kiss you. I want to be in your arms. I want you on top of me. Feel you inside me."

"I don't have any condoms," he rasped.

I sat up. "Really?"

He urged me back down. "I didn't plan on us screwing on the beach. When I make love to you, it's not going to be a quickie ... it's going to be special. Slow and beautiful. It'll take all night."

"Night and day."

"Forever."

His chin rested on my shoulder. Reaching up, I pulled his face to mine, straining for his lips. "Baby. I need to be in your bed tonight." His body tensed. A sigh burst from his parted lips. He felt so hard beneath me, I thought he'd explode.

"I want you more than anything, Jewel, more than anything else in my life. I want you so badly, but I need you to be certain it's what you really want. That it's not just in the heat of the moment. You have to be sure. No regrets ... not now ... not ever."

"You make me so crazy, I can't think straight. All I know is, I could never regret anything I do with you, Indigo."

The salted air made me dizzy, drowning my sense of right from wrong. Regaining my strength, I turned in his arms, pulled him to his knees. I was the victim of starvation, and I couldn't seem to get enough of him. I was feeding off his body, my hands greedily clawing his back, squeezing his buttocks, making their way up the inside of his thighs. I needed to experience his release as much as he did.

I dragged his shirt up over his head. My naked breasts ground into his chest. The throb between my legs was relentless. I brought his hand back to me, guiding his fingers to the ache deep inside, and bearing down.

My palms stroked his erection that bulged beneath his pants. My fingertips locked on his fly. When it unzipped, his cock sprang into my palm. His hand landed on mine, and his deep groan filled my ear. He moved with me, tugging his pants to his knees. Then he was suddenly the clay, and I began clutching, sliding my hand up and down his shaft. When he moaned, I knew I'd found the right rhythm.

We both rested on our knees. Indigo held my face in his hands, the pressure of his palms growing desperate. He buried his lips in my neck. I felt his groan against the side of my throat. When his mouth captured mine, I inhaled his guttural, "Jewelia."

"Don't come yet," my voice was a breathy whisper. "I want to taste you."

His body jerked, and as he got to his feet, a sigh rushed out with the uneven breath he exhaled.

Slowly, I slid my hands up the inside of his thighs. Reaching his balls, I cupped, gently massaging. Brushing my lips lightly over the head of his cock, I lifted my eyes to watch him shudder. I ran my tongue around the base, dragging it to the tip, drawing a lazy circle. From the look on his face, I thought his legs would buckle. He let out a sound between a growl and a groan, then tangled his fingers in my hair, pressing me closer, while my knees sank deeper into damp sand.

I worked my tongue along his cock, flicking the smooth tip until he drew in a noisy breath, then took the head into my mouth, rolling my tongue around it.

With a slackened jaw he watched me, the blue of his eyes barely visible. "Holy shit, Jewel," he groaned, his grip on my hair tightening, urging me to take him entirely.

I dug my fingers into his ass and pulled him into me, until his throbbing cock almost hit the back of my throat. I sucked until I heard his low gasp, breathing out one of my own. Bringing my hand to the base of his shaft, I increased the pressure of my lips, my fingers gliding, as I caressed his sack with my free hand.

The harder I worked, the more he moaned, until I felt him contract in my palm, pulse on my tongue. His balls tightened in my hand, and he released with a trembling gasp.

"Christ," he mumbled, dropping down beside me. Pulling me into his arms, he buried his face in my hair. "You really kicked my ass, Sunshine."

I drew back and gazed into his eyes which were not entirely open: he still had that dreamy, just loved look which gave me a chill. Everything that had happened between us, bringing us this far, flashed through my mind. The excitement of being with him, becoming this close, filled me with happiness ... and fear.

"You better get used to it, baby, 'cos the best is yet to come," I promised, sweeping tousled locks of his hair off his forehead.

I took his face in my hands. My mouth found his and remained there until I heard distant voices grow near.

Ring Around My Finger

Emma was calling me, her voice growing near.

We scrambled for our clothes, giggling like adolescents as we brushed sand from our bodies, hopped from leg to leg, bracing one another as we quickly dressed. "Hold on, you." Indigo stopped me before I could face the beams of flashlights pointing in our direction. "One more kiss."

"You're insatiable," I whispered, happily obliging.

"But only for you." While his lips caressed mine, I kept my eyes open, watching the softness of his face, wondering when he would tell me he loved me.

Fingers locked, arms swinging, we met up with my friends who had patiently partied without us. I felt a twinge of guilt when I looked into Emma's eyes. "Sorry," I whispered, "We kind of got caught up in things."

She smiled, her expression knowing. "It's your mission, Jewel. Enjoy it." She winked.

With Em and me lagging behind, Indigo showed everyone to the guest house, which was an adorable stone cottage surrounded by walls of hedges. In the distance, I could still hear the thundering breakers crashing on shore.

"It was absolutely amazing," with a hushed voice, I confided.

"You didn't actually ..." Emma's eyes caught the moonlight, sparkling like chocolate diamonds.

"No, but almost." I squeezed her arm. "He's just too perfect to be true, Em. I'm so gone, it's pathetic." I groaned into her shoulder.

"Did he tell you he loved you?"

"No." At that moment, I hated the word, hated to admit it. At the concept that my entire world was beginning to revolve around this man, fear took hold. Then at the possibility that my universe could come crashing down at any moment, my stomach sank. "I should pull back," I said to Em so quietly, I barely heard my own words.

"Ride the wave, Jewel. There's really only today."

Gone was the psychologist I relied on to lift my mood. Standing before me was a pessimist. I recoiled. But, she was right. No one knew what tomorrow would bring, but whatever it was, it would have to be dealt with. Just as I'd dealt with losing my grandma and being abandoned by Nikos. With each loss, I'd thought I would perish, but life went on, and I was stronger.

With everyone settled into the cottage, arms secured around one another, Indigo and I went back to the main house, which by then was deserted. The patio lights were dimmed, and only two interior lamps glowed, lighting the path to the second floor.

We crept up the stairs and stood before the doorway to Indigo's room. On the beach we'd been wilder than the ocean. But in the sobriety of the surroundings I suddenly fell subdued. I stared at Indigo, reliving the intimacy we'd just shared, the pleasure our hands had provided. My eyes questioned his.

"I have something for you," he said softly, opening the door and leading me into his room. Moonlight filtered through the tailored curtains, but when he clicked a wall switch, a table lamp stifled the glimmer of the outside world that I longed to sink back into.

He brought me to his bed, where I sat at the edge. "Close your eyes," he said.

My lids shut obediently, and through silence I heard the faint creak of polished hardwood as his bare soles crossed the floor. I heard a drawer slide open, quietly close. Then he was on his way back to me, and I felt the rate of my heart increase, my fingers twist nervously in my lap. The next thing I felt was Indigo as he knelt before me, his hands sliding over my thighs.

"Okay. Open your eyes." He sounded like a little boy.

I looked down at his face. His eyes were glistening. Dear Lord. Was he about to propose? My breathing grew faint. He must have noticed my confused expression, because he quickly slid onto the bed beside me and placed a small box into my trembling hands.

Speechless, I simply stared.

He smiled. "It's your graduation gift."

"Oh, Indigo. I didn't get you anything ..." My bottom lip rolled down.

He gripped my chin, his thumb soothing. "Believe me. You've given me all that matters," grinning, he added, "and I'm not referring to sex, either."

"I know you're not, baby." I held his face in my hands, my heart filling with emotion.

"Go on, open it," he said excitedly. "I hope you like it. Believe me, it took me weeks to find the perfect one for you."

With watering eyes I gazed down at the box, which was now a red velvet blur, and when I lifted the lid, gathered tears tumbled down my cheeks.

Indigo plucked the heart-shaped rose gold ring from the plush lining, and slipped it on my right pinky. He dabbed my face with a tissue from his nightstand, then kissed each cheek.

"There," he said, "now you can see."

"Jimmy," I cried, his real name bringing me closer to him. "It's so beautiful." I held my hand out before me, tilting and leveling, watching the sparkle of the centered diamond. "Now

I have a pink heart right beside the rose from my dad." I brought my hand to my breast.

"*Mi corazón es tuyo.*" Indigo whispered the words, "My heart is yours," directly into my ear, as if sharing a secret.

"Oh, God, baby ..." My eyes burned into his. I almost said: "I love you ..." but with trembling lips, the sacred words remained locked in my throat. I threw my arms around him, knowing I was the luckiest girl in the world. "Thank you so much," I covered his face with a flurry of kisses, "for the party ... for the gorgeous ring ..." *And for being you ...* something else I locked inside.

The clock on his nightstand read four-thirty. The night had been magical, unforgettable, absolutely overwhelming. Despite my happiness, I was about to fall over with exhaustion.

"Come on, honey," he said, tugging me to my feet. "I'll tuck you in next door."

Standing before the open door of what would serve as my room for the next several hours, we paused for one more kiss. "I don't want to let you go," he murmured against my throat. "I've never come this close before ... I know now, I can't be without you."

I cradled his face with my palms, whispering, "I'm not going anywhere." My eyes searched his, bewildered by the staunch determination staring back at me. Was he trying to convince himself? I was tired. I was insane. It was all in my head. I shook free of the concern that gripped my midsection, making a mental note to have Emma analyze me during the bus ride home.

"I hope not." Indigo had barely spoken when my ears rang from an annoying pitch.

"James," Elizabeth's voice was sharp, instantly parting us. "Are you just getting in?"

"I better make like a ghost and disappear," I said, mumbling beneath my breath, "before she gets her broom." We were like two kids, snagged by the shrew who was about to lock them in her tower. On the verge of laughter, I almost fell into the guest room.

Indigo rolled his eyes. "See you soon, Sunshine," he whispered, planting a kiss on my forehead.

I heard him say, "Good night, Mom," and listened to the snap of his door.

I wanted to dance around the room, scream to the world, but sank against a gleaming mahogany armoire, recovering my breath, my fingers caressing the ring he'd just placed on my finger.

Fighting For You

Manhattan Again

$\mathcal{A}$ salty breeze burst through the open window, filling the room with aromatic sunshine; with the help of wavering daggers, I was prodded to a semi conscious state. Grudgingly, I opened my eyes, squinting through halos of brightness. Drugged by exhaustion, for a moment my thoughts were fuzzy, and I had to scramble to remember where I was. Then reality shook me to my senses. Smiling with contentment I stretched and burrowed into the queen sized mattress and silken sheets, bringing my hand to my face to admire my ring.

I'd left my cell phone on the nightstand. The LCD said it was after nine. I also found his message: *You're probably sound asleep right now, dreaming about me, I hope. I already miss you. - J.* Sighing, I held my phone to my chest, then replied to his text: Just woke up. I'll be thinking about you while I shower. xoxo

I lounged for a few minutes, considering our plans for the day, and what I would wear. I wondered if Indigo was awake, thinking about me ... about the romantic night we'd spent in each other's arms, growing closer than I'd ever imagined.

I rolled out of bed, bundled my arms with towels, and

headed for the connecting bathroom. Discarding my clothes on the floor, I stepped into the shower, luxuriating as I twirled in the stall, indulged by five surging streams of pulsing water that hit every single part of my body at once. It felt delicious. Still reeling from the night, I imagined Indigo beside me, replacing the showerheads with his hands.

I brushed my teeth, dried my hair, then rummaged through my backpack, pulling out navy shorts and a crimson top. My sandals were nowhere in sight, so I stuck my feet into a pair of running shoes and exited on tiptoes.

I looked down the hall, at the rows of white painted doors, at the peacock window exploding with sun, edged with clear blue sky.

"Sneaking around the halls?" Indigo came up behind me, squeezing my shoulders. "It's about time you showed up, sleepyhead." His breath washed across the back of my neck, followed by a trail of kisses.

I almost jumped out of my skin. "Hey!" Turning, I held my voice low. "I just woke up."

"I know that. I've been waiting for you for hours."

I sank against his chest. "You scared me."

"I'd never want to do that." He nuzzled my neck. "I thought about you the entire time, just down the hall, all alone in that nice soft bed. I was kinda hoping for a wakeup surprise."

"Believe me, I would have loved to ... if your mother wasn't right across the hall." I stole a peek at her closed door. Imagining her ear glued to the other side, my whisper grew fainter than a breeze, "I thought about you too," I gazed into the intensity of his eyes, "and that nice beach down there ... where I must have lost my sandals."

"We'll have to retrace our steps then ..." He looked so sexy with partially lowered lids, the mint shirt he wore faceting grays and blues in his sleepy eyes. "Maybe reenact ... would you like that?"

He lifted my arms over my head, a strong hand pinning me to the wall while he teased my lips with the tip of his tongue.

We'd come to know each other's bodies beneath the clothing we wore, and the precise targets that would elicit a groan, which I attempted to restrain when his hand ran across the front of my shirt, then tried to slip between my thighs.

"You know I would, but baby," I breathed into his ear, "not here." My knees were locked tightly together.

"Why so tense," he whispered. "They should all be downstairs by now. This is a house of early risers."

"How long have you been up, anyway?" I noticed he looked well rested, wondering how he managed to look so handsome with so little sleep.

"Since about seven." His breath minty, he blew a stray lock of hair from my forehead.

"We didn't get to bed till almost five. Don't you sleep?" I ran my fingers around his collar, down the buttons of his shirt.

"I told you. I don't need much ... just short naps ... and you." His lips played with mine.

As much as I didn't want to, I squirmed. "To be honest, I'm not comfortable here."

He angled his head. "You're trembling."

"I just need a cup of coffee ... maybe some breakfast?" Smiling, I squinted up at him.

I didn't mention that part of the reason my body shivered was because half of my mind was waiting for his mother's footsteps on the stairs, or even worse, Vanessa's. The thought then struck. Where was she? I braced for her intrusion, her creepy, smirking glance.

"I'm sorry, honey. I can understand how you feel." He ran his tongue along my throat. "I'll have to sneak you into the E.R. one of these nights. We've got these great padded exam tables." He sucked my neck so hard, I swore he was drawing blood. Did the hospital have that effect on him? If so, I definitely needed to be admitted.

"Maybe I'll pay you a visit ... when you're on duty ... and it's dark ... and sexy." I nibbled his bottom lip, moving to his neck.

"I'll be sure to text you when a room is free." His throat vibrated beneath my lips.

"Don't tempt me." I giggled. "I might just turn up in admitting."

"I wish you would." His fingers kneaded my ribcage.

I screeched, but his mouth silenced mine. Right after I moaned as loud as I had the night before, I heard a door creak open and slam shut. I instinctively jumped from Indigo's embrace, in time to face the source of the slamming door. Vanessa brushed by us, nose in the air, eyes focused straight ahead.

"Hey, Ness," said Indigo. "Get a good night's sleep?"

"Just fine." Her words were clipped. "And you?" She paused, faced us, shot him a bogus grin. When her lime green gaze shifted to me, she looked demonic. Her demeanor sent a chill down my spine. Did she really hate me that much?

If Indigo noticed, he didn't mention it. In silence, we followed her down the stairs.

Someone had cooked up a breakfast fit for a king, and we all gathered around the banquet table in the formal dining room where we were served. Apparently the caterers hadn't yet left.

We spent the day touring the Atlantic on Indigo's boat. Derek blasted a portable radio, and we all drank the beer we'd stocked in coolers. The girls and I had packed leftover party goodies, so we snacked, enjoyed the sun, now and then dipping our hands and feet over the side of the boat into the water.

Around us gulls swarmed, ducking into the waves for fish, or the bread we tossed overboard. Derek caught the first buzz and dove in, yelling, "Roast bird for dinner."

"That's disgusting, Derek," said Emma with a grimace while she held out spoonfuls of mousse to Bill who lounged on a padded bench at the stern, dangling a leg over the side.

"Derek, get your brown ass back into this boat," Yvonne yelled, turning to me with frustration. "I don't know what's wrong with that man. He's got a career in his sights, and he's being stupid with the fish. Suppose he drowns?"

We all laughed at the fuss she was making, but when she panicked and started screaming, "Shark!" Indigo threw Derek a life preserver and against his will, we dragged him back onboard.

Pete and Casey brought a deck of cards, and became caught up in a poker marathon. As if the only ones on the boat, they ignored the rioting taking place around them, even when Yvonne and Derek's dancing threatened to overturn it.

"I just know the summer is gonna be over in the blink of an eye," I complained to Indigo.

"Yeah, but look at it this way, Sunshine. By August, you'll have a spot in the academy, and I'll be starting my residency. Aren't you excited?"

"Of course I am. But our time is gonna be so limited." I pouted.

" We have our entire lives ahead of us. Patience, my little tamale." He kissed my pout. "I can see it now. I'll be patching up the criminals you arrest and send to the E.R. before they even get a chance to see the inside of a jail cell."

"They'll need a lot of patching up after I get through with them." I laughed. "I hate criminals."

For as hard as we tried to stop time, the day flew. After paying respects to his mother, we all left the main house, ready to amble down the driveway, sad to be leaving, but anxious to get home.

"Thank you so much. I had a wonderful time," I said to Indigo as I gathered my belongings, taking a last look around the barn. "I can't believe the weekend's over. It's so hard to say goodbye," I complained as we walked out the same door we'd entered only twenty-four hours earlier. On our way down the driveway he carried my backpack in one arm, the other was around me.

He fell out of step, walking backward, shushing me with a finger on my lips. "I'm coming back to the city with you." His smile filled my stomach with butterflies.

"On the bus?" I thought I'd explode with joy.

"Right next to you." He nuzzled the front of my throat, which almost seized beneath his moist mouth. "How could I let you go home without me?"

"What about the Wrangler?"

"It's home in Manhattan. I hitched a ride out here with friends."

I was thrilled. I threw my arms around his neck. We'd soon be back on friendly turf, and all would be well once more. I wanted to tuck the Hamptons into the back of my mind: remembering the beach, forgetting Elizabeth and Vanessa. Theirs was a world I wasn't a part of ... with no desire to be.

Before we made it to the end of the driveway, to where our taxis filled the pristine street with fumes, two distinct voices rang out. In my peripheral, I glimpsed the shrew and her disciple.

"James ... Where are you going?" Elizabeth's words flew through the air like a flock of squawking birds.

"Home to Manhattan. I'll call you during the week." He tossed a wave into the air, his head barely turning as we continued our stride, somewhat faster after his mother's voice broke the calm.

"Jim Jim," Vanessa nasalized, "you mother's car absolutely has to be in Briar Ridge by tomorrow for service. You were supposed to drive it back after the weekend. Have you forgotten?"

"Christ ..." I'd never heard Indigo sound so annoyed. He stopped and spun. "You can't drive the car to Westchester, Ness?"

"I don't drive standard," was her whiny reply.

"How did you get here, anyway?" He lashed out at her.

"I drove out with your parents." At first she looked stunned, then became defensive. "My car is at the house." Her eyelids blinked furiously, then she seemed to gain control. "I'll take you back to Manhattan tonight ... unless it's late and you want to spend the night in Westchester with me, which would be nice."

Why was she addressing Indigo but looking straight at me? My stomach churned.

"I'm not an errand boy for you, Vanessa," he jerked his hands in the air, then shot a defiant look at his mother, "or for this family. You think nothing of inconveniencing anyone."

"Jim Jim," Vanessa's face flushed, "what's wrong with you? I've never seen you act this way before." She looked daggers at me.

"James," Elizabeth interceded, "I can't leave tonight." With narrowing eyes she threatened, "You have obligations, and I'm about to tell your guests exactly what they are."

The exasperation in Indigo's eyes subsided when he turned them on me. "I'm sorry, Jewel." He shook his head. "I guess I did promise." He let out a sigh of defeat. "They're helpless."

I wanted to throw myself at both of the bitches, scream at the top of my lungs to let Indigo live his own life. I had a feeling his *obligations* had a lot to do with his weird mood swings. "It's okay, Indigo. Text me when you can. I don't want to miss the charter. The others are already in the cabs," I pitched my head toward the exhaust fumes that were burning my throat, "I better run." I absolutely had to get out of there or Lord knows what might have spewed from my mouth. I didn't want to make matters any worse for him.

The brilliant sun heated my face, giving me reason to pull my sunglasses down, cover the disappointment pooling in my eyes.

Instead of meeting us halfway, Elizabeth stood her ground and insisted on screaming, "Derek. I'll phone you when the ensemble is ready for fitting."

"I've got your number too, Mrs. Ballou," his reply was obedient, and loud.

"You'll have to drop whatever you're doing when I call. You understand, correct?"

"I'll be there, ma'am, at the drop of a hat," he replied.

"Does this mean another trip out here?" I asked Indigo before climbing into the taxi. The thought weighed heavy on my mind. For as lovely as the home was, the atmosphere was depressing. No wonder Indigo preferred his apartment in Manhattan. No wonder Indigo had his brooding moments.

While he worked his jaw, his face became wrought with frustration. "I doubt it. The show's on Fifth Avenue. They'll more than likely get together at the house in Briar Ridge." When he said, *the* house, it told me a lot about his childhood, and his adult emotions.

We shared a discreet kiss. Waiting for me to settle in, he shut the door.

You should be sitting beside me ... my mind cried.

An awkward barrier stood between us. I held up a hand as the taxi pulled away. As he waved goodbye, Indigo's face looked worn, watching our departure like an abandoned soul, unsure of which side of the road he belonged on. I knew he was struggling with something monumental, and suddenly his struggle became mine.

On the drive back to the charter, the beauty of the night was invaded by thoughts of Vanessa and Indigo driving to Westchester, and the possibility of him staying the night. My jaw clamped shut. I was inconsolable on the ride home.

Breaking The Ties That Bound Me

"Shrink me," I said to Emma, who sat beside me on the bus, a comforting arm around my shoulders.

Stiff back, turning in the seat, she stared, but didn't speak.

"I'm freaking," I lamented, "I don't think this is gonna work out." Looking out the window, watching gliding sailboats and diving gulls, I sighed, unable to believe my own words. "Let me rephrase that. It's not working." I fixated on the night we'd spent on the beach and was filled with overwhelming love, agonizing emptiness. I thought I'd convulse with disappointment, loneliness, and frustration.

Emma's face was sympathetic. "Jewel. I'm usually never at a loss for words," she frowned, "but this time, I just don't know what to say. Your relationship with Indigo seems to be turning into a bad soap opera."

"Crap, Emma. I thought you'd console me. What's up with the sudden negativity?"

"Hun," she rested her head against mine, "from the outside looking in, he's got you on a roller coaster, not to mention a leash. This isn't you, Jewel." She plucked strands of hair from my lashes. "You're up, you're down, and I can't stand watching you suffer this way. Indigo's a great guy and all, but unless you can take the bumpy ride, maybe you should just hop off the train."

"Oh my God, Em. I can't believe you're talking like this. Are you serious?" My eyes bore into hers. "Is this a test, or a new way to shrink me? Slap me to my senses or something?"

"How much does he mean to you?"

"Everything."

"Is he worth the pain?"

I didn't have to think about the question. My eyes watered. "Yes ..."

"Well, that's your answer then. I opened the door ... you just walked through."

I stared at Em with amazement. "Damn, you're good."

"That's why I'll get $250.00 an hour when I'm in my private practice."

***

But, things didn't turn out as planned. Indigo didn't return to Manhattan that night, or contact me for over a week. A week of pure hell. Emma finally talked me into texting him, to see if something was wrong.

"Maybe he's had an accident," she said, scaring the hell out of me.

So, I texted him. Nada. I heard nothing from him until the following Tuesday, when I read his reply: Hey. Sorry I haven't called. Still at Hamptons. Family crisis. Contact U soon.

"Contact me soon? What is he replying to my job application or something?" My head rolled in my hands.

After reading his text, I over-plucked my eyebrows. I had to get them out of my system: One for Vanessa ... One for Indigo, and so on and so forth. Before I knew it, I looked like a brunette Pamela Anderson ... just the brows.

"He forced my hand," I told Em. After exiting the bathroom, my voice was unbelievably calm. "He leaves me no choice. I'm done."

"I'm sorry, Jewel."

"It's fine," I lifted my chin, refusing to break down, "got my test score ... and my academy date. I start the first week of August."

"When did you find out?"

"The other day."

Her face sagged with guilt. "Sorry I haven't been around much. Bill and I ..." She threw her arms around me. She was sniffling.

"Hey you, don't worry about it," I scrunched my mouth into my own version of the duck face that never failed to bring a smile. "I'm fine. The weight of the world is off my shoulders," my eyes narrowed, "let the bitch have him. Obviously, he realized I'd never fit inside their circle." Between words, I gulped air. "Who'd want to, anyway? Right?"

"Does Pete know about the academy?"

I nodded.

"That explains it."

"Huh?"

"Seems we're going to Maine." She turned her pure white smile on me.

I laughed. "You know, he's been bugging me to go to his family's place. I guess my misery is the perfect excuse, huh?"

"Oh, hun. Things will get better." She hugged me, then her compassion turned secretive. "Don't tell him I told you. He wants to spring it on you himself."

Pete congratulated me in person for placing high on the list for the academy, saying he knew I had it in me, and by the next weekend, we'd be, "Cutting loose with the moose."

"Have you been up there yet?" I asked, "to see your inheritance?"

He slung an arm around my shoulders. "Not for a long time. Which is why I need you guys to help me clean the place up." After a serious stare, he burst out laughing. "I'm kidding. I hired an agency to get the place ready for us. So tell Emma and Bill we're on for this weekend, and if you'd like, you can even bring Yvonne and Derek. Those two are three quarters of the party."

"I'll get everyone together, Pete. I can't wait to see the moose, but I don't want to run into any wolves." I over-tensed my jaw. "Eeeek. We're trippin'. I'm hyped."

Pete hesitated, sounding strained when he asked, "What about Indigo?"

"What about him?"

"Will he be coming?"

"For all I know, he never returned from the Hamptons. I don't know when ... if I'll see him again, Pete." I didn't think my face held much expression, because my voice was dead.

Pete shook his head. I'd never seen him look so sad. Maybe it was because he had Casey. Emma had Bill. Yvonne and Derek were inseparable. And I was alone.

He put his arms around me. "You've got us, Kit Kat. We'll stand behind anything you decide. I'm always here for you, honey." He drew a breath. "The dude did seem okay ... so into you." He ran a palm across his five-o-clock shadow. "I saw the way he looked at you." He shook his head.

I drew in a bolstering breath. "Things aren't always as they seem, Pete."

He looked thoughtful. "Don't try to figure out a guy. Hey, let's get outta here for a while, Jewel."

Pete and I took a ride to Poughkeepsie on his bike. Helmets always made me claustrophobic, but I loved the freedom of the open road. We spent a great afternoon with my family, who always fussed over Pete. Who didn't love Pete? My mother sent us home with another care package, which was slung over my shoulder in a canvas bag, insulated for the ride home.

When I walked through the door, Emma had a nervous look on her face.

"What's wrong?" I blurted. My stomach hadn't seized that severely since the Hamptons.

Her mouth tightened. "Indigo was here."

"What?" My eyelids flew up to my brows. "When?"

"You just missed him." Her eyes were wide, expectant. I

knew she was waiting for me to freak out. And I did.

"What did he want? Why didn't he text, or call me? Why did he just barge in?"

"He did try to reach you. Apparently, your phone's turned off. Check it."

"Damn. I forgot to take it off vibrate, and it was stuffed into my bag."

Sure enough, there were three missed calls.

"So, what do you plan on doing?" Hands on hips, Emma looked like my mother on a bad day behind the bakery counter, when the place filled with afterschool kids who tried to lift wrapped cookies from the tables.

"Nothing." I set my jaw.

"Are you at least going to return his call?"

"I'll think about it," I said on my way into my room. I quietly shut the door, sat on my bed, and let pent up teardrops slide from my face to my shirt. What did he want from me? If his intent was to drive me crazy, he was certainly doing a great job of it.

I took a long hot shower, and didn't turn the water off until I'd made up my mind.

Sitting on my bed, my back braced against a pillow and the headboard, I dialed his number. For this confrontation, texts wouldn't suffice. He answered on the second ring.

"Hey." He sounded so anxious, his breath short, as if he was pacing.

"Hey." The greeting rolled off my tongue, but my lips were quivering.

"How are you?" he asked.

"Where are you?" I countered.

"My place. Just got back." The breath he drew was ragged. With the way he sounded, I wondered what he looked like, and if his tan face was pale and forlorn as it had been when my taxi had pulled away.

"What's up?" My voice was so cold, I pulled the spread over my trembling body. My teeth were almost chattering.

"You're angry with me ..." he pulled in a breath, "with good reason."

"No fucking kidding," burst through my lips, then I realized coldness could hurt more. "Why ever would you think I was angry, James?" I willed my voice to not shake as my limbs were doing. "After all, it's only been two weeks."

"Can I see you tonight?" He sounded desperate.

I blew my response into the phone. "I can't. I'm busy packing."

Desperation turned to alarm. "Where are you going?"

"To Pete's place ... in Maine. I'll be back on Monday .. or Tuesday ... or Wednesday."

"Jewel ..." His voice cracked. "Baby ..."

"Don't call me baby!"

"Okay, okay. Jewelia. Please let me see you before you go. I can explain everything."

"Everything? As in why I received one text from you? And a vague one at that. Family crisis? Did Vanessa stub a toe or break a fingernail?"

"It had nothing to do with Vanessa, bab ... Jewel. If you let me explain, I think you'll understand. At least, I hope you will. There was no way I could leave. It was so messed up, I couldn't even call. I ..."

"What good are apologies when you're constantly fucking up?"

"Just hear me out ... please."

He sounded so sincere, so torn up, I wanted to sail through the phone, hold him in my arms. My hard shell cracked like an over-boiled egg. Stepped on. Scrunched. Scrambled. Totally emulsified, like the wall I'd managed to build around myself.

"I got into the academy." I couldn't seem to iron out my voice, no less the situation.

"That's fantastic ... but I knew you would."

"Yeah, so, we're going to Maine to celebrate. We can talk there, if you want." I held my breath. If he declined my invitation, I would throw the phone at the wall right before I died, or had a nervous breakdown, whichever occurred first.

In a subdued tone, Indigo accepted, agreeing to show up at my apartment the following morning by eight a.m., packed and ready to roll. I had planned on driving up with Emma and Bill, who were hitching a ride with Yvonne and Derek, but because of the seating arrangements, we decided Indigo and I would take his Wrangler, along with the coolers and some of our gear.

Sorting Things Out

Emma and I waited outside our apartment, bags piled between us on the sidewalk. The day was sweet and warm. It was summer. I should have been lighthearted, but I wasn't. When I saw the Wrangler pull up to the curb, my heart started racing. When Indigo stepped from the car, came to my side, leaned in and kissed my cheek, I almost passed out from hyperventilation.

"All set for camping, I see." He scanned our possessions, attempting a grin, but discomfort was obvious. Of course, he was putting up a front.

Everything hit me at once, and my heart broke for him. *What is wrong with you, Jewelia? Why can't you be hard?* Because half of your heart is standing here, staring at you.

"Hey," I said, unable to remove my eyes from his. "You okay?"

He was as handsome as ever, but looked so worn, with circles of stress beneath his eyes, and tiny lines visible at the corners. Lines I'd never before noticed.

"I'm good, hon." He put up a hand to avoid the strong rays of sunshine that rose above the high rise buildings aiming at us from across the street. "Are you?" Shoving his hands into his pockets, he looked like a solemn little boy waiting to be reprimanded.

"Feeling better." My lips were taut, but I managed a smile.

"That's good to hear." His voice softened.

As I watched his face turn pensive, dormant butterflies sprang to life, scratching away, just like old times. My hands threatened to tremble, so I locked them behind my back, but nothing could brace my legs that so badly wanted to wobble.

I had to put myself in another place, engage my mind so I didn't fall apart. Just seeing him again made my chest swell with excitement. I felt all tingly, and my lips threatened to freeze, my jaw to shudder. The academy, Jewel! Think about where you'll be in just a few short weeks. Starting a new life. Living your dream. He's not your life, silly girl, not the world around you. That world crashed on a Southampton street.

So I told myself all the lies I needed to get me through the moment. And it worked. On the outside, anyway. Inside I was crumbling.

"Should we get this show on the road?" I said with a cocky grin. Unlocking my arms, I grabbed my bag and a cooler.

Emma, who had retreated to the narrow porch five steps high, had to have been silently observing us. When my eyes finally traveled to her, she was smiling and Bill was standing beside her; an arm around her, he also looked pleased as Indigo and I stood within two feet of each other. Emma gave me an inconspicuous thumbs up and headed down the stairs.

Pete and Casey showed up on their motorcycles, dressed in fatigues and olive drab T-shirts and hiking boots. They were hunky and adorable. Pete wore a lightweight black jacket; Casey's was chocolate brown. Unhitching their bags, they threw their belongings into the Wrangler's trunk, then greeted Indigo with *hey mans* and handshakes. Pete even patted Indigo's arm with what I judged to be compassion. As soon as Yvonne and Derek drove up in his parents' Escalade, Emma and Bill hopped into the luxurious back seat.

Heading out of the city we formed a convoy, with Pete

and Casey the point guards, Indigo and me the center, the Escalade bringing up the rear. Since Pete was the only one who knew the way, we had to be careful not to lose sight of him. At some point our cell phones were bound to die as we climbed the mountains of Maine and we'd be out of touch.

"Have you ever been to Maine?" I asked Indigo, who drove with both hands on the wheel. He wore aviator sunglasses, which made him look irresistible; I knew his eyes mirrored the smoky lenses that shielded them, because the unbuttoned shirt he wore over his heather tee was peppered with gray and black.

"I've been to Bangor. It's beautiful country, especially this time of year, with everything blooming and all."

He seemed to be wired tighter than a time bomb. I ran my fingers down his arm, trying to relax him. He must have read my mind, because he said, "Once we get out of the city, onto the highway, the traffic will thin ... we can talk."

I sat in a favored position, knee bent, half facing him. I watched his profile relax, only to tighten again as he drove. "We don't have to talk yet. Concentrate on driving. Want a bottle of water? Soda? Coffee? I have a thermos in the back."

"No thanks. I'm good."

The ice inside me had melted, and I had a feeling, regardless of what he told me, I was falling deeper in love with him, dangerously fast.

We merged onto Interstate 95 and he sank back into his seat, left hand on the wheel, while his right hand reached for mine. I remembered the night he'd pulled me onto his lap, and how he'd made me feel: so wanted, so hot. That night had started with an argument. I thought of the first night he met me at The Prestige, which almost ended in an argument.

Holy shit, was that our destiny? To be two bickering people? Bitter and old? I gripped his hand tightly, vowing I would do everything possible to make things work.

But, should I have to try? Shouldn't it come naturally? *Grandma, did this ever happen to you? Please ... give me a sign.*

Am I handling this the right way? Can you make raindrops fall ... just for a minute, so I know you hear me? How about whipping up a little wind to give me the okay? Would that be possible?

The sun kept right on shining, and the only wind came from my partially open window, a result of traveling sixty miles an hour on the Interstate ... and the air remained dry.

"I could barely function without you," Indigo said softly, his voice almost inaudible above the road noise. "I missed you so much."

"I missed you too." I squeezed his hand. A lump tightened my throat. "You know. We have a hell of a track record." I suddenly burst out laughing.

For a moment, he took his attention off the road to glance at me. Behind his sunglasses, I saw the furrow of his brow.

"Do you realize we've had almost as many arguments as dates?" My shoulders shook, tears flooded my face. I'd never been hysterical before.

"Oh baby, don't cry." He reached across the seat, pulling me as close as possible with the console between us. "If I could put you on my lap, I would. You're breaking my heart. I'm sorry, baby. I never meant to hurt you like this."

I covered my face with my hands, sobbing, "It's okay. I'm sure you had a good reason. I'll be fine. I just need to get it all out."

The minute Pete coasted into a rest stop, Indigo cut the engine and pulled me close. He held me so tight, breathing was difficult. "God, it's good to hold you again," he whispered. "I was so afraid you'd never talk to me again."

"I was so afraid I'd lost you."

"Never." His mouth closed over mine.

We kissed with fury until Pete tapped on the window. I'd never seen him gripped with such emotion.

"Sorry to break this up, kids." He leaned an arm above the driver's side window, acting just like the cop he was, only he was smiling. "We're almost there, but I need to take a serious piss right now or I'll be leaving a trail."

Pete disappeared and Indigo sighed, then started laughing. "Oh, Jewel. We can't ever let this happen again. This separation almost ruined my career."

"What do you mean?" Stunned, I stared.

"It was just as hard on my patients as it was on me. Do you know the penalty for mixing up charts? Trying to take someone's temperature with my pen?"

We laughed so hard, possibly as a form of relief; my too dry eyes would have normally watered, but there didn't seem to be any tears left inside me. When I pulled down the visor and looked in the mirror, I almost passed out. Two swollen, red-rimmed circles stared back, and with mascara coating half of my face, I looked like the grim reaper.

"I look awful," I groaned. Not wanting Indigo to see me that way, I stared out the window past outdated gas pumps, through the glass front of the store that appeared deserted. The scene was isolated, missing life, the frightening way I'd felt without Indigo.

He brought my face around, ran his thumbs under my eyes and gently kissed each lid. "You look beautiful." His touch, his careful tone, told me he knew we were teetering on the edge of something so tenuous, denial was a better way of surviving should we fall. And although we'd just kissed as lovers, we hadn't yet resolved the issues that could have easily destroyed us.

So, we didn't say another word about the past two weeks, or the gremlin riding between us, and when Pete returned, we followed the bikes down winding dirt roads, over wooden bridges, into a forest so thick the only defining characteristics were the colors of the branches, limbs and boughs.

"What is this? No man's land?" I said with disbelief, as our journey seemed never ending. I tried to call Emma, but after dialing her cell all I heard was my carrier's pre-recorded message. "Great. No reception."

We were surrounded by monstrous forms of vegetation, some stretching skyward, others spreading into a bushy carpet of spindly undergrowth. The woodland was so dense, shafts of sun would never be able to penetrate. I thought of every horror movie I'd ever seen, and was swept with waves of apprehension. I scrubbed my arms till they warmed. "I can't believe we'll be stuck out here with no phone. Suppose there's an emergency?"

"Don't you think there's a phone at the house?" Indigo tried to calm me with optimism.

"Pete didn't say. And since no one's been living there, most likely not." As we traveled the bumpy terrain, I stretched my neck as far as it would reach, peering into the woodlands, wondering if I'd see a moose. "There's no way I'm hiking in there. It's too creepy. Did I ever tell you I used to have nightmares about being lost in a forest?"

"I'll protect you, Sunshine." Indigo's chuckle sounded light, as if he'd forgotten the tension, or had deliberately buried it. If I didn't try to do the same, heading back home would have been a better option.

"You'll protect me from wolves?"

"Two legged?"

I smacked his arm." I'm serious. I'd wake up to them howling."

"Your neighbor's dogs?" He smirked.

"Well, I'm sticking close to the house. We shouldn't have bothered bringing the bikes."

"Look. If there's a medical emergency, you've got me. And if there's an intruder, or a wolf, Pete to the rescue. So stop worrying. We've got everything covered."

"Why am I still uneasy?" I groaned, sliding my hand down his thigh.

"I don't know, but this must be it," Indigo cut into my cynicism as we stopped before a steep driveway.

"I would think so, since it's the only house we've passed on this Godforsaken road."

"We'll be fine. And where there's a way in, there's a way out. Don't worry."

"You make such sense." I exhaled a sigh, for a moment

forgetting we were here to work things out, until I analyzed his words: *We'll be fine. Where there's a way in, there's a way out,* which could have pertained to our relationship. My heart was heavy.

He mumbled something that sounded like, "I only wish that were true." But when I asked him to clarify, he said it was nothing and clammed up.

The A-Frame In Maine

Following Pete and Casey, the Wrangler crept up the driveway. The Escalade sailed in behind us. Derek idled his vehicle in front of the garage, stuck his head out the window, yelling, "Open the door, Pete. I'm pulling her in. This baby's been garaged since day one. I'll have my head handed to me if I bring her back with even a scratch."

"It's full of stuff," Pete replied. "Your vehicle will be safe in the driveway, Derek."

"Yeah," I said, walking around the Wrangler, "Like someone's gonna come running out of the woods and steal it? We're probably the only humans within fifty miles." I shuddered, suddenly missing Manhattan like crazy. Then the thought struck me: *What else could come running out of the woods? Or creeping would be even worse.*

We gathered on the hardened mud driveway, speechless, heads rotating every which way.

"What are we looking at?" I said. "There's nothing around but mountains and trees."

"You've got a point, Kit Kat," Pete laughed, "let's check out the inside of the shack."

"I wouldn't call this a shack, bro," said Bill, "this is the biggest cabin I've ever seen."

"It's not a cabin," said Emma, "it's an A-frame. It's so rustic. I love it."

I stood back, admiring the fieldstone foundation, wraparound decking, and the suspended chimes that greeted us when a breeze kicked up. The roof pitched over the front door, diving dramatically down the sides of the two-story structure. Standing before it, the house seemed to stretch up as high as the trees. "It's a nice place, Pete," I said, thinking: *Maybe it won't be so bad here after all.*

"I'll start cleaning out the trunk." Indigo unwound his fingers from mine as we stood beside his open door.

"I'll give you a hand," Casey said, placing his helmet on the back of his bike. He smoothed his hair, then brushed dust from the legs of his pants.

Yvonne was already hanging over the front porch railing. "Derek, get your brandy butt up here," she yelled at her boyfriend, who was making certain no tree limbs or branches would be able to reach the Escalade's fenders, even in a strong wind, should there be one.

"Coming, princess." He took the weathered steps two at a time, in cutoffs, his long legs flexing rippling muscles.

We all helped carry, and dumped our bags in the center of the large living room which was paneled with the same rustic cedar that wrapped the outside of the house. At times, Indigo seemed like a square peg in a round hole, not really fitting into the occasion. Although I'd been the injured party, my heart went out to him. I eased him into a corner, ran my palms up and down his chest, enjoying the feel of him. "What's wrong?"

"Nothing. I just wish we were alone." His stare, ranging from desirous to desperate, was unsettling.

"I'm gonna bring in some firewood." Pete stood before the fieldstone fireplace, a hand on his hip, the other rubbing his chin. "Gets chilly up here at night."

At the thought of nightfall I shivered, for more reasons

than one. Each time I glanced at Indigo, he seemed to be drifting deeper into another place, far away and separate from me, Maine, the others around us ... our predicament. I wondered if we'd end up having a discussion or another argument. Why was I feeling like this was the last stand?

"I'm starving," said Derek. "I'm gonna go out and set up the barbeque." He grabbed Yvonne's hand. "Come on babe, help me."

"If you think I'm cooking," she examined her long polished nails, "you're crazier than I thought. Grilling is man's work." She strutted across the floor, poking her head down the hallway.

"So is cleaning and driving and shopping," Derek grumbled as he headed for the door.

Indigo and Casey carried the last of the bags into the house, while Yvonne perched on a barstool, watching the rest of us work. Bill appeared with his guitar, and from that moment on, Arkana became his official tag.

The guys congregated outside, grilling burgers and hot dogs, and drinking beer. Emma and I rummaged through the cooler, pulled out the perishables and stashed them in the fridge. We'd brought plenty of paper goods, and piled two plates high with potato and macaroni salad.

After filling our bellies, we crashed on the sofas. With dusk fading, Pete lit the logs in the fireplace. I almost jumped out of my skin when lightning flashed and thunder crashed in on us, with torrents of rain beating the windows. "What's that?" My back sprang off the cushion I had napped on.

"Haven't you heard thunder before?" Pete lifted his head and gave me a stupid look.

"No. Don't you hear it? The howling ..."

Indigo seemed almost back to himself. Seated beside me, he pulled me against him. "It's only the wind." His breath was flavored with the beer he'd been drinking.

"No one said it was going to storm this weekend." I argued.

"You need a drink." Pete let his head fall back against Casey's shoulder.

Casey, who had been the quietest of the group agreed, easing himself off the sofa to pass out refills of beer. At Casey's suggestion, we moved to floor, gathering around the fire. Indigo sat cross-legged. I snuggled inside the pocket his thighs formed. Lifting my face to his, I offered my lips. He nuzzled my neck, "I'm happy you let me come. We need this time together after the past few weeks."

At that point, I wasn't sure I even wanted to hear his explanation. In my opinion, whatever had been so taxing on him, couldn't have been drastic enough to keep him from at least sending me a text. I felt the rise of anger, and had to shut off my mind. The fire was heating my face enough; I didn't need my emotions adding to my uncomfortable flush.

It was getting late and I wondered what the rest of the night would bring. Indigo must have felt my vibes. "Let's go upstairs," he whispered. "I really need to talk to you."

My stomach knotted with such anxiety, I could barely stand it. I stood and stretched, raising my voice to capture Pete's attention from Casey, who was talking a mile a minute. "Hey, what are the sleeping arrangements?"

"There are rooms all over the place," Pete slurred. "Take your pick. I'm thinking about crashing down here, right in that chair over there, which I'm about to pull over here in front of this fireplace." He turned back to Casey. "I might just get used to country living. Maybe put in an app for a job as sheriff."

Casey laughed. "Yeah, okay, Peter. Tell me that in the morning."

Yvonne kept shaking Derek, trying to wake him, whining about how tired she was, and that she wanted to go to bed. I saw her whisper something into his ear, and as his lids rolled up his mouth spread into a smile. Then he pulled her face down to his.

"Em," I perched on the landing, my gaze strong, "you guys coming up soon?"

"In a few. You get settled in." She seemed caught up in the

evening, and her Arkana. With her head on his shoulder, her body gently rocked as he strummed his guitar and sang ... for only her.

"How many showers you got in this place?" Derek yawned. "I need rejuvenating. You hear that, woman?" He said to Yvonne, who swatted the side of head, saying, "Dance for me and I'll consider it."

Sex And Surprises

I followed Indigo up the stairs, each of us lugging our bags, our emotions. Indigo seemed to be bursting at the seams again, and I felt as though we were facing a prison sentence, rather than romance. We chose the master bedroom suite at the far end of the hall. When we closed the door, we locked the rest of the world outside.

The storm still raged, more menacing upstairs, drowning any trace of sound the others might have been making on the first floor. Indigo and I were suddenly alone, facing the weather, facing each other, facing the fact that we had important issues to work out.

"That's a lot of racket out there, I hope we don't lose power," I said, my voice quivering. "Did you by any chance bring a flashlight?"

"Yep." He pointed to his bag, then his arms went around me.

"Ahh." I cuddled against his warm chest. "You feel so good," I murmured, my face buried beneath his chin. "Cozy."

"I've been called a lot of things," I felt the vibration of his voice as he spoke, "cozy not being one of them, but I suppose we could try that one out."

"Mmm. You taste good, too." Gently sucking, I tugged on his bottom lip.

Arms locked around each other, lips meshed, we worked our way to the bed, letting our bodies sink into the mattress. After releasing me, Indigo settled near the edge. His mood was all over the place, desire and despair struggling for victory.

I kicked off my shoes and crawled up behind him, running my hands up and down his back, each stroke lifting his shirt higher as I smoothed my palms over his skin, brushed him with my lips, then my tongue swept his ear.

He pulled me around and onto his lap, cradling me in his arms. "You have such beautiful hair." He loosened my braid, ran a finger up my jaw line, studying me as though he'd never seen me before. Then he began touching my face. "Your eyes have such sparkle." His finger moved up the bridge of my nose and across my brow. "The color is amazing, like a delicious mixture of chocolate and mint." He kissed just above each lid, then whispered, "and your mouth ... I love your mouth." His finger ran around the line of my lips, parting them, dipping inside. "I love kissing you. I missed kissing you." With his thumb, he pulled my bottom lip down. "I want to kiss you, Jewel."

I went completely limp in his arms. "Kiss me ..."

"There's just one problem ..."

"Problem?" My mind had shut down, and I had trouble finding my voice.

"I want to do more than just kiss you." His fingers left my mouth to trail across my neck, followed by his eyes.

He drove chills up and down my spine so intensely, the tingle actually bit into my skin.

"Are you okay with everything?" he whispered, returning his eyes to mine. "You're not pissed off at me, are you?" His fingers played at the base of my neck, his thumb stroking the hollow. "I hope you're not. I don't want to do anything to piss you off ... separate us ... lose you."

Practically speechless, I managed a weak, "You'll never

lose me." My words sounded like they came from a mouth filled with cotton, and he chuckled softly, his eyes never leaving mine.

"How about that shower we never got to take at your place?" My words grew stronger. My aggression surprised even me, but the misery I'd tried to elude during our separation was crashing down on me, as were Emma's words, "Make the most of today." I was about to make the most of the night, the seclusion, the shower, the bed, while I gave my very best to Indigo.

Gaze locked on mine, he studied me. "Are you sure, Jewelia?" His eyes narrowed slightly. Darkened. For a moment, I worried, faced with the reality that he might falter, and disappointment filled the hollow inside me that cried out with need. "We don't have to. That's not why I came up here," he was whispering and I was angering.

"What, you don't want to be with me?"

"Does time ever stop?"

"What kind of question is that?"

He rubbed my cheek with his, almost purring, "I'll always want to be with you."

"Right now, then." My body was in high gear. I couldn't take another tomorrow wondering, waiting, worrying. "No more fighting. No more talking. Let's not waste anymore time."

After a look of deliberation, he tried to grin. "I'm curious," again he ran a finger over my bottom lip, "is that a closet, or maybe the door to a bathroom? Hopefully, with a nice big whirlpool tub ... because I could sure use the relaxation."

"If you're looking for relaxation, check in at a rest home," I quipped, brazen on the outside, freaking out internally.

"Not unless you're my nurse." In the dimness, his eyes were burning slate, blue and white rays shooting sultry sparks.

A breath caught in my throat. Concealing a shiver, I separated us, rising from the bed. "Guess there's only one way to find out." I felt the heat of his stare as I padded to the door and swung it open. I was suddenly a temptress, an arm and a hip pitched against the doorframe, lips parted, inviting him inside. "Will a shower suffice?"

In three strides he was at my side, tucking strands of hair behind my ear. Then his lips came down on mine and my heart throbbed so, my chest began to ache.

Every ounce of blood in my body seemed to be gathering in my head, leaving my vulnerable limbs lifeless, but Indigo made it easy, comfortable, kissing me the entire time he undressed me ... I undressed him.

Beneath glistening overhead light, I instinctively wrapped my nakedness with my arms as we faced one another. But the intensity of his eyes didn't stray from the fragileness of mine. Without words, he reached into the stall, adjusted the shower, and pulled me in beside him. There we stood, instantly saturated, moist with shower, moist with passion.

The next thing I knew I was in his arms, and we were enveloped in steam which rose, glazing the glass walls, filling the air we breathed, and I felt like I was in the lushness of a rainforest, experiencing the world for the very first time.

Indigo's mouth was crushing mine, our glossy bodies, like our lips, sliding back and forth, up and down. The water coursed, its gauzy mist a blindfold. Molded against him, I needed no sight; I felt every mouthwatering inch of him. His hands said he felt the same.

Beginning with my shoulders, he searched, he caressed, his fingers deftly slipping to my waist, my hips, my buttocks. He clutched and stroked, pulling me so close, between the rushing water and his mouth, I could barely draw air.

Drenched by the shower, by Indigo's passion, I was dizzy, I was floating. The world spun around me, and I was the discordant nucleus the mind of man had never infiltrated. Our mortal forms were no longer solid: we were souls, spirits, weightless entities, but every shred of being, every electrifying nerve ending cried out.

His fingers came between us, sliding from my breasts to my belly, dipping into my folds. I felt my legs being nudged further apart and his fingers enter; heard myself scream, and scream again. My nails raked the length of his neck, dug into the muscles of his arms. I slipped my hands between his thighs, gripping his cock and stroking until I felt him tighten and was certain he was about to explode.

In slow motion I was spun, pinned to the wall, where my body sank against wet tiles, and he was behind me, bringing himself closer. Had he not been holding me, I'd have crumbled to the floor.

Moaning, I clutched the steel support bars, nearly collapsing with ecstasy. I heard my voice in my ears, felt his body collide with mine, then he was rubbing against me, sliding his cock between my ass cheeks, his hardness almost sawing me in two. Through the sound of rushing water, I heard his staggering moan. His hands roamed my body, lifted my wet, clinging hair, clearing a shoulder which he kissed, bit down on. And then he was positioning me. Following the touch of his fingers, I felt his blunt tip at my opening, and with a cry, my lungs emptied of air.

"Baby," he groaned, grinding against me. One arm slid around me, securing my tummy, bending me forward. I felt the condom graze my skin, enter inch by inch, and in moments, he was inside me.

I gasped. "Oh God, Indigo." My mouth hung open, gathering droplets of water, my lips sliding across the smooth surface on which I was braced. Sensations slammed my body, my head, faster than my brain could process.

His free hand massaged, fingers plucking my nipples, the sweet friction rippling through my aching breasts, stoking the heat between my thighs. A thumb slipped between my folds, stroking the almost unbearable ache; all the while he pumped with a matching rhythm, working me into frenzy.

His hands moved with the same fury as his rolling hips, which were tight and powerful, each thrust met by a groan. I threw back my head, turning my face, searching for his lips.

As he kissed me, his hands moved to my hips, holding me firmly in place, as he rammed his cock again and again. Then one arm went around my waist, and the fingers of his other hand rolled my clit. While he fucked me, I lost every ounce of air in my lungs, gasping with the intensity of my orgasm.

Water seeped through my parted lips. I was being suffocated by the shower, devoured by Indigo, and I almost passed out with pleasure and pain, at the time, synonymous.

Before I could catch my breath I was spun, crushed against his chest, kissed, lifted. I felt my legs become tangled around his hips, and together we sank to the floor. The shower filled with the turbulence of rushing water, our coiling bodies, our moans.

Palms pressed to the wall, on my knees I straddled him, filled his mouth with a breast and I pumped and cried out until there was nothing left inside me but Indigo. The shower beat down on us, our chests heaved, inaudible words were murmured, and then there was silence.

Suddenly, I was standing, wrapped in his arms, swaddled in a towel, and held as though he thought I might break. If not for the surging adrenaline racing through my veins, I would not have been able to move.

With nothing but terrycloth slung around our hips, we walked to the bed, and he was hugging me, telling me how beautiful I was.

"It was amazing," he said softly, pushing my hair from my face, nibbling my shoulder. He spun me, backed me into him, and his hands began massaging my breasts. "I love your body."

"You're amazing. And yes, I believe you do love my body." Stretching, I lifted my arms, locked my wrists around the back of his neck, and resting my head on his chest, pressed against him, squirming. "I hope I met your expectations." With the way he was touching my breasts, I was becoming breathless. I pulled one of his hands down the front of my body, guiding him to my thighs.

"Beyond anything imaginable." His breath came in gasps as his teeth moved to my neck. His fingers found a rhythm, clutching and sliding until my body weakened with another orgasm.

"Did I make up for all the suffering you endured?" Turning

in his arms, I recovered against his lips, nibbled on his earlobe, then gnawed on his neck.

He ran his tongue up my throat and along my jaw line, then held me out before him. "Hmm. I'm not sure." He cocked his head, then cupped my breasts. "Let me think a minute." He closed his eyes, pretending to concentrate, then his lids slowly opened. "Did I ever mention, I love your breasts? And as a physician, I know just what to look for."

"Yes, I know you love my breasts ... and you are so naughty." I giggled, and I slipped my hand beneath his towel, cupping him as firmly as his palms held me. "I'll make putty out of you yet." I tucked up the side of my mouth. "Hmm. Maybe I already did?"

He laughed. "Recovery, woman. I need recovery time. Or as Derek so eloquently said, I need rejuvenating."

I rested my hands on his, pushing my breasts into mounds, forming a deep valley. Guiding his eyes with mine, I watched his gaze fall, whispering, "Next time, baby."

"Christ, Jewel. You *are* out to get me, aren't you?"

"You have no idea." I grinned. "And thanks to you, I worked up some appetite. I have some chocolate chip cookies over there." I flicked my head toward our bags. "Interested?"

"Only if they're moist and delicious ... like you." His cupping palms squeezed my ass. "Have I told you, you have the most delectable cheeks? And everything else to go along with them?"

"More than once. You're such a bad boy," I giggled, "and you could become very fattening."

"And habit forming, I hope."

"Oh yeah. High in calories and very addictive." Lifting my face, I sucked on his lips, "Should we bother to get dressed?"

"Hell no." His voice was huskier than I'd ever heard it. He dropped his towel, tugged at mine, then swept me off my feet. We tumbled into bed, diving beneath the sheets. I cuddled against the warmth of his body, a contrast to the cool bedroom air that surrounded us.

Once Is Never Enough

Indigo lay on his back. Tucked between his arm and chest, I was the first to break the silence. "I thought I heard you ... in the shower ... say ..."

"All I heard was the floodwater in there, and you moaning and groaning," he teased, his arm tightening around me, his lips brushing my forehead. "And then with that storm out there ..."

"Be serious." Playfully elbowing his abs, I felt compelled to insist. "I could have sworn I heard you mumble ..." The words came out in a breath. Immediately, I drew another.

"Are you asking if ..." I felt his lips run through my hair, then move across my cheek. His tongue swept my ear. "You want to know if I said I love you?"

My heart thumped. "Did you?" Lifting my head, I gazed into his eyes, deep and the color of pewter. "Was it in the heat of the moment?"

My gaze inched from his, to watch the gentle movement of his lips, to witness the shape of his mouth murmuring the words I'd longed to hear. I felt his breath as he whispered, "I love you."

Melting inside, I climbed onto him. "You love me?" On all fours, I posed above him.

"I do."

"Say it again."

"I love you, Jewel." His arms came around me.

"I love you too ... Jimmy." I brought my lips to his, murmuring, "so much."

Positioning me on my side, his fingers traced my face, moving to my neck, my breasts that longed to feel the moistness of his mouth again. "I love making you scream." His voice was so raspy, he sounded as though *he'd* been the one screaming.

"You weren't kidding when you said you know how to bring a woman to a screaming climax." I brought his hand to my face and sucked his fingers, one at a time. "I just had several."

"You could've fooled me." His laugh was soft. "Years of practice."

"What?" Once more on top of him, my head strained above his.

He chuckled. "Textbooks, my baby."

"Ah ha. Okay, I'm letting you slide on that one, but just this once, you hear?"

Our foreheads pressed together, a sheet covering our bodies.

He ran a hand down my spine where it came to rest at the small of my back. "Tell me again."

"I'll let you slide?"

"You know what I mean." He urged me closer.

"Jimmy," I breathed, "I love you."

He rolled me onto my back, propped on an elbow, and gazed down at me. "That morning in Kelly's. It was crazy. I felt an immediate connection." His lips played with my ear, the curve of my neck.

"You did?" I turned to face him, winding a leg around his, while my fingers brushed his chest.

His hand trailed idly up my thigh. I was certain he had no idea what his fingers were doing to me. "I did. Those dark eyes of yours flashing messages. I thought you were feeling it, but then again, I wasn't sure if I was just another guy hitting on a beautiful woman, until you came over."

"Until Vanessa, you mean."

"I put her in her place, but when I turned around, you were gone."

"I figured you were taken."

"I was ... by you. I thought I'd never see you again. I felt awful."

"Believe me, so did I." I squeezed him. "I almost fell over when I saw you looking at me. Your eyes were like silver magnets ... like they are now."

Repositioning, he cradled me, tucking my head beneath his chin. "I'm sleepy, but I could love you again, and again, and again." He sighed contentment.

"Love me more tomorrow," I giggled, "right now I'm so exhausted I need to sleep or you'll be performing CPR."

"I wouldn't mind in the least.

***

I must have drifted off to sleep, because my next conscious thought was, *holy shit*. Lightning shattered the room like an exploding bomb. Was it howling wind or a freight train slamming into the house?

"Did you hear that?" I whispered, straining to hear through the racket beyond the bedroom windows.

"Hear what?" Indigo's words weren't quite formed.

"Were you sleeping?" My breath came fast.

"Baby, what's wrong?" He snapped awake.

"There it is again. Didn't you hear that? The clunk ... something hit the house." I was up and off the bed faster than the strobes of electricity clobbering the yard, snatching the flashlight Indigo had placed on the nightstand. I lifted the window, stuck my head out and saw a jagged tear in the trunk of an evergreen. "A tree hit the house," I said, inhaling the night, the clean, pine scented rain. "It must have been struck by lightning."

The flashlight revealed a limb stretched across the walkway, needled boughs like broken wings. With crumbling bark, I imagined it to be a pterosaurs, a prehistoric reptile that had fallen into this time from another era. I wielded the light like a beacon, checking for damage, and in the strong beam I saw them; dozens of eyes reflecting back at me. Red and evil and glaring.

"*Dios mío*," I shrilled, "*Manada de lobos!*"

"What the hell's going on, Jewel?" I had to concentrate to distinguish Indigo's words.

"There's a pack of wolves out there."

"Honey, it's the storm ... and you've got an overactive imagination. Come back to bed." He held up the sheet, inviting me into his arms. "You're safe in here with me."

I sucked in a breath, slammed the window shut and stood frozen, naked in the flashlight's glow. Indigo was propped on an elbow. I felt his eyes on me, warm as his hands had been. I dropped the light and dove into bed beside him, snuggling into the curve of his body.

When he pressed against me, thoughts of lurking creatures were quickly erased. "Mmm, you're nice and warm," I whispered, running my palms across his chest, "and hard." I giggled.

"Very observant," he murmured, his lips brushing my ear.

Pushing him onto his back, I nibbled his neck, then my tongue licked a path straight down his chest.

"Baby," he whispered, his fingers tangling in my hair. "You're asking for trouble."

Knees folded beneath me, I hovered over his erection, gazing up at him, meeting his eyes with longing. "I sure am. Now it's your turn, baby," I said, my voice gritty. "I want to hear the same sounds coming out of your mouth that came out of mine in the shower. I want to taste you ... every inch of you."

I pressed his hot cock to my cheek, circling my open mouth with the head. He gasped and I felt him shiver.

Fighting For You

I watched his jaw drop, heard the ragged breath he drew. Moaning, he sank deep into the mattress. I teased his cock with stroking fingers, and when my mouth came down on him, he held my hair off my face, groaning, "Fuck yeah ..."

My fingers caressed the length of his shaft, while my tongue whirled around the smooth tip. I sucked in rhythm with my sliding palm, while his body bowed.

Knowing exactly where, and how to touch him, I had him practically growling, fisting my hair, curling his toes. My lips buffed his pulsing cock until he was about to come. I ached for him so badly, selfishly wanting him inside me while he was still big and hard.

"God ... don't stop," he grunted the moment I lifted my lips.

"Ssh." I grabbed a condom, smoothed it on, then straddled him, slowly dropping my hips, gripping the headboard to brace myself. I sank onto his cock, watching his head roll from side to side. His lips were parted. Thick lashes curled above his partially closed lids. Watching his pleasure intensified mine.

Hovering inches above him, I was held by my breasts, my nipples abraded by his palms. The ache between my legs exploded, and when he reached behind me, I thought I'd pass out with the sensation. My moans turned to gasps, then cries as I came.

But he didn't come. Instead, he flipped me onto my stomach, covered my mouth with his hand, and after aligning our torsos, slammed his cock into me from behind. Drawing up my knees, I offered better access. He was like an animal, finally set free. My heart beat wildly.

He slid in and out smoothly, then frantically pumped. Exploding inside, my muscles gripped him hungrily. I felt a rush reach my brain, clawed at the covers, my body squirming furiously. As he guided my hips, he nibbled my neck. When his teeth grazed my shoulder, I felt him tense, and after a final thrust, he collapsed beside me. Sinking into the mattress, his chest heaved.

"Christ. You almost killed me tonight." Drawing deep breaths, his words were hoarse.

"Me?" My throat burned, my raspy voice foreign to my ears. "Much more and you'll be pumping my chest instead of my pussy." My wildly thumping heart began to calm, but the laugh I attempted turned into a strangled cough.

"I love you," he whispered, "and I love making love to you." He lay on his back, with me tucked between his arm and his chest. "I love the sounds you make. And I love your pussy." Exhausted, his slur was comical. I wondered if he realized what he was saying.

I was delirious. I was groggy. "I love you," I murmured, drifting on a euphoric wave of slumber. In the distance I heard more whispers of his love, then I went out like a light.

Revelations

The blood curdling scream woke me from my dreamless sleep. While I wrapped myself in a sheet, Indigo pulled on his jeans. I flipped the wall switch and the nightstand lamps glowed rudely, blinding my sleep deprived eyes.

"Holy shit," I cried out, "what the fuck's happening now?"

My eyes adjusting, I ran to the door. Indigo pulled me beside him, his voice a harsh whisper. "Hold on, babe. Let me go first."

We rushed from the room to find Bill and Emma perched on the landing. They were fully clothed, just as we'd left them, but now their mouths were stretched into huge smiles. Her eyes glistened. His sparkled.

Suddenly, the hallway grew louder than the storm-filled night as doors flung open and we aimlessly assembled. We looked like wanderers who'd lost their compass, circling, bumping into each other, the walls, rubbing sleep from our eyes.

"Are you just coming upstairs?" I asked Emma, running my hands over my face, through the tangles of my hair. "What time is it?"

"About two, maybe three." Emma looked blameless and lovely, dressed in her own special glow.

"It feels like it should be morning. What's up, Em?" I knew I sounded annoyed, but geez, how about some peace and quiet, people?

"Look, Jewel." She stuck her left hand under my nose, proudly presenting a brilliant diamond solitaire radiating with fire on her ring finger.

I grabbed her hand, examining it closely. "Oh, Em, it's gorgeous," I mumbled, then threw my arms around her. "You're engaged. You're engaged! Oh my God!" I felt her tears on my shoulder, then mine began to fall. "I'm so happy for you." I sniffed. "When are you getting married?" My fingers dug into her shoulders.

"November 15th," she wheezed in my ear, "I'm so excited I can hardly stand it."

"Holy shit, Em. You don't waste time. It's less than a year away." I pulled back, my eyes widening. "We've got a lot of planning to do." When I brought her in for another squeeze, she whispered, "You know you're my maid of honor, right?"

As Yvonne and I blabbed with Em, Indigo's stare caught my attention. I flashed him a bleary-eyed smile and shrugged, mouthing, "I can't believe it."

Before congratulating Bill, the guys teased him with the usual ball and chain comments, then shoved Yvonne and me aside to reach Emma. That's when I realized I was standing in the middle of the glaring hallway, looking like I'd just rolled out of a Toga party.

"Let's go back to the room," I said to Indigo, pulling him from Bill's side. With a look of relief, he took my hand and followed me down the hallway to our room. "Who can sleep after this?" I mumbled, shutting the door with my hip as I continued to chatter away. "You're awfully quiet. What's up with that?"

While I uncoiled from the sheet, I watched Indigo slip out of his jeans and settle at the edge of the bed. He was a solid mass of beautifully carved rippling muscle. It was the first time I had a chance to examine his exquisite body in bright light.

"I like your ink," I said, referring to the black Byzantine cross bulging with his triceps. I shook out the sheet, letting it parachute to the mattress. "They are one happy couple, that's for sure. Did you see the look on their faces?"

His delayed response shocked the hell out of me. "I'm sorry things have been so rocky, Jewel. You deserve more." He sounded like he was in a confessional.

I hopped onto the bed and crawled up behind him, throwing my arms around his broad back. Pressing my bare breasts against him, I kissed his neck. "I happen to think things are just fine," I whispered as I nibbled, "and I do believe I got what I deserve," I giggled. "I doubt I could take much more. I'm sore."

"That's not what I meant." He let out a long breath, then slammed me with a rush. "If you want what Emma and Bill have ... I'm not sure I can give it to you." Confession over, defeat dug into his voice.

"What are you talking about?" I peered over his shoulder, analyzing his grim profile.

"I thought I could handle it ..." Stripped of emotion, he shook his head.

Dropping my arms, I stiffened. As my mouth fell open, my feet hit the floor. "Exactly what can't you handle?" I marched around the foot of the bed, not caring that I was naked. I was angry all over again, ticking reasons off on my fingers as I faced him. "You called and apologized for disappearing for over a week. You came to Maine. You fucked me and said you love me. So what the hell's the story?" My chest heaved. "What is it now? Because I'm on my last nerve with this on and off bullshit."

"It's got nothing to do with fucking you, Jewel. Or loving you." His tone chilled the room. "You're the only good thing in my life. It's everything else that's wrong."

I was losing grip of who this man was, and it was freaking

me out. "What's so wrong? You're scaring me, Indigo." I settled softly beside him, my heart fluttering.

"I shouldn't have said anything. It's not your problem." His gaze went beyond the window.

"Hey. You can't say stuff like that and then just blow it off ... blow me off." Although I sounded tough, he was turning me inside out. "Talk to me." My voice shook.

He faced me, but seemed to be looking through me. "Talk," his laugh was creepy, "what good does talking do? It doesn't change anything. Nothing does. Just forget it." He actually turned his back on me.

"You're a boyfriend and a stranger at the same time. You have to let me in. If you can't confide in me, or even explain yourself, then I guess there's really nothing to say." I couldn't believe the wall was back, and I had to think before I said something I'd be sorry for. As I stomped to my own side of the bed, the ink pouring across the contour of his shoulder blades caught my eye, and my antenna went up. "Unusual tattoo." I came up behind him, running my fingers over the intermingling bodies of two snakes rising in a braid to the nape of his neck, their horned, dragon heads rearing. Beneath the tattoo was a line of black mumbo jumbo. "What's it mean?" My voice was as cold as his skin.

"A symbol of medicine." Without facing me, he spoke quietly, hesitantly.

I found it hard to believe I was prancing around naked in the same room with this stranger who was making me feel like spending the rest of the night on the living room sofa. Better yet, I was about to throw *him* out of the bedroom. Wasn't that how it usually worked?

"What's the writing mean? What language is that?" I demanded, not caring if I acted like a bitch. What the hell? We were probably breaking up anyway, yet again. Would I become desensitized? When I looked at him, the answer pounded inside my chest. I could never feel anything but love for this man, no matter what happened.

"It's Latin." He seemed to be wound tighter than Bill's

guitar strings.

Indigo had two levels of consciousness: hot and cold. And at that moment, he was below zero. I knew something had to be very wrong, so without the attitude, I slid off the bed and stood in front of him. That was when I noticed the pensive expression that had been chiseled into my memory from day one.

My insides clenched as tight as Indigo's lips. In the lamplight he looked ghostly, shadows of sadness crossing his face. I took a gulp of air, released it, and swallowed hard, waiting for the world to crash around me. This time for real, because he was sitting right in front of me, we'd just made love, and instead of climbing the walls with happiness, he seemed to be withdrawing ... wrestling with a demon. Was it me?

His brooding gaze washed over me, dark and unnerving. He teetered at the edge of the bed, and elbows on knees, he placed his head in hands.

"Indigo?" I began to panic. "What's wrong?" Kneeling before him I lifted his face, cautiously peeling away his fingers, holding their coldness to my lips, clutching them to my breast. I tried to stare into his eyes, but his eyes were no longer mine. "Did I do something?"

He barely looked at me, and I couldn't seem to drag out a response. He just kept shaking his head. I stroked his hair, dropped a kiss on his cheek, whispering, "Baby, what's haunting you?"

His jaw was set, but tears pooled in his eyes. I ran my hands up and down his arms, trying to warm him, bring him back to me. My stomach churned. I felt close to losing everything I'd eaten.

"What the fuck is going on?" I ran my fingertips over the red heart on his chest, scrutinized the Byzantine cross on his arm, bearing the text: *Souls In Flight, As Brothers We Fight.*

"Brothers we fight," I repeated the black ink phrase. "Is that from a fraternity?"

He was closing his eyes to me, or to whatever evil gripped

him. He uttered an eerie, "No." His detachment was paralyzing. What was the meaning of the messages he'd permanently stamped on his body? As permanent as his misery seemed to be.

I ran my fingers through his hair, kissed his neck, praying: Dear Lord, don't let me lose him, not now, not ever. My touch had no effect. Sitting close beside him, I ran my palm over his back. "What's this writing mean?" I whispered, my fingertips lingering on the text beneath the dragon tattoo: *Fratrem meum - qui confidunt in me. Puritate et integritate vobis servabo vitam meam doctrinam.*

"Something like the Hippocratic Oath ... my version." His laugh was low and self-deprecating, pushing me to the brink of something I'd never felt before: sheer terror.

"What's the translation?" I prodded, my words catching in my throat.

Avoiding my eyes, in the same self-loathing tone, he replied, "*For my brother – and those who put their trust in me. In purity and honesty I will guard you with my life and my knowledge.*"

I lifted his chin, forcing his gaze to mine. He had the chilling look of death in his eyes.

"I had a brother, Jewel."

"Okay ..." I braced for the worst.

"He died when he was just a kid."

My hand flew to my mouth, covering the breath I sucked in. "I'm so sorry. Was it an accident?" I wondered if Indigo was somehow involved in his brother's death and couldn't forgive himself.

"It's complicated. It's been rough for all of my family, which is part of the reason I couldn't get in touch with you after you left the Hamptons."

He was completely blowing me away, bending my mind. What the hell was the deep dark family secret?

"In case you wondered, you didn't meet my father that weekend because he was locked in his den, blasting himself to hell, yet again. Just one of the reasons my mother's the resentful," he struggled with his words, "bitch that she is. It all stems from Danny's death."

His stare was cold, hard granite.

"Danny was your *younger* brother ..."

He snatched his wallet from the nightstand and flipped it open. Inside was a photo of an adorable little boy sitting on a flight of wide concrete steps. He was plastered to the side of Indigo, who appeared to be a teen. Indigo's arm was draped protectively around the grinning boy with a missing front tooth.

I held his wallet, staring at the photo, my heart breaking. "What happened to him?"

Indigo was turning on me, shrinking away as though I was an invasion of privacy, and not the woman he'd just held in his arms. My stomach knotted, and I had to steady myself. Once more I knelt before him, taking his face in my hands. "Baby, you've got to talk about it. Unload or it will eat at you for the rest of your life."

He drew a deep breath, and I watched the muscles in his face strain as he worked his jaw. "Danny contracted childhood leukemia. He passed away shortly after that photo was taken." He closed his eyes tightly, as if darkness would erase the memory.

"Talk to me." I grabbed his shoulders and shook him as though trying to bring the dead back to life, streaming tears reaching my chest.

When his eyes finally opened, I knew he was unreachable. "My parents were absent more than they were home when we were kids – and of course they weren't around that day." He muttered in broken phrases. "They never had the best marriage. My mother was modeling in Europe, on a trip she said couldn't be postponed, and my dad, well, he fixed a lot of brains in his day, but couldn't do anything for my brother, so he withdrew into himself. I was the closest thing Danny had to a parent. We did everything together. I did everything for him. I promised him I was going to be a doctor, and if he'd hang in there, I'd make him well. I swore I could help him ... I promised ... and he believed me. I believed me."

He touched the place on his chest where the tattoo rested beneath his heart. His eyes sought peace, my understanding, escape from the self-inflicted punishment that was destroying him. His eyes said so many things, I feared he'd explode at any moment as life came rushing back into him.

"This is for Danny?" I pressed my lips to the heart on his chest.

"Everything is for Danny. I'd give up my life to bring him back. To keep my promise."

I pulled him to the floor beside me, and there we sat, two naked souls. In sobs, his secrets spilled onto my lap, along with warm tears.

"Danny died in my arms, Jewel. There was nothing I could do. Afterward, my parents *really* hated each other, each blaming the other for Danny's illness, for not being there when ..."

"Oh baby, I'm so sorry." If my arms, my love, could have eased his pain, he would have looked into my eyes with peace, not the darkness that chilled my soul. He was suffering so badly, I wondered if anything in the world could ever help him.

"After you left the Hamptons that day, my parents had a blowout. Nothing unusual. My father took off and didn't return that night. Again, not unusual." Working his jaw, he spoke with bitterness. "We called the police two days later, and eventually found him slumped across Danny's grave. He'd been lying there for over forty-eight hours and was in such bad shape, we called an ambulance to take him to the hospital, where they dried him out." His cheeks were as red as the rim around his eyes, the circles beneath them scary purple.

While he bared his soul, a fist squeezed my heart. We stood at the edge of a rocky ledge and I couldn't let him fall. I couldn't fall. But were there any words of consolation for someone whose life had been shattered? How could I help him pick up the pieces?

"How is your dad now?" I asked, my voice cautious.

"He's been sober a couple of weeks. A landmark record for him. We've been walking on eggshells, hoping to keep it that way." When he shuddered, my arms wrapped him tighter. Once he began talking, it seemed his story was an endless road of pain. "He stopped practicing medicine after Danny's death. Accepted an appointment as CEO of a drug company. A position he's barely holding onto."

"That's promising, baby. It's a start." I tried my best to soothe him. "Healing has to start somewhere. Maybe with your dad ..."

His life was being torn apart, and mine hung in the balance. The storm raged beyond the windows as Indigo walked through his nightmare. His laugh was frightfully sardonic, chilling me to the bone. "After Danny died, my mother attempted suicide. I found her lying in a pool of blood, her fingers wrapped so tightly around a knife, I had to pry them loose."

Stunned, shocked, horrified, I had no idea what to say other than, "I'm here for you." My voice was light as a feather, my lips pressed to his ear. "I'll do anything I can to help you. Just tell me what to do, Jimmy."

"Danny was the only one who ever called me Jimmy. Until you." When he looked at me, his eyes were deep, once again mine.

"I'm sorry. And now I have my whole family calling you Jimmy. It's like an invasion."

"No." He put a finger to my lips. "It's okay." His throat sounded as raw as his emotions. "Danny was the most important part of my life. I loved him more than anything. After I lost him, I couldn't get close to anyone. I didn't want to. I buried myself in medical books. Then you came into my life. It was difficult to take the risk of loving you ... losing you."

The wheels in my head turned, and I realized why he'd been teetering on a seesaw. "You haven't managed to scare me away yet." I tried to put a smile on his face, but it wasn't working. "Danny wouldn't want you to suffer this way." I smoothed furrows from his forehead. "Or your parents." I began to understand his mother's behavior, although I could never accept it. "You can't blame yourself for anything. You were a kid, taking on all of the responsibility."

"I hear what you're saying, but," he frowned, "this is why I want to be the best doctor ... I have to be. If I can help just one child, save one life ..." he drew in a sob, "but I'm not sure I can."

"What do you mean?"

"There are things you don't know about me. Things I could never admit to anyone. Especially you."

My heart actually flipped in my chest. "Are you a thief?" My brows reached for my hairline. "A murderer?"

"Of course not," he snapped.

"Oh wait, you're a pimp. Better yet, you pimp yourself out," I said, sarcastic. "Is that the secret you can't share with me?"

He didn't return the smirk I expected, so I tried another angle.

"If every couple knew absolutely everything about the other, not only would the relationship be boring, it would be fucking crazy."

Staring straight ahead, he deadpanned. "Boring is one thing being with you is not. Fucking crazy ... maybe."

"I think we've had enough for one night." My lips quivered as I kissed him softly. "You're like ice. Let's get you into bed."

I snuggled against him, pulling the covers around us. My nerves were so fried, my body shook at unpredictable intervals.

As his body relaxed, he sighed. "I'm sorry to unload on you, Jewel. I came up here with you to straighten things out between us, not make them worse. The last thing I wanted to do was involve you in my shit."

"I meant what I said. I'm here for you, whenever you need me, no matter what, I love you. I'll never let you down."

"What would I do without you?" His arms were around me, and he was holding on for dear life.

"That's one thing you never have to worry about."

"I'll get through this."

"We'll get through this."

I hugged him so tight I felt the beat of his heart. After whispering, "Good night," we didn't speak again. I couldn't fall asleep. His anguish preyed on my mind. I imagined how horrible it must have been for him, then realized there was no way I could imagine how he felt. I heard his even breathing and pressed the side of my face to his back.

"Grandma," gripping my cross I whispered, "I hope your eyes were closed tonight, and you weren't listening." My cheeks flushed. Then it hit me: If anyone understood passion, it would have been my grandmother.

Morning ... After The Storm

Indigo's lips on my shoulder, his warm palm circling my butt, awakened me from the sleep of the dead. I uncurled my legs and stretched my sore muscles, shielding my eyes from sunshine filling the room. I lifted my head and squinted, seeing only the side of his face as he lay behind me, propped on an elbow.

"It's finally morning?" I groaned, pulling my arm from beneath me, shaking out pins and needles, then rolled onto my back.

"Yep. You okay?" He untangled strands of my hair that had wound around my neck while I slept. "You were moaning." His lips touched my throat.

"You were rubbing my ass." I ran a finger along his jaw line, hoping our issues had dissolved with the night, hoping my breath wasn't dreadful. "How about you?"

"I'm good, babe." He dropped a kiss on my forehead. "Thanks to you. Getting things off my chest was the best thing that could have happened. I honestly feel better ... optimistic. Having you makes all the difference in the world." To my relief, he looked down at me, smiling as though the anguish of last night hadn't occurred. Was he burying it, or was it really over?

"How'd you sleep?" He tweaked my nose, then kissed it. "My little angel."

I threw my arms around his neck, sank my lips into his smooth skin. He sighed into my hair, held me tight, and when I felt his erection, I knew everything was fine. I came up for air. "How much did I sleep is more like it." I giggled. "Yvonne and Derek were going at it last night. They were so loud, they woke me ... scared the living shit out of me."

Indigo's eyes widened. "Arguing?"

I lifted a brow. "If that was arguing, we should try it. They were pounding the walls."

He chuckled. "So you didn't get enough last night?" His fingertips dug into my ribs. I started laughing, and then we were rolling across the bed, and the next thing I knew we were making love on hands and knees on the floor. Afterward, Indigo lay on his side, leaning on an elbow, stroking my hair, gazing down at me as my breathing normalized. He ran a fingertip around my ear, tucking my hair behind it. "Yesterday was one fucked up day, huh? Are you sure you're good with everything?"

My fingers tiptoed across his chest. "I'm fine if you're fine, which I kind of just got the feeling you are. And what a feeling it was ..." I slid my knee up the inside of his thigh, ran a finger over his lips. "Hey, you never curse. You're starting to sound like me."

He was playing with my hair, lifting strands, threading them through his fingers. "Is that a compliment?" His voice was easy. The way he looked at me, how his fingers traced my face, the outline of my breasts, told me I had become as big a part of his life as his family, his career.

"I don't know, but if you start cursing in Spanish ... we're in trouble." I plucked his chin.

I'd never felt so secure. I heaved a sigh, my spirit so airy, I felt like it could float across the room, out the window, into the wilderness and never stop climbing. I was high on love. "Stick with me baby. I'll teach you all there is to know about four letter words."

Indigo chuckled softly, then buried his face in my hair. "I'm stuck. So what do we do now?"

"Shower."

Party's Over

We all congregated in the kitchen. Pete had made coffee and set out cups and plates. We sat at the butcher block counter, plastering bagels with cream cheese and jelly, recounting the night before.

"Kit Kat," Pete said, slapping his palm on the countertop. Shaking his head, he guffawed, repeating, "No way were those wolves. You may have been sleeping with one," he smirked at Indigo, who looked uncomfortable, then his gaze traveled a full circle, landing back on mine. "I doubt any wolves hang out in the driveway, Jewel. Not as pets or houseguests," he chuckled, "what you must have seen were the walkway reflectors."

Taking my hand, he pulled me to the window which was directly beneath the bedroom where Indigo and I had slept ... made love. The rapture of the prior night still filled me, I looked around the room at my friends, at Indigo ... My life was perfect.

I stared up at Pete, relief spewing through my lips. "Your reflectors almost gave me a freaking heart attack. I can deal with anything in the city, Pete. You know I'm not a wuss, but creepy woodlands are not my thing."

"That's alright, Kit Kat. We can't all be up for a promotion." He ruffled my hair. I swatted his arm. He grabbed a bagel and threw it at me. I picked up the cream cheese, and the food fight was on until Emma stood between us, yelling, "Hope you two have fun cleaning the mess while the rest of us are relaxing."

"Wait ..." I stood in the middle of the kitchen, a wet sponge about to be launched from my fingers, "you're up for a promotion?"

"I'm losin' the blues, baby." Smug, he lifted his chin.

I dropped the sponge and threw my arms around him. "When did this happen? Why didn't you tell me, Pete?"

"I've been waiting for the right time." He grinned.

***

Bikes hitched, cars loaded, we left nature and the A-frame on the dusty road behind us.

In the Wrangler, we followed Pete and Casey onto the Interstate. After riding in silence, Indigo reached for my hand. "All things considered, it was a nice getaway. I needed it." Again, wearing aviator sunglasses, he looked hotter than ever, and relaxed.

"Does all things considered mean us?"

"Everything, I guess. I feel so much better, Jewel. It's got to mean something ..."

"Huh?"

"What we've been through ... our ups and downs. We care enough to disagree and not just walk away."

Sunlight pulsed through the trees, piercing the windshield, my eyes. I pulled my purple shades down from where they'd been resting on my head. "Things got rocky for a while, but we're solid," I said lazily, peace falling over me. I gazed at Indigo, then looked out the window, watching civilization reappear and dwindle as we passed rest stops and small towns.

"The weekend flew." I was so mellow, I could have drowned in the beautiful wave of exhaustion sweeping over me. Closing my eyes I let myself drift, leaving my present, my future, in Indigo's hands.

The good times usually do." He cradled my hand. "In a way, I'm sorry to see it end. It was fun sleeping with you."

"So that's what you call everything we did ... fun?"

"You know what I'm talking about." He clicked his tongue. "You and that temper. You're always ready to attack me." His hand dropped to my kneecap and he squeezed, which made me scream. "You love stirring the pot, don't you?"

"You're so cute when you're trying to defend yourself, and I just love making up with you." I giggled. "And you have to admit ... you do have a way with words."

"Are you implying I need a lot of understanding?"

Shaking my head, I sighed. "Is climbing Mt. Everest a challenge? Speaking of which, I'm ready to answer that question now."

"Now you're really confusing me." He didn't turn his head, but I was still able to see his smile.

"Join the club." I laughed. "Remember our first date?"

"How could I ever forget? You scared the hell out of me."

"As if." I burst out laughing. "After getting to know you better ... you *are* a challenge."

"I was being honest." He ran his hand up and down my thigh. "I liked having you in bed with me. I don't know how I'm going to sleep tonight without you."

I studied his face to see if he was serious, but he was unreadable. I gulped. "I guess I could get used to it too."

"Hey, how about dinner tonight?"

"Sure." I was thrilled he wouldn't be dropping me off at my apartment and leaving. I'd been giving quite a bit of thought to the walk of shame, wondering if things would be the same between us once we got back to the city, and here was my answer. He didn't want to leave me any more than I wanted to leave him.

"I'll cook for you." He glanced at me and smiled. "Sound good?"

"Sounds great." I burrowed into my seat, clutching his arm,

feeling so content. "What's on the menu?"

"To be determined." He chuckled, running his palm over my thigh. "And ..."

"And what?"

"I was thinking. How about staying the night?"

"You've been thinking, huh?" I giggled. Excitement escalated, along with my butterflies. "The worst thing about a getaway is going home with the blahs, you know what I mean? Like the holiday letdown."

"Is that a yes or a no?"

"A definite yes. I'd love to spend the night at your place. I'd be lonely ... after ..."

"Tell me about it." He squeezed my hand. "Yeah," he sighed, "things are looking better and better ..."

"I'll drink to that. How about some tunes?" I reached for the radio, flipping through stations until I heard something I could fall into. "Ahh. Now that's relaxation." I tossed my hands around, singing, really hamming it up. I grabbed my travel mug from the cup holder and toasted to the beat.

Indigo stole several glances, shook his head, then began to laugh.

"What's so funny?" I sang to him, bobbing my head.

"You have to ask?" As his fingers tapped the wheel, he started rocking out.

"Look at you, all cool and rockin' over there." I laughed. "Is that how you looked in high school? All hot and handsome. An arm hanging out the window, picking up girls?"

Shaking his head, he looked too hysterical to even drive. I reached for his abs, and he shoved me away. "Stop it or I'm gonna have to pull over."

"Truth or dare."

"No."

"How old were you when you bagged your first female?" I reached for his abs again. "Did she wear one of those cute little school uniforms with a pleated skirt hiked up to her panties? Showing off her bum bum?"

"What's in that mug?" While steadying the wheel, trying to keep his eyes on the road, he grabbed for it.

"Coffee. So you went to a private school right? With all those proper rowdy people?"

"Actually, I went to parochial school and at one time, I thought about becoming a priest."

My eyes bulged. "Oh my God. No way."

He burst out laughing.

"I almost believed you." I swatted his arm. "Now you're in for it ... pull over ... you're gonna get it." I sank my fingers into his thigh and tugged.

"It's gonna have to wait until after dinner, babe." He smirked.

"Now that you bring it up ... does that dinner you're cooking include dessert?"

"Of course. Actually, we can start with dessert if you'd like ... your phone's ringing."

"Huh?"

"Someone's phone is ringing." He tapped the pocket of his cargo pants. "Not mine."

"Boy, you've got good ears." I turned the radio off. "Yay. Service." I grabbed my cell from my bag. "It's Yvonne," I relayed her message as she spoke. "Your mother just called Derek. She reamed him out for being out of contact. She wanted him there yesterday." I watched Indigo's face tighten. Refusing to let him drop back into the dismal zone, I rested my hand on his arm, my fingers caressing. "She wants him there today. Something about the show being moved to Friday and she needs time to fit him and coach him."

Indigo sighed and I could see the curtain fall. The poor guy couldn't even enjoy a weekend without someone in his family brewing up a storm. My heart went out to him, along with kisses I mouthed and blew, trying to raise his spirits, but my actions were hopeless, like the look on his face.

"How much do you care about Derek?" His voice held that deflated tone that made my stomach almost turn inside out.

"Huh?"

"Whether or not he's in the show ... does it really matter?"

"Oh geez ... he's so hyped, he'd freak if it was called off."

"I guess we're going then. Have Derek tell her we should be there before dinner. Try to get a hold of Pete and tell him to point us in the direction of Westchester."

Chaos In Westchester

When we reached our exit, Pete and Casey slowed, threw out hand signals, then sped ahead. As we made the cloverleaf turn I watched them disappear and something resembling emptiness scurried across my tummy. After one glance at Indigo, the feeling retreated, but I wasn't happy about the tight look on his face.

The Briar Ridge house was another mansion, the backyard overlooking a golf course. It was white, had all kinds of angles and peaks, resembling a fortress surrounded by hedges and wrought iron fences. We parked in the circular driveway edged by rows of plants and shrubbery. The grounds were a horticulturist's haven: lush lawns wrapping walkways, creeping past fountains, leading to a conservatory.

Indigo parked the Wrangler, and the Escalade crawled to a stop at our bumper. Derek and Yvonne bounded from the car. Derek was yelling, "Let's get this shit rollin', people. I'm about to be famous." He started dancing across the driveway.

Yvonne rolled her eyes, but her smile was huge. Running to catch him, she pulled him to her side, laughing. "He's been driving me crazy all the way home."

I was happy for their company, the fortification, not wanting to face the looming place before us, one on one. I motioned for Emma and Bill to join us. When they didn't move from the back seat, I tapped on the window, coaxing, "Come on, Em."

She shook her head, and Bill put his face in front of hers. "We'll sit this one out, Jewel."

My eyes went from his to Emma's. I angled my head. "But ..."

"We have things to talk about." Bill grinned.

"Wedding plans to make." Emma's voice was muffled behind him. "Don't worry. We'll be here when you get back."

She didn't realize that was not what I was worried about. They looked so cute and cuddly in the back seat. I sighed, assuming remaining in the car was Bill's way of sparing himself and Emma the misery that lurked inside the lovely home.

"Let's go, babe," Indigo said, pulling me from Emma's eyes, "before Derek breaks the door down."

Indigo's fingers wrapped mine protectively when Elizabeth opened the door, her face forming its usual pinch. Without mincing words, Derek was led upstairs and without invitation, Yvonne automatically followed him, leaving Indigo and me standing in the foyer.

"Hey," I said, "your house is beautiful."

His lips twitched into a grimace. "Come on, I'll show you around." Softening, he kissed the knuckle of my every finger that was joined with his, then taking both of my hands, he towed me behind him.

The place was immaculate and silent, like a museum, with statues on pedestals, gold-framed pictures, vases filled with floral arrangements. The soles of our shoes squeaked upon marble floors merging with crimson carpeting. The vaulted ceilings were high, and when I lifted my gaze, I realized the forest we'd just left seemed to offer more comfort.

"So that's the end of the tour ... and here's my room." Indigo led me to his bed and kissed my forehead. I knew he was trying to appear upbeat, but one look at the strain on his face told me he was putting on one of the biggest acts of his life.

With a king sized bed and gleaming dark furniture, the room reminded me of his apartment bedroom, but not half as warm. It looked like a showroom, rather than a place one would use for relaxation and a good night's rest.

"I'm gonna hop in the shower." His eyes tested mine. "I won't be long, okay?"

"Sure, I'll be fine." I smiled and pulled his face close. "You okay?"

"I'll be better when we're out of here." He lifted a brow, then rolled his eyes. "I'll be right in there if you need me." He motioned to the half open door of the adjacent bathroom. "Or ... if you want to join me." He didn't pull his grin off very well.

"I bet that would go over big." I smirked and waved as he closed the door behind him. While I waited, I sat at his desk, flipping through his medical books. As promised, he returned in a few minutes, wrapped in a towel. I watched him dress, then held out one of his books, quizzing him on the photographs of different diseases that had shocked me. I decided being a doctor might not be all it was cracked up to be. It had to take a strong stomach, and dedication. I knew Indigo had both.

In less than an hour we were joined by Derek and Yvonne, who happily departed the premises to head for home immediately upon dismissal. I imagined things had gone well. As they whisked by, Yvonne said she'd call to fill me in on everything. We were all bone tired and couldn't wait to get home. In a sense, Indigo *was* home, but he didn't look very comfortable.

The aroma of cooking wafted from the kitchen, and Indigo led me into the dining room, where I hesitated. "I wasn't planning on dinner ... here."

"If you're not hungry, it's okay. We'll say a quick goodbye

and take off. Grab a seat." Boy, had his mood changed.

An upholstered barrel chair was positioned on either side of the polished table, a high back chair at each end. It was a no brainer. I chose a decorative barrel chair and started my mental countdown, more than ready to leave that morgue and get back to his apartment.

Sitting across from Indigo was difficult. Not being able to touch him was even harder. My nipples had been sucked raw, and now my emotions. My breasts throbbed against the soft fabric of my bra, a constant reminder of the weekend we'd spent in each other's arms. I'd been loved so intensely, my body still ached with pleasure, and I wanted to share my joy. My legs were much of my height. Extending a foot, I stretched beneath the table, nudging his shoe, offering a smile.

Then Vanessa paraded into the room, her hair twisted and coiled, decorated with sparkling ornaments somewhat matching her foil-like shift dress. I was all for fashion, but she looked extraterrestrial. Her pale face, plastered with makeup, added to her eeriness, her alien attire.

Four additional barrel chairs were lined against the wall. She gripped the back of one, slid it across the floor, and of course, pulled it up beside Indigo. Hands resting on the back, she announced, "I'm introducing the show, and your mother. This is my outfit." Her face curled into a question mark. When we didn't reply, she said, "Well, what do you think?"

I stared in disbelief, certain I was hallucinating: *I think you're all insane* sprinted across my brain.

Indigo gave her a quick once-over, his face displaying the first sign of humor I'd witnessed since walking in the front door. "That's one hell of an outfit, Vanessa. What did she have to do to get you to agree to it?"

Her confusion sprang into a gloat when she said, "Your dad has fantastic news."

My stomach clenched. What was she up to now?

"What news?" Indigo's brows pulled together. His fingers drummed the table.

The atmosphere was so unfriendly, bordering sardonic. I wondered if things had always been this severe, and how the hell he could have taken it all of these years. His parents' muffled voices emanating from the next room shattered my analysis. Elizabeth's face was actually crushed by a small smile as she and her husband entered, side by side.

The dining room was large and echoed. Sapphire draperies drizzling from the half dozen windows failed to insulate the tension. His father stood at the head of the long oak table, directing everyone's attention to me. "I understand you're a friend of James's. I'm his father, Henry Ballou, and I'm an alcoholic." His face was as bland as my brain as he spoke.

Lord, was this man about to cleanse his soul right before our eyes? Indigo hadn't mentioned his father had joined AA. I assumed he wanted to afford the solemn man privacy. His father looked somewhat emaciated, but his facial characteristics were downright handsome. I realized Indigo, who appeared as shocked as I felt, shared his father's features, but nothing more.

"I'm making good on my promises." His father's eyes moved from Indigo to Elizabeth, even touching upon Vanessa. What the hell? What promises? Was he about to say he was going to be a better father? Go back to practicing medicine? Something was making Elizabeth's face crinkle, and we were about to discover what it was. "And the first is for you, James."

I couldn't keep swallowing. My mouth was already too dry.

"In Daniel's name, you'll be taking your residency in Paraguay. You'll be working with children, as you've wanted to since," he held his voice steady, "since Daniel's passing."

My heart flipped. My mouth dropped. My stomach rolled into a ball. Were my ears deceiving me? Or was Indigo? I stared into the panic gripping his eyes. Mine began to tear and plead with him: "What? Why? Why didn't you tell me you were going away?"

I thought he mouthed, "Don't worry. Everything will be okay," with a quick nod of his head. Or was his head just twitching?

At the mention of Daniel, Elizabeth's expression drooped like modeling clay under a blowtorch. I stared at her face, my gaze dropping to her wrists. Indigo had said, after Danny's death, he had found her in a pool of blood, holding a knife. But her wrists weren't scarred. Then it hit me. I focused on her neck, the brightly colored scarves she always wore, realizing what they were concealing. Dear God. She had tried to slit her own throat.

While everything around me blurred, Henry continued with his heartrending speech. Fingers twisted in damp palms, I hid my trembling hands beneath the table. I wanted to cover my face, to scream out to Indigo, for someone to tell me it was all a dream – a bad dream – the worst nightmare of my life. But no one did, and Indigo could barely look at me.

"We're all going, as a family." He smiled at Elizabeth. "I'll be practicing right alongside you, James." His glassy gaze shifted. "And Vanessa. On behalf of your father, my close friend Jon, while James and I are practicing medicine, you'll be writing for the Paraguayan English news. I know you've always wanted to be a journalist. You two practically grew up together ... now you'll be studying together." He was breaking my heart – why was he smiling with pride?

I caught Vanessa's complacent stare. She had known all about this. I wanted to choke. I wanted to vomit. I wanted to jump over the table and strangle her.

"I pulled some strings," Henry was saying, winking as he blew my life to shreds. "It wasn't easy, but it will be worth it."

Gathered with the family, I forced myself to stay in my seat, while with bowed heads, the Serenity Prayer was recited. While my body froze, my mind stuttered, wondering if any of the fanfare would do more than part Indigo and me, possibly bring the family together. Once more, I felt like I was hallucinating, or that I had slipped in to a comatose state, and without knowing, I was suffering in purgatory.

While the maid served the meal, I excused myself and

hurried to the bathroom. My bag was still in the Wrangler, but my cell phone was in my pocket. After dabbing away every single trace of tears, I dialed Pete and gave him the address. "Come and get me, Pete," I held back a sob, "I need to get home – fast."

Pete didn't question or argue. I heard his phone disconnect and before thirty minutes had expired, the Harley roared into the driveway, sounding as mad as I knew Pete would be when he learned what had transpired.

Although I hadn't eaten a bite, I thanked Indigo's parents for the meal and left the table, my parting words, "I have an early day tomorrow. It's been a lovely visit." Attempting to appear unscathed, I did everything but curtsy.

Indigo was standing beside me, saying he'd walk me to the door. Each time his fingers crept around mine, I shook free. He didn't seem to realize the "Goodbye," I said was for good. There was no place for me inside those walls, or in his arms.

I felt sorrow for him. I felt love for him. He was the pillar of strength, at the same time, the whipping post for dysfunctional parents. But there was nothing I could do. The roots ran too deep. I was torn in two: I couldn't leave him like that, but I also couldn't stay.

We stood in the foyer, where the tables of tradition were reversed. I was the hero rescuing the damsel in distress. "Jimmy," I pleaded with my eyes, "don't stay here. Come home with me. Stay the night," I whispered, thinking: *I'll make you forget. Make me forget.*

I was screaming for the crash cart. Stay *with* me. Stay *with* me. He was dying and I was crying out for him to remain conscious.

"They're draining your resources, baby. I can understand your loyalty to your family, but Vanessa, she's like an incurable disease." I fought to keep my voice low, attempting to chip away at his reserve, but he was unresponsive. Hands stuffed into his pockets, he stared at the floor.

"Why didn't you tell me about your plans?" My voice hit

a pitch. My jaw clenched so tight, any more pressure might have cracked my teeth.

Finally facing me, Indigo brought his hands to his head, ran his fingers through his hair before they locked. With elbows jutting from either side, he looked like he was under arrest.

Guilty! Guilty! Guilty! I wanted to scream at him, pound his chest with my fists but instead braced them against my temples, trying to erase all memory of the night, the day, Vanessa, Indigo, Paraguay.

His arms fell to his sides, his eyes the palest blue and watery. "I didn't mean for this to happen, Jewel. I *was* planning on going away, but that was before I met you. I should have told you, but we had so much going on. I never meant to hurt you."

"Famous last words," I scoffed.

He reached for me, but I shook free of his intention.

"So, I was a pastime till you left the country?" Hands on hips, my eyes narrowed.

"No, Jewel, it was nothing like that."

"Everyone knew your plans but me. How do you think that makes me feel?" Grunting, I shook my head. "You should have told me. Leveled the playing field."

"I wasn't playing ... after I met you I struggled with the decision ... but I knew I could never leave you."

"The times we were together. When I was falling in love with you, leaving was on your mind ... and I was a fool."

"You weren't," he rasped. "Christ. I feel like I'm fighting a war."

"And I feel like I'm losing it ... the war ... and my mind."

"I'm sorry you had to find out this way," he cradled his head with his hands, "I'm sorry about everything."

"So am I." I stared at him so hard my eyes burned.

"I'm sorry ..."

"That you're a liar?"

He looked like he'd rather have been hit with a brick than hear those words spill from my lips. My hardest punch wouldn't have hurt him half as much as he'd hurt me.

Fighting For You

"Why didn't you tell him you're not going?" I glared.

"When the time is right, I will. He just stopped drinking. I don't want to cause a setback by starting a scene."

The Harley let out a roar. Indigo opened the door a crack, lifting a hand to Pete who sat on his idling bike. "Can we please talk tomorrow?" He sighed. "I can't leave them now." His gaze took mine to the room from which I'd practically bolted. He sounded broken when he said, "Don't look at me that way."

"Like what? Like I don't know who the fuck you are?" I sucked in a breath. " How should I look at you, Indigo? With love?" I tried to stop my voice from cracking. "Okay, so love me and leave with me ... right now."

His eyes deepened, the gray turning to steel. "They've lost one son. I can't just walk out on them. Regardless of who they are ... what they are ..."

"So, you're gonna be their permanent *on call*?" When he flinched, I knew I had struck a nerve.

"Don't make me make choose, Jewel. Please try to understand. He's just getting on his feet. I can't tell him I'm not going. Not just yet. It was his dream, too."

"Too? Oh, God. So now I'm standing in the way of everyone's dream?" I tossed my hands into the air, bombarded by almost every negative D word in the dictionary: deception, degradation, desperation, disaster, demolished ... demonic.

Like sunshine, a few words broke through my rage: delightful, delicious, desire ... but were instantly overcome by destined, disheartened, doomed ... done.

"I can't rock the boat." His grim face kept talking, while I had trouble comprehending. His eyes were fixed; his jaw was set; he didn't even look alive. "But I want you to know, my feelings for you haven't changed, and I'm not going anywhere. I just need time to sort things out."

Why was he still talking? I wanted to cover my ears and scream. The jerk of his head, pointing to the dining room, dragged me further into hell. "I'll call you," he was still talking, rambling like a broken recording warning of imminent death in World War Three. "I'll call you," the mechanical stranger kept insisting.

"Haven't I heard that one before?" I sounded so cold, I shivered.

Indigo kept proclaiming his love, repeating, "I'm sorry," his eyes filled with remorse, his voice filled with hopelessness as if he didn't even believe his own spiel.

It was too sad to watch, too painful. I longed to close my eyes and simply walk away, disinterested or deaf – two more appropriate D words – choosing whichever would have eased my agony most.

I was angry as hell, but I wasn't heartless, and I had to make the biggest sacrifice of my life. "It's okay." My voice was stiff as I stroked his cheek, running my fingertips through his hair for the last time. "Adios captain, go take command of your vessel and sail." I caught a sob before it could do any damage.

"Jewel," he called after me, following me onto the porch. I knew he was desperate.

Pete hopped off his bike; arms crossed, he took his stance.

Indigo let out a snort and shook his head. "I'm not fighting Pete." The door stood wide open, yet not welcoming. Before retreating inside, Indigo mumbled, "I'll call you later," in such a defeated tone, a chill swept over me.

In the corner of my eye, Vanessa's shadow flickered. I had a feeling she'd been listening to our entire conversation. Moments later she appeared in the foyer, smug, pink lips forming her sick little smile, her voice loud enough for me to hear. "Jim Jim. Dessert is being served."

Did she literally have no heart?

I watched Pete retrieve my gear from the Wrangler, strap it on his bike. I donned the helmet he'd brought for me, and hopped on behind him. Once Indigo closed the door, I didn't feel his eyes on me again, but I did hear him scream louder than I'd imagined possible: "Get the fuck out of my face, Vanessa!"

On the ride home, a flood of tears covered the back of

Pete's jacket. He escorted me into the apartment, to my room where I dumped my belongings, and my soul. "Oh, Pete." I snuggled against his chest, my chin burrowed beneath his neck. A bristle of beard grazed my forehead, then came his tears.

"Jewel, I don't get these guys. You're the most wonderful ..."

I sobbed harder.

"You know, if things were different ... if I didn't love Casey, I'd never leave you."

"I know, Pete. But you'll never leave me anyway, right?" My sore eyes strained into his.

"Never." His arms closed around me.

Emma slept at Bill's place that night, and Pete stayed with me. We snuggled on the sofa, just like old times, only this time he kept patting his chest, his voice so gentle, saying, "Let it out right here."

I cried half the night.

The following day, Indigo delivered the cooler I'd left in his car, and my bike, but I made Emma tell him I wasn't home. I knew it was over. He'd realize it too.

No one knows why, but sometimes even the best of things aren't meant to be.

Fighting Heartbreak

The days were long, the nights longer, and unbearably lonely. I'd lie in bed, reliving the last moments Indigo and I were together. Reevaluating possibilities, alternatives. Never did a single detail of his beautiful features fade. The facets of his eyes, their potent expression and hues, were unforgettable. My anger had abated, lifting the weight of betrayal, leaving in its place a hollow nothing could fill. A constant craving not a thing in the world could satisfy.

Plagued by *what if's*, I couldn't wrap my mind around the fact that our relationship had ended, and wondered if I'd reacted too harshly. On my journey through the stages of grief, I ended up blaming myself. I knew we were broken, but had no idea how to make repairs. I knew in my heart Indigo was an honest, loving person. Strange things happen, I told myself, striking without reason out of the blue. It was part of life; who was I to question? But was there really a *reason* for everything?

Curdling loss still clawed at my stomach, and in the solitary of my room I'd speak Indigo's name aloud, in different tones, pretending he was beside me, which helped keep me sane. Sometimes I'd curl up into a ball, my insides so tight, I thought

I'd never make sunrise.

I worked as many hours at AMA as possible, read a lot of books, and studied the police manual until I could practically recite each chapter verbatim. Pete and I practiced hand to hand combat on a regular basis, while Casey sat in a chair watching TV, or us. We shared hours of conversation, and many cups of herbal tea.

Indigo repeatedly texted me, but I never replied. I deleted his many messages without reading them. My phone was turned off most of the time, and I never listened to the voicemails he left.

One day I accidentally opened one of his texts, reading his words: *I won't stop calling until you talk to me.* I was longing to know what he had to say, but I couldn't. It would have killed me to hear his voice. I'd experienced life, matured beyond my years, and now had to stop myself from dying prematurely.

So I turned my cell off permanently, shoved it into my dresser drawer, and bought a trac phone. I'd formed a habit of never answering the door, so I was safe on all fronts. Eventually, his attempts grew fewer, further apart. Part of me suffered sorrow, part relief. For as much as I yearned to be with him, the past had proven a future would be impossible.

I'd be in training for approximately five months, and planned on giving the academy my all. The first mornings I stood in formation at roll call were among the most exciting times of my life. As days passed, I realized how difficult becoming a police officer would be. Pete looked over my shoulder though, and almost every night we'd relive my day, in person or by phone, with him coaching me through any rough spots.

"The calisthenics are a killer, Pete, but I'm a pro at defensive tactics, thanks to you."

"How's your aim?"

"Great. How's yours?" I teased. As I brewed tea, I gave him a rundown of my day. "We went to the range to practice today and next week we'll be in the pool, learning how to tread water while we remove our pants or shirts and tie them into life preservers."

He nodded appreciatively. "When are you visiting the Medical Examiner's office?"

"Ugh. An autopsy is one thing I'm not looking forward to."

"Well, be prepared. It's gross." He flexed his chin, then arched his brows. "Wait till EVOC. It's awesome."

"Oh yeah." I scrubbed my palms together. "I can't wait to hit the course, not the cones." I giggled. "I've been practicing my high speed maneuvers on my dad's Jeep ... and Tony's video games when it's not."

Pete rolled with laughter. "Anything's better than nothing, Kit Kat."

"I've been riding my bike in parking lots when no one's around. Weaving around cars. You know, to get the feel of the wheel."

"Leave it to you." He shook his head. "You're resourceful, gotta give you that much. Don't dent any fenders." He planted a kiss on my forehead before walking out the door.

* * *

The weeks flew by and Indigo's efforts to connect with me were so infrequent, any attempt threw me for a loop, and back into the past. I thought a lot. I dreamed a lot. I cried a lot. I missed him so much, I'd bury my face in my pillow and sob. Emma tried to console me, saying in time I'd forget, but some things were simply unforgettable. Indigo.

I assumed he was well into his residency, and busy as hell. Was he still in Manhattan? When would he be leaving the country? At the thought of him relocating to Paraguay, the clench of my gut caused physical distress. The loneliness, impossible to deal with. Had I permitted my mind to take the journey for which it longed, I might not have made it back to reality.

Then one Saturday, a knock at the door almost blasted me

out of my self-contained sanctuary. As usual, I didn't answer the buzzer. While I sought refuge in my room, Emma replied to the caller, and the doorbell. "Thank you," I heard her say, her words light, wistful. "Jewel," the tone of her voice was then cautious. "Come out here, please."

Was it her caterer delivering a sample menu? The arrival of her dress? Wedding plans had wrapped her in a continual state of bliss. Chaos had become a frequent visitor.

Filled with expectancy, and a rush of adrenaline, I half expected, half hoped, to see Indigo standing in the middle of my living room. He would take me in his arms and the nightmare would be over. What I found, however, was almost as unnerving, surprising, irresistible.

A long glossy box, wrapped with my favorite color of purple, sat on the counter. A hand flew to my mouth; I sucked in a breath, and tears came faster than Emma's words. But she didn't have to tell me; I knew it was from Indigo. My trembling fingers stroked the satin ribbon, and I hesitated. My heart was inside that box. Could I risk opening it again?

"Oh Jewel." Emma put her arms around my vibrating shoulders.

"It's been hell, Em. I never thought it would be this difficult. That day when I left him there, calling my name. I was so angry. Something inside me snapped. Maybe my pride. I couldn't turn back. And then it just escalated, and the anger was replaced by fear, and I just couldn't ... I couldn't go through that again, Em." I sobbed so hard, the collar of her shirt felt damp beneath my chin. "What should I do?"

"It has to be your decision." She drew back, a strained look on her face.

"Em, you look like you're about to deliver bad news. Don't tell me something happened to him?" With balled up fists I covered my ears, tears still streaming down my face. As I watched her concern escalate, the knot in my stomach grew. "I don't want to know."

"Okay." Her voice was quiet as she reached for a mug.

"I'll make us some tea."

I was the earth, and emotions bombarded me like a meteor storm. I felt my body revolving. Everything my eyes fell upon wavered. I steadied myself on Emma's shoulders and put my body in front of her, my fingers still gripping. "What, Em? What is it?"

She drew a troubled breath. "There's nothing to tell. I was hoping you would have come to terms with this by now, but you don't seem to be any closer to a resolution." She let out a breath.

"Have you seen him?"

"No."

"Heard from him?"

"No, but he's reaching out to you." Her gaze shifted to the counter. "Maybe you should talk to him."

"I don't know if I can. There's this thing inside me, like a wall I can't seem to get over." I shuddered. "It was such a roller coaster."

"I understand. I had hoped you'd be able to move on by now. Are you going to open the box?"

After a soulful moment, I took the deepest breath of my life, and slid the ribbon off the box. After wrapping it around my hair, I lifted the cover. A dozen crisp white rosebuds were buried beneath tissue paper. Carefully separating the stems, I brought the sweetness to my nose. The fragrance almost swept me off my feet. Roses cradled in my arms, I read the note:

To the part of my world that shines brightest;
Jewelia, my joy.

Love is a gentle song which leads a heart to a meadow
The fragrance of paradise, a thoughtful hand on a shoulder
Love is every perfect note in the sound of your voice
The lifetime I've spent in search of you
Each breath I take missing you
Your sigh when you're fast asleep

Fighting For You

Memories I'll forever keep
Love is your eyes when they gaze into mine
A traveler of sorrow, a soul lost in time.
I love you, Jewelia.
Always, Jimmy

Prime Suspect

My beautiful roses found a place in an antique vase on my bedroom dresser. Before their delicate petals wilted, I pressed them in a favorite book. Each night before bed I read Indigo's note, then slid it back under my pillow; I knew the words by heart, but savored them just the same. All the while, I fought an internal battle. Could I handle the risk – or should I close the door forever? Maybe I just wasn't cut out for love.

While struggling with my demons, I continued to work at AMA on weekends, while I excelled at the academy. I was chosen to be the leader of my squad, which meant I had to ensure that everyone was squared away with their uniforms and other incidentals, and that they were present and accounted for at all times. I also had the responsibility of making sure everyone completed their tasks properly. The wheels were in motion. I seemed to be on the right track and things were looking fantastic ... academy-wise.

Then, without warning, my new world in the making, began to fall apart. One Saturday evening, after I'd left my shift, there was a break-in at AMA. When I heard the news I was astonished.

The security in that place was so tight, I couldn't believe anyone would have the nerve, or be dumb enough to try it. But someone did, managing to remain under the radar. The thief was slick: dressed in black, face shadowed by a wide-brimmed hat. And smart. The alarm system had been successfully disabled. Someone had done their homework.

We discussed the case in class, learning the camera had captured the perpetrator's image, still the police weren't able to make an ID. The videos were grainy, but with the help of the lab, might be enough to pin the crime on someone, if they had any leads. The story was all over the papers, and apparently, he or she had made quite a haul.

The following weekend at work, I stared at the newly replaced jewelry cabinets. A major aspect of my life, I had a loyalty to AMA. I lifted my eyes to the ceiling, analyzing at the camera lens embedded into the corner, shaking my head. I felt personally violated. Refocusing, my gaze washed over the sparkling new glass counters, and I noticed the empty velvet niche. Had the necklace I loved been sold, or had it been part of the heist? How dare they! My stomach churned.

A few weekends later, another high-class store was burglarized further uptown, and the pattern appeared to be the same. Money was never taken. Valuable electronics weren't touched. All the thief seemed to be interested in was gold, gemstones and diamonds. The cameras had captured the profile, and back of the thief's head, but the face remained well disguised by the brim of a hat. Still, authorities were able to match the videos and the consensus was the same individual had committed both crimes.

We had a serial burglar roaming the city. Security was beefed up. Besides being headline news, the case became the topic of lectures at the academy, where all hell broke loose after a third break-in occurred in another upscale department store.

Not long after, I was called into the office of my superior. Two NYPD officers stood at attention beside the door. The captain scrutinized me, then dropped the bomb. "Ms. Delarosa, we seem to have a problem."

My heart sank. "What's that, sir?" While my legs trembled, I managed to maintain an alert stance. "I've been on time, been keeping my squad intact." My mind raced, attempting to grasp exactly what I'd done wrong.

"It's come to our attention," his voice was gruff, "that you're a prime suspect in the recent string of burglaries." His eyes traveled to the officers and back. Shock ebbed from his face, only to be replaced by disappointment.

"But. What? Oh my God. I would never ..." Every ounce of blood drained into my feet, which felt like they were filled with lead. "Am I going to be fired?"

"Not at this time, but we'll be keeping a watchful eye on you, until you are hopefully cleared and not charged. These officers are going to escort you to the station."

"I'm being arrested?" My entire being tensed. Pooled blood rushed to my face, throbbed in my head.

"I didn't say that." The intensity in his brown eyes softened, but only slightly. "You're being taken in for questioning."

"I can't believe this!" Outraged, I fought to control my reaction. The worst thing I could do would be to fly off the handle with those controlling my future.

"Take it easy, Delarosa. You're not under arrest yet."

"Yet?" About to flare, I gritted my teeth as the captain showed me to the door.

The officers escorted me to a patrol car and transported me to the station where I was interrogated by two detectives who handed me composite drawings created from the video clips. The pictures were of someone with long dark hair. The suspect seemed to be close to my stature, with a similar profile, and wore a floppy hat I'd never include in my wardrobe.

"I'm sorry, detective," I protested, "but this could be anyone. The features are indistinguishable. The photos are blurred and they're murky. Skin color is undeterminable, as are the eyes. I don't understand why I'm being accused, and I resent being–"

"This isn't all we have, Ms. Delarosa," raising a hand, and his voice, the stocky man cut me right off. "Is there something you want to tell us, or do you want us to continue? We can make this easy, or we can make it difficult."

"This is ridiculous." Of course my mouth hung open like a stretched out rubber band ... I was powerless. My lips barely moved. "I have nothing to hide, and nothing to say other than you have the wrong person."

"We have a witness who swears to have seen you wearing one of the stolen items."

"What?" I almost fell off the chair. My heart thundered in my chest. My life was on the doorstep of catastrophe. I fought to organize my thoughts.

"A gold necklace. The description matches an expensive piece of jewelry taken from AMA, the store where you work. Sound familiar to you?"

The second detective, young and wiry, addressed the first. "Makes sense to me. She knows the system, the layout." He acted as if I wasn't sitting right in front of him! Condemning me for a crime I hadn't committed. Treating me as worthless, he sized me up, shook his head and let out a chuckle sounding more like a snarl. His demeanor made me long to shrink out of my uniform, or crawl beneath his desk, a more plausible alternative. I was being framed, possibly kicked out of the academy, and thanks to some so-called witness, might be losing my job, too.

I burst into tears, then I called Pete. From his end of the phone he vouched for me, swearing I'd been with him every Saturday night. His voice was so harsh, I heard it through the receiver the detective held an inch from his ear.

* * *

"Pete. It's her." I told my *plain clothes* best male friend as he took me home. I was in bad shape. My legs were so weak, he half carried me up the stairs and into my apartment.

"It's her? You mean Vanessa?"

"Yes, Pete. It has to be her. Who else would set me up?"

"But you and Indigo broke up. What reason does she have to stalk you?"

"She hates me. Isn't that reason enough? We've got to catch her in the act." My eyes narrowed, the wheels in my jumbled brain turning. "Beat her at her own game. She's got the stuff, Pete. I know it in my heart. If we can pin it on her, I'm vindicated."

While we stood in the kitchen, Pete scrubbed his chin. "Okay. But we've got to think this through. We need to put a tail on her. Someone we can trust."

I lifted a brow. "I'm free every night. Who better?" My head filled with scenarios.

"Ah ah, Kit Kat. I'm not sure about this. If anyone found out, it could land you in more hot water, maybe even prison. There are laws protecting witnesses."

"She's not a witness! She's a liar!" I backed against the wall, burying my face in my hands.

Pete's arms went around me. "Hang in there, Jewel. I'll do what I can."

For the rest of the day I sat stiff in a chair like a chunk of ice, which is how Emma found me when she returned from work. With a horrified look on her face she listened to my story, angered, then bunched an afghan up to my neck. Together we sat for hours, nursing chamomile tea and my nerves.

Pete called that night. He'd been able to obtain Vanessa's address, and we learned she was living in a seedy part of the city. The next evening, armed with sandwiches and lattes, we configured our stakeout.

"Why would an heiress live here, Pete?" I said, considering she might have rented the apartment as a cover up, moseying back to Park Avenue after each crime.

"You've got me, Kit Kat. Maybe she leads a double life. Maybe she's looking for excitement. Maybe she's just a lunatic."

Scanning the area, I commented, "I could think of a million other places to find excitement. Look at the overflowing dumpsters. The dog do on the sidewalk. The bars on some of the windows."

Hidden in shadows, Pete and I hung out across the street from the rundown apartment, spending most of the time tucked into an alley. It was Pete's night off. A steady breeze brought a chill to the night. While I held down the fort, Pete walked to a nearby deli and returned with hot coffee. We surveyed the front door until three a.m., but saw no sign of Vanessa either entering or leaving.

"Let's hit the road, Jewel. I doubt she's gonna show." Pete blew warmth into his hands.

My frustration escalated. "If she's not planning a robbery tonight, she's probably not here," I complained. "I'm not so sure this building is her permanent residency. This is bugging the hell out of me. I can't figure her out."

"I'd tend to agree with you, but the source of this info is reliable."

Before leaving our stakeout, Pete said he'd be pulling a nightshift the following week, so I'd be on my own. "I hate leaving you alone, Jewel," he said. "Are you sure you'll be okay?"

"I can handle it, Pete."

His arms were crossed. I watched a scowl grow on his face. "Remember, I'm just a phone call away." He drew in air through his nose, releasing two vapory streams like a snorting bull. "Make sure you keep your cell phone on."

"I will." My face was rigid, not only from the cold.

"You're unarmed and emotionally involved. Keep your head on straight." Pete looked like he was taking a deep drag on a cigarette, this time, exhaling dissatisfaction through his pursed lips. "Don't take any risks."

"I won't," I promised, but knew inside, I'd do whatever was necessary to beat Vanessa at her own sick game.

Stakeout

During the first few nights of surveillance others came and went, but Vanessa didn't show her face. I did, however, see someone moving around inside her apartment. With bright lights and no window shades, living on the eighth floor didn't ensure total privacy. Still, from the distance, I couldn't be sure the wavering shadow was even hers. I made a mental note to borrow a pair of binoculars from Casey, the bird watcher.

Filled with garbage bags and cartons, along with seclusion, the alley offered a distinct odor. On more than one occasion, my stomach rose to my throat. Sitting lightly on the cleanest piece of cardboard I could find, my mind flew in multiple directions. I had to reel it in so I could concentrate. While I observed, through anxiety and frustration, Indigo was always with me. I had so much time to think, so many regrets. I should have been more understanding. Instead of stomping off, I should have comforted him. *Back up, Jewel, you tried.*

I was bored. I was angry. I was tired. I was on the verge of a nervous breakdown. Waiting for Vanessa's next move was agony, and when she didn't show, I was so discouraged I felt like taking the next flight out of the country. I didn't know how much more I could take. Each night I'd wait for hours, hoping, and when she didn't show, I'd slip my makeshift seat into the safest place I could find ... between the wall and a rusting drainpipe clipped to its side ... so it would be ready for the next watch.

The robberies had all occurred on Saturdays, close to midnight, so the perpetrator had earned the name of the midnight thief. Leaving nothing up to chance, I decided to watch the place on a daily basis, making bicycle drive-bys, staked out in the alley every night.

The sleep I was able to find was fitful. On probation at work, under surveillance at the academy, I felt like an outsider, not to mention a loser. Stress showed on my face, and I lost weight. Emma worried, pleading with me to rest for a while with my family in Poughkeepsie, and leave solving crimes to the authorities. "I'm the authorities," I told her with a hug. "Besides, my parents have no clue as to what's happening." I scrunched the side of my mouth, uncertain but determined.

For two weeks I holed up, waiting, hoping. Feeling like I was wasting my time and optimism, I started drifting into a state of desperation. The weather was turning, and the news predicted rainstorms and falling temperatures for the weekend. I'd have to pull myself together so I'd be alert, thinking, "If this doesn't end soon, I'm gonna lose my mind!"

Between her job and wedding plans, Emma focused on me, begging me not to go out that particular Saturday night. First she said she had a bad feeling. Then she offered to accompany me, but there was no way I was getting the soon-to-be-bride mixed up in any legal issues ... or danger.

"Grandma," I whispered as I pulled a black knit cap over my head, zipped my insulated sweatshirt to my neck, slipped on gloves and unhitched my bicycle from the lobby's bike rack. "Please have my back. I'm really scared, Gram, but it's something I have to do. Don't be mad at me. I have to clear my name. My entire life depends upon it."

The sudden thought occurred to me, and I ran back up

the stairs.

"You're not going?" Emma looked relieved when I burst into the apartment.

"I forgot something," I panted as I rushed into my room and pulled open my dresser drawer. I grabbed my cell phone and turned it on. "You're coming with me," I whispered to Indigo. He'd always made me feel safe, and at the moment, I needed him more than ever.

As I headed back down the stairs, I thought of my family, longing to see them again. I couldn't burden them with my problems, so they had no clue as to what was going on. Besides, they would have locked me up had they known what I was about to take on. Only Emma and Pete personally knew of my plight, and my plan.

I put my cell on vibrate and stuck it into my pocket. I'd need it to photograph Vanessa in the act. As I clunked through the lobby door, bumping the wheels of my bike down the stairs, the paralyzing thought struck me. If a patrol car passed, for certain I'd be arrested. Dressed all in black, my face half hidden, I looked every inch a thief in the night. And with what they had on me, I'd be charged for sure. I needed to be careful, staying on back streets.

Tonight was the night. I could feel it in my bones, along with the chilling wind as I rode through lightly trafficked sections of the city. Halloween decorations hung on doors, jack o'lanterns sat on porches. I thought of how Teresa would be trick or treating in a few weeks; Mom setting dinner on the table; the warmth of the living room fireplace, and my stomach contorted. Where did I go wrong? Was I serving this sentence simply because I fell in love?

A cold drizzle pecked at my face, and I pulled the hood of my sweatshirt over my head as far as the fabric would stretch. All that was visible were my cheeks and mouth as I hunkered, protected by the alley. The front door of Vanessa's apartment, and the dingy windows, were the objects of my undivided attention. Of course she'd hang a witch and black cats in her windows. I wondered if she'd come flying out on her broomstick. Then again, maybe Elizabeth had it tonight.

The lights were on, which I felt was a good sign, and it became even more encouraging when I detected movement. My eyes clung to the eighth floor, and what had to be Vanessa's floundering silhouette.

Music blared from passing cars, a few residents walked dogs, but as far as I could tell, no eyes breached my cover. "Let's go, bitch," became my battle cry, and I repeated the phrase again and again. The day was right, and so was the time: thirty-five minutes before midnight, and there hadn't been another burglary since the last which had taken place several weeks ago.

I crouched, frozen to the bone, my neck stretched and aching. The wind made its way through my lightweight gloves as I shielded my face from what had evolved into pelting rain.

A film of gloss covered the road, which I assumed was ice, and from beneath the corner streetlight, I watched its erratic fall. Leave it to you, Vanessa, to pick a night like this, flashed through my head as the front door of her apartment building flew open, inched closed. She emerged, dressed much like me. My breath quickened. I willed my limbs to find peace.

I had no idea Vanessa traveled by bicycle. Of course, automobiles had license plates and identifiable features, were traceable, but city streets hosted thousands of bikes, easy to conceal, to flee off road. As she tore off past me, it appeared she rode proficiently. *So, she's assuming my entire persona while she turns me into a two-bit thief?* Two-bit? The amount of jewelry she'd lifted was rising to a charge of grand larceny.

I didn't move a muscle until the distance between us felt safe, then I tracked her. She rode in the right lane, where an intermittent flow of traffic trickled by. Now and then her wheels hit puddles, which I avoided. We appeared to be heading uptown, in the direction of my neighborhood. What, was she going to rob *me* next?

Possibly feeling the heat of headline news, she altered her

course, selecting a quiet area in which to carry out her crime. I followed easily down side streets, but my heart rate grew turbulent when we approached corners, where I'd pause, holding my breath, concerned she might have noticed me and was lying in wait, concerned if I didn't accelerate, I'd lose her. We seemed to be riding in circles then squares, or was it my imagination? Was she carrying a weapon? Did she have more on her mind than framing me? I wasn't putting anything past Vanessa. She was evil, and she was out to get me.

Eyes straining, ears acute, I never let her out of my sight, and when I heard her tires crunch grit, hitting my brakes I coasted. In the distance, where the main road intersected ours, headlights occasionally swept through mist, but the street we were on was deserted.

With Vanessa secured in my sight, I scanned the area, attempting to fix the location, planning my victory, fearing my demise. We ventured into an industrial graveyard, and a patchwork of structures fell to the wayside as we sped past warehouses, garages, small shops caged with bars. There was no moon, no stars in the city, especially on a night like this. With the scarcity of streetlights, illumination was minimal, and accumulating fog challenged visibility.

I had been bullied into a scene from a horror movie. With the exception of Vanessa, not another soul existed in my nightmare. I corrected my assumption; Vanessa had no soul. I longed to be home, or accompanied by Pete, better yet, be safe in Indigo's arms. Any place but this hellhole. Pitched through the air, the only sound other than the rumble of thunder came from the lungs of a dog howling in the distance. Soaked and chilled, I felt his anguish.

My adversary appeared to be heading toward a storefront office, where a single light wafted through the window and its painted sign: Diamonds – Gold – Bought – Sold. The dreary building was backed into the shadows, sandwiched between two others.

I probably followed closer than I should have, but anxiety

bordered panic: slowing my heart, my pedaling feet, was nearly impossible. Governing my breathing I paused, wide-eyed as Vanessa hopped off her bike, pushed it into the alley beside the brick wall where water coursed through a gutter.

Should I forge into the unknown? Should I hold out a moment longer? Forced to make a split second decision, my stomach rose to my throat. My straining stare pulsed with the same blood that pounded my temples.

I focused so intently, my vision grew dim; misty air clung to my face making matters worse. While inhaling dampness, my eyes blinked away shuddering circles and black static snow, created by the nerves in my eyes.

Before leaving home, I'd strapped on a wristwatch, and I timed her. She'd been gone for less than two minutes. I'd give her sixty seconds more, and then I'd head down the alley in search of her. Although I yearned to catch her in the act, I couldn't risk her disappearance, for I knew there would never be a night like this again. No such luck. But what kind of luck was this? I was cuffing her, reading her rights, counting my chickens before they hatched.

While I debated, she emerged, a bag slung over her shoulder. Something broke from the shadows, and it was beside her; two slithering phantoms. What the hell? The figures merged, divided, reattached, unbraided.

My eyes followed the burning tip of a cigarette. An illusion or accomplice! I was so not prepared for this. But I'd gone this far; there was no turning back now. I quickly pounded Pete's number, but my trembling fingers misdialed. On my second attempt, the call immediately went to voicemail. As I left him a breathless message: "Where are you Pete? Here's where I am … Something's going down," my mind screamed, "It's not going to be me."

Vanessa's double flicked the cigarette and began to shrink, vaporizing into one of the cloud formations floating around us. Unable to discern the direction of her partner's retreat, Vanessa's outline claimed my sole attention. Wiping rain from eyes, panic from limbs, I watched her slide along the wall, past the storefront, to a door on the opposite side of the building. Starting my count, I held my breath. I'd give her a few seconds, then make my move.

After calling Pete, I'd held onto my phone. Before sliding it into my pocket, I started snapping pictures, hoping the camera would capture her in dim light. I glimpsed the steady fall of rain in the glow of the corner streetlight, but saw no trace of Vanessa's companion. The thought of someone sneaking up behind me was chilling, and I fought the urge to revolve in circles, protecting my own back. What had I gotten myself into? Mine could be the next body found lying face down in an alley. This was even worse than being the discarded candy wrapper, ground to shreds beneath the heels of the detectives' shoes. This was life-threatening ... this was reality ... and it was suddenly sinking in.

I began to fashion my own fate: I hoped it wasn't Pete who found me. Back up, Jewel. If there's a breath left in my lungs, God, please let Pete find me, but if I'm stiff and bloodless ... I couldn't put him through that. Vanessa's sudden movement curtailed my runaway imagination.

Crouching, she pulled something from her pocket and went to work on the lock. The realization hit me. Her accomplice disabled the alarms, while she gained entry. Holy shit. Where had she learned this stuff? Certainly not in prep school.

I can't let her break in, mingled with the other reasoning rounding like a halo inside my head. And I can't let her get away. My hiding place was only a few yards away, behind the cover of a utility pole. Angling my bike, I sucked in my breath, trying to make myself invisible.

I prayed Pete would get my message soon, and magically appear. I considered the size of her stocky accomplice. How was I going to handle both of them?

"One, two, three. Are you ready Grandma?" My cross lay buried beneath my clothing, so I patted my neck where I felt the heirloom pressed to my skin. I mounted my bike, devising my strategy. What strategy? I carried no weapon; my saddlebag contained only a pair of handcuffs. What had I been thinking?

My mind went into overdrive. I'd do a combination drive-by, tripping the guy, and tackling Vanessa, knocking them cold with one swift blow. I knew enough hand to hand to take care of two creeps at once. The only problem was, I had no idea of the location of her partner. Switch to plan B, which was ... pure animal instinct.

Then my mind slipped into reverse. Creep? Vanessa? Holy shit. Could it be the rude guy who she'd been with that night at The Prestige? After the run-in we'd had, I'd gotten a taste of his strength. It wouldn't be like in the club. I wasn't wearing heels, and I wasn't bombed. Still, a shudder hit my legs first, then targeted the rest of my body.

Pull it together girl. You're a rookie cop – at least you will be, soon. Dear God, if you get me through this, I promise I'll never sin again.

I'll repent, I'll repent, I'll repent. I hopped on my bike, sped down the road, wheels slipping on the slick pavement. My jaw clenched; my ears sang. Every ounce of power concentrated in my legs, I gained as much momentum as possible. With the weather and stress everything around me looked smeared, but I managed to lock onto the shock on Vanessa's face as I reached her side, head down, wild eyes lifted, fingers gripping the handlebars as if they were wrapped around her neck.

Startled, she dropped the object she'd been holding, threw her hands out in front of her, rammed her hip into my bike and took off. "Shit!" I wobbled to a stop. She could disappear down any alley. I could lose her. Not now. Not when I'm so close. She was leaping off the curb, splashing through water gathering in the gutter, and I was in pursuit.

I was inches away when my tire hit a rut. I remembered thinking; Shit ... next thing I knew, the wheels of my bike were spinning, I was flying over the handlebars and headlong into Vanessa, who immediately crumbled. While I body slammed her, my bike took its own flight.

Disoriented, I scrambled to my feet, frantically looking around. She was gone. How long had I been out? I hopped on my bike and launched into the night. Fueled by adrenaline, I was pumped. And I was on a mission. Without the need for anonymity, I snapped the headlight on and the glare washed both sides of the road. *This can't be happening. I'm almost there. Please, God. I need help!* Not to mention coffee and a hot shower. I was so cold I could barely feel my fingers, my toes. I licked cold rain from my stinging lips. Everything was happening in slow motion: my movements, my mind. Was I about to pass out?

Vanessa couldn't outrun me. Her wavering outline shimmered not more than five feet ahead of my light. Then I was rolling alongside her, leaping off my bike, tackling her before she had a chance to veer off in another direction. As I landed beneath my bike, my head hit the curb. Stunned, I had no idea of where I was until I felt her beside me. Her recovery came a moment sooner than mine. Her boot hit my side which exploded with mind-numbing pain, literally knocking the breath from my lungs.

I heard myself scream, "You bitch," as I reached for her ankle, yanking her down beside me.

She ripped off my hat, snatched fistfuls of my hair, fighting me like a girl. It would have been humorous had my neck not been on the line. Her body covered mine and she grunted, clawing at my face. Our limbs tangled, we rolled, my calf muscles bracing my weight. I heard her yelling, "Bitch," calling out, "help me Lenny." I felt my forearm dig deep into her throat, jerked her head back, and easily flipped her. On my knees I began pummeling her jaw. Her eyes were closed, her mouth a gaping cavity filling with rain, with blood. Next thing I knew, strong arms were pulling me off, and I was in bathed in the beam of headlights.

"Kit Kat!"

"Pete?" Disoriented, I shook my head to clear it.

"I'll take it from here, babe." He set me aside.

"No," I argued as my tongue swiped my teeth, my mouth flavored with the taste of blood gushing from a wound just above my right eye, where my head had slammed the curb. "She's got an accomplice." Out of breath, I panted. "He could be in the alley next to the pawnbroker." I gasped for air. "Go get him, Pete, before he gets away."

I watched Pete hesitate. "Go! I've got this." He must have caught the determination in my eyes, urgency in my voice, because he backed off. "I need this, Pete. Please."

My gloves were soaked and a hindrance. I ripped them off, let them fall to the pavement. Dropping to my knees I cuffed her. I heard Pete's car door slam, his cruiser pull away. And then there was nothing but street lights and rain and a shooting pain in my pounding head. Exhausted, all I wanted to do was fall to the ground.

Vanessa's cruelty boiled in my mind, stabbing like a knife, like the pain in my side. The smugness on her face glistened and bled, and I fought the urge to pound her head into the pavement. When I lifted her arms, she moaned. When I grabbed the collar of her jacket, something cold and hard, like Vanessa, pressed against my palm. And as I hauled her to her feet, a sliver of gold fell into my hand; I balanced weight against worth, realizing it was nothing. Why such importance was placed upon items said to be precious was beyond my comprehension. Life, family, love, Indigo: they were precious, irreplaceable, unable to be purchased; meant to be treasured more than gold.

"Busted," I said. As my mouth was in the process of swelling, I creased one cheek as I slid the AMA necklace into my pocket.

She was on her feet and I was dragging her to the corner where I read her her rights. A search of her pockets revealed valuable bracelets and multiple rings.

"Are you carrying everything you robbed?" My anger blew against the side of her face.

Feeling as if I'd been branded by the tip of her boot, I wondered if she'd cracked a rib. My eyes burned, my head hurt, and I was dizzy, but I wasn't going down. I was about to enjoy one of the best moments of my life. "Busted, busted, busted," suddenly elated, I sang. "So, how does it feel?"

Her face was swelling, and bloody. She was mumbling something like, "Go fuck yourself."

Headlights broke the darkness. Red bubbles circled above a patrol car as it rolled to the curb, followed by another. Before shoving Vanessa onto the seat, I said, "After you, *puta*."

Her accomplice was cuffed and slumped inside the second patrol car, shooting daggers at me. Remembering his face, I blew him a kiss, then climbed in beside Pete, listening as he called in to the station. We arrived, delivering an agitated Vanessa, who I threw onto the desk of a detective on duty.

Emergency

"Here's your midnight thief." I slapped the gold necklace down in front of the detective, then shook out Vanessa's pockets. "I'm Jewelia Delarosa, a cadet at the NYPD Academy. She's the one you're looking for."

The detective's eyes grew. "Yeah, so I see," he grinned, "I heard about you."

I wanted to vomit, to collapse, to laugh and to cry, all at once. Pete watched me with sympathy, pride and concern.

Since Vanessa was in possession of stolen property, any question of guilt was nil. Following an hour of questioning, she implicated the guy, confessing to the break-ins and her intention of gaining access to the lobby of my apartment building, planting the jewelry in the saddle bag of my bike, and reporting me to the police, who would have had all of the evidence they needed to put me away for four to seven, maybe more. She would have then been as happy as I was at the moment.

Her partner turned out to be an employee of a security alarm company. He was booked; so was Vanessa, but shortly thereafter she was driven to the hospital. Although I insisted my injuries were minor, Pete transported both of us to the E.R. in the same car, with me in the front, Vanessa behind the cage. By then she was awake and sobbing, cursing, and moaning.

Pete stopped at the entrance of the nearest hospital, left us in the car, reappearing with an attendant, a wheelchair and a stretcher. While I was plopped into the chair, Vanessa was rolled through the door.

The E.R. was quiet, but for a few patients occupying the sizeable waiting area. Most suffered minor illness. One man seemed to be cradling a broken arm. Our incident had been called in prior to our arrival, so attendants were prepared.

Strapped to a gurney, Vanessa idled in a hallway like a shattered mannequin in line for repair. I was parked beneath the receptionist's window, which she slid open to ask my name. I heard her respond to the person she dialed, "Yes. One was beaten. Both are conscious. The other one went over the handlebars of a bicycle. Ah ha, you got it, head over wheels."

Pete was in the process of returning my handcuffs, and I'd been watching the receptionist, musing at the stark red of her hair, when a door to my left flew open. From the corner of my eye I spotted him. Back to me, he posed with a sexy hands on hips stance, competent, relaxed. I almost died when the well-built doctor in scrubs turned around.

"Holy fuck," I whispered to Pete, "It's Indigo." I felt like I was about to convulse.

Looking from me in the chair with syrupy blood clotting on my cheek and chin, to Vanessa whose head rolled back and forth on the gurney, her entire face colored with blood and moaning, shock and confusion fought for control of his face. Without a word, he reacted as a professional, pushing Vanessa through the doorway from which he had emerged.

"So that's that," I said, a lump forming in my already swollen throat. The curb had also done a number on my neck. I reached up and felt the painful tissue expanding beneath my ear.

"I'll be back soon," said Pete. I knew it was his duty to

accompany Vanessa.

So there I sat for approximately five minutes, until the door swung open again, and Indigo strode to my side. An odd look crossed his otherwise unreadable face when his glance slipped over my cuffs Pete had slung over the arm of the chair. I wondered if he thought I was under arrest as well.

"Jewel." It was amazing to see him, to hear him call my name. "What the hell happened?" After he wheeled me into a room, his expression eased.

He helped me onto a table and started peeling off my clothes, examining every part of me. "Where does it hurt?"

"Everywhere," I groaned, shock and expectation muddling my brain.

The events of the night were beginning to register. My brain was a web of disorientation: dazed, sad, elated. Every emotion in the book slammed me all at once.

"What are you doing here?" Were the first sensible words I uttered.

"I work here." Without facing me, he continued to assess my injuries. By then I was covered by a sheet, as well as his eyes.

"So, you didn't leave?"

"Obviously not, because I'm here." Scrupulous and thorough, he acted as though he was attending to a child.

"Are you happy practicing here?" Under bright light, I squinted up at him.

"Couldn't be happier." He palpated my stomach.

"Why didn't you try to find me?" My voice almost broke, like my heart.

"Are you serious?" That's when he met me square in the face, his eyes a combination of disbelief and concern. Their pewter glimmer said they were attempting to morph into something else. "You should go undercover – you're great at hiding."

I tried to laugh, but my ribcage hurt. "Get x-ray in here," he said to a nurse when he saw me flinch. Leaning over me, he brushed blood-soaked hair from my face and began cleaning my head wound, his breath flowing down on me, and my immediate instinct was to pull his lips down to mine. But I didn't.

"Do you undress all of your patients?" I made my voice, and my eyes, as sultry as possible, given the situation. I managed to deepen one dimple, but the other side of my face was too swollen to move.

He looked uncomfortable. "The nurses normally do that."

"So, I'm special?"

"Yes."

After giving me a good going over, he stood back and crossed his arms. "I recall saying you'd send me the battered and I'd patch them up, but after tonight I'm not sure I'm liking this."

My hand flew to my hair, my face. "I look like crap, huh?"

"You look beautiful, but I worry."

"I can take care of myself, doc."

The same nurse burst into the room with a bowl and set it on the bedside table. She looked to Indigo as if to ask, "What next?" but he dismissed her with a nod, so she left the room as quickly as she'd burst in. Accomplished without the need for words, I imagined it was some kind of hospital communication. For some odd reason, the thought struck me as funny, and when my lips spread into a smile, the pain shot into my jaw. "Ouch," I whimpered, bringing my hand to my face.

Indigo removed an ice pack from the bowl, sat on the bed beside me, and gently ran a finger across my cheek and around my lips. "Look at your mouth." His eyes, blue as his scrubs, watered. "It's so swollen," he whispered, then held the ice pack to the side of my face. With his other hand, he stroked my hair. "You really did a number on yourself, didn't you, Jewel."

"I had no choice ... and look who's talking ..." I mumbled.

He moved the pack to my mouth. "Keep your mouth shut ... if that's possible. Let me get rid of some of this swelling."

"I can hold it." I replaced his hand with mine.

"You're so stubborn."

"Speaking of ... Where's Vanessa?"

"Being treated in another room."

"You came back for me. Why didn't you treat her?"

"You're my priority." Running his hands up and down my body, he prodded gently.

Old feelings crashed in on me. I melted under his touch.

"Where'd you disappear to?" he asked in the same disciplined tone. But I thought I noticed the *something* in his eyes evolve as they lifted in a stare, inches from mine.

"The academy. Why are you still here? I thought you'd be in Paraguay by now."

Most of his tan had faded, leaving his face clear and smooth, his flush easily detectible. "When you didn't answer my *many* messages, I realized you needed to work things out for yourself, without me screwing with your head ... while I worked out my own issues." Even in his bowed position, I detected his frown. "But I kept in touch with Bill to see what was going on, and make sure you were alright."

"You cut your hair." As he listened to my heart, I reached up to run my fingers through the lush sandy crop.

"No one cared if it was long or short."

I brought a hand to my chest. "So, is it beating?"

"You've got incredible rhythm, Ms. Delarosa."

"Ms?"

"That's what your chart says. I try not to become too chummy with my patients."

"Is that a hint or something?" Praying it wasn't, my insides clenched.

"I sent you flowers." His voice was flat. "What do you think?"

"The roses were beautiful. Thank you. And the note ..."

His flush deepened. "I meant every word of it, Jewel."

I put my hand on his chest, searching for his heartbeat, my voice all too loud when I exclaimed, "I'm in love with my doc ..."

When his hand clamped lightly over my mouth, my brows

met the bridge of my nose. "Ouch! This is at least the fourth time you've silenced me," I mumbled beneath his palm.

"Some things are necessary ... stop with the eyes ... you look like a bruised bug."

"Hey!"

He shook his head. "I don't know anyone who's as full of life as you are, Sunshine. God, I missed you." His eyes swept mine, and I was certain the memories were as constant for him as they were for me. "I'll tell you what, we'll get a cabin in the woods." His face softened so, he looked ready to lose the cool that made the physician so hot.

I grabbed his hand. "No!"

"Okay, how about a place on the beach with no one else around. Then you can scream as loud as you want." A sexy grin broke the stoic look that seemed difficult for him to maintain.

I remembered his groans and a chill ran down my spine. "I want ..." When he leaned in close, I brushed his cheek with my fingertips.

His face was beside mine. He was whispering. "How do I know you won't disappear? Break my heart all over again."

"Oh, baby. I had no idea."

His head lifted, and he stared into my eyes. "So ... What do I have to do? Have them issue a warrant for your arrest?"

"Vanessa already took care of that."

"There's always house arrest." His tone deepened. "I'm sorry about what she's done to you." He stood, ran a hand through his hair and let out a breath. "After her father drove off that bridge ..."

"Drove off a bridge? I thought her parents were killed in a plane crash in his corporate jet on the way to Europe for a meeting?"

"Where'd you hear that?" He leveled a puzzled grin.

"Around. In circles." I giggled. "Like what my head's doing right now."

"You're dizzy?" He brought his face close to shine his

penlight in my eyes again.

Blinking him away, I said, "It's been a hell of a night. I just need some R & R. Is Vanessa okay?" I disliked her, but didn't want to be the one to cause her hospitalization.

"Bruised but she'll be fine." Hovering over me, he stroked my hair.

"She said her name was Whitehall, but at the station they booked her as Simpson?"

"That's her name ... Simpson. I feel responsible. I should've clued you in on all of this, but I had no idea you'd be affected." He frowned. "She created her own world, started rumors that stuck, I guess. Her dad ran a small construction outfit, but it was nothing like she built it up to be. He'd sometimes take us to his yard when we were kids ... let us play on the machines. He was a nice guy. It was unfortunate that he lost his business."

"And she lost her mind. I can't believe I'm saying this after what she's done, but I actually feel sorry for her. She's out there Jimmy, blasting off to her own private planet."

"No one's called me Jimmy since you." His eyes, lively blue and gray, clouded. "I've tried to get her help, but like my father, there's not much you can do for someone unless he or she wants to help him or herself ... other than watch them kill themselves."

As he reflected, I held my breath, waiting for the brooding curtain to fall, but not an ounce of the painful past crossed his handsome face. He finished swabbing my head with antiseptic, and I tried to sit up. His hand on my shoulder held me.

"How's your father?" I smoothed my palm up and down his arm. He felt as delicious as ever.

"Doing well. He's back in neurology. He and my mother are trying to put their lives back together. Things changed after that day." His eyes burned into mine. I sensed the months had been as bad for him as they'd been for me, possibly worse.

Tears stung my eyes. "I'm sorry you had to go through all that."

After placing a bandage on my forehead, he kissed it.

"Hopefully they'll work it all out, and Vanessa will finally get the help she needs as well. I'm sorry she dragged you into our mess."

"We weren't together. Why did she do this to me? Why does she still hate me?"

"They almost had to use the crash cart on me," he shot me a quick glance, then his gaze accompanied his fingers to the lump on my neck, "on more than one occasion."

I gasped.

"I'm joking," he said, adding almost shyly, "she knew I was in love with you. Maybe that was the reason."

My heart skipped a beat. "Was? As in past tense?"

His brows furrowed and he cocked his head. "I think you know better than that."

"Why do you sound so serious? Not what you're saying," I quickly corrected, "the tone of your voice."

He shot me a look of disbelief. "I'm at work, remember?"

I giggled.

"You think it's funny? If you weren't lying on this table, I'd show you how upset I've been, and exactly how serious I can be."

"Promises. Promises," my grin was lopsided, "Hey, where's that padded table I was promised?"

His shoulders lifted with a soft chuckle. "You're something else. You should be out of here in a couple of hours." He checked the wristwatch he wore. "And I'm off duty at eight. I'll hang around and take you home."

"Nurse me back to health?" I caught his hand before he left my side. "Your place or mine?"

"Getting back to your arrest, where did those cuffs go?" Grinning, he pretended to scan the room.

"I told you. The case is closed. I'm a free woman. And I'm on the loose." I felt delirious, seductive, and madly in love with him.

He caught himself before he laughed. "This is another offense. Better yet, give me the cuffs, I'll do it myself. This is a citizen's arrest."

"What are the charges, doctor?"

"Theft."

"I don't know," I squinted up at him, "You're gonna have to do better than that."

"Okay. How about grand larceny?"

"You got proof of that?"

He covered his heart with his hand.

"Ohh."

"Ohh nothing. You have the right to remain silent Delarosa."

"But."

"No buts."

"Anything you say may be held against you."

"You."

"Me?"

"You should be held against me."

Carefully drawing me into his arms, his lips touched mine.

January Valentine

Epilogue

After a week of rest, with a passionate kiss, my doctor cleared me to return to work, and training at the academy. My class erupted with cheers and applause the minute I entered the room. I assumed catching the midnight thief had transformed a prime suspect into an overnight celebrity.

Emma's Wedding

Beneath a radiant sky, and canopy of autumn-tinted foliage, Bill and Emma lived out their dream. Indian Summer in upstate New York blossomed into breathtaking reality, their day a gilded page in a fairy tale.

Indigo looked out of this world gorgeous as he stood beside Bill, both men dressed in white tuxedos and plum ties, sweet William tacked to lapels.

On the manicured grounds, bow-topped seating filled with loved ones while violinists played heavenly songs. Knockouts in pinstriped suits, Pete and Casey settled in front row seats.

As I walked toward the pedestal that served as an altar, I watched Pete's arm go around Casey's shoulders, and when he whispered something, they both smiled then focused on me. Casey winked, and Pete mouthed a kiss as I glided by wearing lavender silk, ankle length and drizzling, violets trimming my braided hair. With a slow blink, I returned his smile, then my eyes fixed on Indigo, and the warmth in his.

Colorful leaves cushioned the earth beneath the white carpet on which Emma, satin gown flowing to her toes, gracefully approached her husband-to-be, to exchange vows they had written. She looked like a princess, the beaded wreath upon her hair glistening with slivers of sunlight peeking through trees.

The reception would be held in a carriage house on the grounds of a stately mansion, weekend host to the romantic affair. Music and waiters weaved through guests during two sensational hours of cocktails and hors d'oeuvres. Mimosas in hand, Indigo and I mingled with others on the veranda.

A voice shattered the aura of refinement. "It's been a long haul, but we made it! Time to party!" I spun to see Yvonne's arm lock around Derek, who held a bottle of champagne in one hand, two glasses in the other. She waved frantically. Her humor contagious, he danced around her. They reminded me of Maine, and memories began to build.

"How's your career going, Derek?" As I called to him, I raised my glass in toast.

"I got me an agent! You'll be seeing my face, maybe even more of me, on magazine covers." A smile reshaped his entire face.

"Maine will never be the same." Returning my attention to Indigo, I rolled my eyes.

"Neither will my mother," he chuckled, "she loves that guy."

"I'm happy everything worked out for everyone. And relieved. I'm almost afraid to breathe and ruffle the air." I sipped my drink, my head filled with Indigo, my stomach with anticipation.

"Feels like we're in another world." Indigo's gaze was easy, his movements precise as he set our glasses onto a waiter's tray.

Sweet air filled my lungs, its effect much like the alcohol flowing straight to my head. "You look temptingly handsome today, doctor. Every day actually." I ran a hand over his jacket, the fabric smooth as my words. "Emma should dress you more often."

"And you look ravishing, Officer Delarosa. I'm kinda partial to your sexy uniform, though." He winked.

"Almost officer. Six more weeks, baby, and I can legally arrest you." My laugh was soft, but my mind churned over the past. "Standing here today ... with you," I focused on Emma and Bill, smothered by loving family, "I can't help but think of all we've been through ...what we've been able to put behind us." Hands braced on his shoulders, on tippy toes, I caressed his lips with mine.

"Life seemed impossible for a while, didn't it?" He ran his hand down my back as he stared over my head to where the tree line thinned, yielding for the Hudson River.

I sighed. "But we managed to work it out."

He nodded. His arms, encircling my waist, swayed me. "You know how much I love you."

"Not half as much as I love you." I smiled up at him.

Releasing his hold, he took my hand. "Come on. Let's take a walk." His words were mellow, his eyes crystal blue, seductive as the day.

I recognized their sparkle, the one that made my body tingle, my insides quake. I wondered if we'd be searching for a barn housing bales of hay, the mere thought triggering my wild imagination, irrepressible sensations.

"Be right back ..."

"Okay ... be that way ..." I heard him chuckle as I flew across the veranda.

"Psst. I need to talk to you." Cornering Emma, I pulled her around a banquet table scattered with samplings of delicious food, wedging myself between the table and a potted plant.

"What's the big secret?" She gave me *the eye*, which looked a little tipsy from champagne. I was happy to see marriage hadn't changed her ... yet.

"I'm gonna take off for a while," I whispered as my eyes raked her face.

"No! You can't leave ..."

I gripped her shoulders, excitement radiating through my fingertips. "Indigo and I are taking a quick hike into the woods to get laid."

Her eyes left mine for a moment, then returned with shock, "Holy spice cake ..."

"Holy spice cake?" I burst out laughing. "In all the time we've been together, haven't I taught you anything?"

"Holy shit ... spice cake on the table? Who the fuck ordered spice cake?"

I threw my arms around her. "I love you, Emma. See you later."

As I turned to rush back to Indigo, she patted my backside: *"Mierda santa guarra hermosa. Lance una pierna a su cabeza para mí."* [*Holy shit beautiful slut. Throw a leg over his head for me.*] I stopped in my tracks and whirled. "When you get back from Phuket ... Spanish lessons Mrs. Arkana. I'll make a Latina out of you yet."

Grinning, Indigo watched me return. He reached for my hand. "What are you up to now?"

"Not much." I grinned back. "I just had to tell Emma something. So ... where are you taking me?"

"On a nature walk." When he winked, my stomach did flips.

Leaving the others behind we strolled the grounds, slipping beneath boughs of perennials clinging to vines, until the lawn grew lush and wildflowers sprouted knee-high.

In the distance I saw the horizon, the flaming glow of the slowly descending sun. "The scenery is simply amazing," I breathed as we brushed past bridal gazebos that had been reserved for rain, abandoned in sunshine.

"You are." Indigo lifted me and whirled me in his arms. Head angled, eyes barely closing, his parting lips captured mine in a kiss that made my body throb.

When he set me on my feet, I was shaken. "Wow," my shallow voice drummed with the blood in my ears, "what was *that* all about?"

"Do I need a reason?" The look in his eyes heightened the intensity of the moment.

I shook my head, blinking, suddenly oblivious to the meadow spreading around us.

"So, you've lost a roommate." His eyes searched my face as they'd done so many times. They still held the magic – rousting butterflies in my tummy. "What will you do now?"

"Huh?" My struggle to comprehend fell as flat as my reply.

His face was eager, his eyes soft, and now he was ambushing me with this secretive tone. My already whirling brain was short circuiting, leaving me with no means to consider the seriousness of his intentions.

"With Emma married ... and Pete taken as well, you're on your own, Sunshine." He pursed his lips, clicked his tongue, stroked my bottom lip with the pad of his finger.

"I can carry the apartment on my cop's salary." I squinted up at him, my heart thudding.

"What about me? About us?" Starbursts, fragile and silver, flickered with his gaze.

"I don't think I can afford you." Deliberately lightening the moment, I teased, tapping the tip of his nose with a finger. I needed time to gather my thoughts, my strength.

His stare, questioning, evoking, refused to free mine.

Deciding to take the plunge, I drew in a breath. "I don't know, baby. Moving in together is a big step." I made my words leisurely as I drank in his nearness, his love.

He tilted his head, his eyes burning, and my limbs felt inadequate. There was nothing I could do to stop the rush of blood pooling in my cheeks.

"That's not what I'm talking about." His fingers slid across my throat, grasped my delicate cross, examining the gold, while his eyes examined mine.

We edged deeper into the countryside, through lofty vegetation, colorful and sweet-scented, where he pulled me into a swift embrace before the wide trunk of a tree, its writhing limbs forming an umbrella. I was backed against the crispness of bark, and his hands came down on either side, the sleeves of his jacket grazing my face, his arms barricading me.

The biting scent of pine was overwhelming. Much more than earthy heather filled the air. The woman inside me sensed the need of the man holding me captive with his eyes, his heart, his hands. Breathing deeply, I tucked my head against his chest, lifted my face.

"The very first day I looked into your eyes," he whispered and moved his head slowly side to side as if to digest what boiled inside him, "I knew there was something about you ... something special."

"Donuts?" Brows arched, I waited for the tickling to begin, well expecting more. My eyelids fluttered with a will of their own.

His feathery laugh brushed my face, balmy as the breeze. "I knew I could fall in love with you– " His piercing eyes refused to blink.

My already whirling head was short circuiting, leaving me with no means to think.

"Crazy in love with you, Jewelia."

"I ... We're ..."

"Like you said in Maine, we're solid." He smiled.

My stare didn't move from his face. In shock, I willed my jaw to remain closed, but my lips parted, my breath all but ceased.

"Marry me ..." his breathy whisper filled my ears with an unexpected joy I had never imagined possible.

My legs almost gave way and I leaned into him. "Jimmy," I whispered against his lips as tears rolled down my cheeks.

Stunned, I drew back, clutching my chest, certain I was about to have a coronary. "¡Oh, Dios mío. ¿Va en serio?" *[Oh my God. Are you serious?]*

"Sí " *[Yes]* He bit his bottom lip and grinned. "Casarse conmigo, mi amor. *[Marry me, my love]* In the spring ... right here," twirling strands of hair loosened from my braid, he drew a breath, "we'll gather right here, around this tree. Share our happiness with everyone." His eyes released mine to sweep the day, the sky.

I threw my arms around him, pressing so close, his neck pulsed against my cheek. My voice trembled with excitement. "Yes. Yes. Yes." The tips of my fingers wound through his hair. "I love you so much," I murmured between kisses. Then I drew back, smiling. "I can't believe I'm marrying a doctor."

He almost squeezed the air out of me as he lifted me off my feet, then set me down and cradled my face in his hands. "I can't believe I'm marrying a detective."

I eyed him curiously, mindlessly scrunching the side of my mouth, control impossible. "Detective? Do you know something I don't?"

"I know one thing for sure." His lips curled into the cutest smirk. "You always manage to land on top."

"If you're complaining, I'll start taking the bottom."

"What am I getting myself into?" He shook his head.

"The best you ever had." I grinned.

"Close your eyes."

I tried to obey, but couldn't resist the urge to steal a split-second peek in time to see him reach into a pocket of his jacket. Holy shit, my mind screamed. Is this really happening? Pinch yourself, Jewel. Bite your tongue. Do something to make sure you're not dreaming.

"You can open them now." He took my hand, kissed every fingertip, then slipped a diamond onto my left ring finger.

I almost died when the glitter hit my eyes. "Oh – my – it's gorgeous." Stunned, I sucked in a breath. "It's a cushion cut. How did you know I love this shape?"

"I know a lot of things, sweetheart."

"Yes you do ..."

A sudden gust of wind plowed across the meadow, the force pressing me closer to his chest, lifting my dress, whipping the silk around the backs of my legs. The ferocity stole my breath, the flowers from my hair. Scattering leaves, swirling petals, cascaded like a shower of dazzling snowflakes caught up in turbulence.

"Jimmy," I breathed, "it's like a tornado." Through a downpour of foliage, I looked up at heaven, thinking: *Grandma, is that you? Are you telling me you're as thrilled as I am? And all along, this is how you knew it would be?*

Tears burned my eyes, and I closed them. Danny's face flashed across my mind. His essence was so strong, I felt I could almost touch his features. My eyes sprang open, my face darting in Indigo's direction. Wind parting his hair, he stared at the sky, and I wondered if he felt the same connection with Danny as I did with my grandma.

"This is incredible," I whispered. "They're smiling down on us. I can feel them."

"I believe they are." Reading my mind, he sounded wistful.

Our eyes brimmed with emotion, teardrops dried by a mild breeze replacing the sudden whirlwind. In the distance, chimes sounded like tinkling wedding bells, and Emma's voice carried through the air.

"I think they're looking for us." I loved Emma, but the last thing I wanted to do was return to reality. I longed to bury myself inside these precious moments I'd treasure for the rest of my life.

"I wonder how those rooms are." Indigo's prudent gaze led mine in the direction of the mansion turned bed and breakfast.

"I saw the bridal suite. It's beautiful." My hand tightened around his.

"I don't need frills. Just a nice soft bed."

"And a shower, the island in your kitchen, the front seat

of the Wrangler."

He laughed. "I don't know about you, Jewel. Your mind is always in the ... Hey, did you bring your cuffs?" His eyes darted to mine.

"Yup. Did you bring your stethoscope?"

"I did."

"Clamps?" My hand flew to my mouth at the thought.

He nodded, his eyes clouding with what I knew was me.

"Did you remember to bring your scrubs, doc?" A chill ran down my spine.

"I memorized your list, Jewelia." He chuckled, pulling me to his side.

"Chocolate roses, flavored oils, everything the authorities ordered?" I giggled.

Smiling, he nodded, then checked his wristwatch. "We've got about a half hour until the start of the reception." He lifted a brow. "What do you think?"

My mind exploded with memories: the first time I set eyes on him, the bike ride in Central Park, velvety grass, cloudless sky, his hands, his lips, his eyes, his voice ...

"Jewel ..." My name was an airy rush. "I doubt we'd be able to hang together out there," he motioned to the wheels spinning past us, "but Bill and I usually stop at Kelly's after riding." Those deeply faceted eyes were vibrant as they caressed my face, slowly, seductively.

He didn't have to speak, or move. Just standing before me with that look on his face, the purse of his lips still molded with my name ... was enough to push me over the edge.

Lifting my long dress to my knees, I bundled the silk in my fingers, kicked off my heels. Squinting up at him, I grinned. "Race you back." I was breathless.

As we dashed to the mansion, our laughter left a musical trail.

No one knows why, but ... sometimes what seems impossible ...works out best.

January Valentine

About The Author

January Valentine is the pen name of Victoria Valentine, New York writer, indie book publisher, and blogtalkradio show host.

Victoria uses January, her birth month, when writing romance and thrillers. Children's books and poetry are written under the name Victoria Valentine. Victoria hosts her radio show, *Away With Words,* every Wednesday @ 6:30 p.m. EST on blogtalkradio.com, where she interviews writers and poets.

Her books include:

Wheel Wolf (werewolf horror) Amazon Best Seller

Fighting For You (new adult)

Newly Bred With Magic (erotic short)

Seven Day Wonder (erotic novella written as Lana Lundon)

Love Dreams (contemporary romance)

Sweet Dreams in the Mind of a Serial Killer

Snowed In (5 author anthology)

At the Stroke of Midnight: 24 tales of terror

The Cutest Little Duckie (color storybook)

Desert Noon (romance poetry collection)

Running From Regret, Indigo's story, will release in 2014.

Find January Valentine & Victoria Valentine on Amazon.com, Barnes & Noble, Kobo, iTunes, and Water Forest Press Books.

Amazon Author Page
JanuaryValentine.com
VictoriaValentine.net
WaterForestPressBooks.com
http://waterforestpress.miiduu.com (Bookstore)
http://www.blogtalkradio.com/aww1 (Away With Words)
http://januaryvalentine.blogspot.com/ (Blog)
http://victoriaskyline.blogspot.com/ (Blog)

I love to hear from readers. :-) If you are interested in receiving updates and promotional alerts, please sign up for my mailing list. http://www.victoriavalentine.net/VictoriaValentineMailingList.htm
Contact:
waterforestpress@aol.com
Connect with me on Facebook:
https://www.facebook.com/VictoriaValentineBooks
Twitter:
https://twitter.com/VictoriaSkyline
Linkedin:
http://www.linkedin.com/pub/victoria-valentine/41/120/812

Acknowledgements

Until you actually sit down to compose an acknowledgment page, you don't realize just how many people have been an incredible influence and monumental help before, during, and after the creation of a book.

Although I've been writing longer than they've been around, I have to thank my three kids: **Phaedra** for her valuable input and for pushing me to the verge of hysteria, **Tommy** for his "time" and "bugging out on me", and other cool stuff, and **Cindy** for her sensitive ear and uplifting feedback, and to all three of my blessings who cheered me on when I suffered through bouts of inadequacy and OCD. My kids don't aspire to be writers, but with their talents, they really should be.

Thanks to Liz for her "blah ja blah" and other mumbo jumbo, Matt (our future pharmacist) for his "Apple" skills, and Nick for being so damn cute.

Thanks to Sil, my inspiration for hot and sensitive heroes, John for delectable meals, and Judy because she's my sister. :D

Thank you to my cousin, Mimi, (Maggie Schmidt) the fantastic artist who sketched the most *guapo* "Indigo".

There are some very important others I'd like to thank, beginning with Shellie Hedge, my good friend and monumental support system who proofread my revised chapters and cheered me on when my eyes blurred. Keep growling & howling, girl. Can't wait to read your new book :-)

A huge wolf hug and howl goes out to the fantastic ladies of my street team.

I'd be lost without! You guys get the word out. I can't thank you enough.

TEAM GO WOLF!

www.ingramcontent.com/pod-product-compliance
Lightning Source LLC
LaVergne TN
LVHW051620080426
835511LV00016B/2086